David Jayne Hill
and the
Problem of World Peace

Hill in his later years. Date uncertain.

DAVID JAYNE HILL AND THE PROBLEM OF WORLD PEACE

Aubrey Parkman

Lewisburg
BUCKNELL UNIVERSITY PRESS
London: ASSOCIATED UNIVERSITY PRESSES

© 1975 by Associated University Presses, Inc.

Associated University Presses, Inc.
Cranbury, New Jersey 08512

Associated University Presses
108 New Bond Street
London W1Y OQX, England

Library of Congress Cataloging in Publication Data

Parkman, Aubrey, 1918–
    David Jayne Hill and the problem of world peace.

    Bibliography: p.
    1. Hill, David Jayne, 1850–1932. I. Title.
E748.H54P37   1974   327'.2'0924 [B]   72–3530
ISBN 0–8387–1259–2

The author wishes to thank Appleton-Century-Crofts for permission
to quote from *The Rebuilding of Europe* by David Jayne Hill,
Copyright © 1917 by The Century Co., and from *Present Problems in
Foreign Policy* by David Jayne Hill, Copyright © 1919 by D. Appleton
and Company.

To Jean

Contents

Preface

The idea of writing this book came from an investigation of
the David Jayne Hill Papers. An extensive collection covering
fifty years, they offered a storehouse of untapped material on
educational, diplomatic, and political developments in the United
States between 1880 and 1930. In these developments, Hill played
a significant role. As a young college president during a period
of revolutionary change in American higher education, he
revitalized two small and failing universities. As a diplomatist,
first as Assistant Secretary of State under John Hay and then as
United States envoy to Switzerland, the Netherlands, and
Germany, he was closely involved in the century-old arbitration
movement that reached its climax in the two decades before World
War I. Finally, as a publicist, he became one of America's most
influential spokesmen for foes of progressivism and opponents of
United States membership in the League of Nations and the World
Court. Although Hill's interests were wide and his activities
diverse, one concern stood out above all others. That was how the
United States could best contribute to the establishment of world
peace. In writing this biography, I had three aims in view. One was

9

to portray as accurately as possible the public life and personality of a remarkably able man. Another was to show Hill's place in events and issues of importance to his times. My third purpose was to add whatever relevant pieces I could to the broader history of this era.

Acknowledgments

I am deeply grateful for the helpful suggestions offered by Dr.
Glyndon G. Van Deusen during the early stages of writing
this book. I must also express my appreciation for the valuable
assistance given to me while reading the Hill Papers by Mrs.
Margaret Butterfield Andrews, Mrs. Margaret K. Toth, and
other members of the staff of the Rush Rhees Library of the
University of Rochester; for the kindnesses of Mrs. Blanche
Baughman, Mrs. Dorothy Union, and other librarians at Bucknell
University and Tufts University who helped me find material; for
the courtesies extended to me at the Cornell Library, the Rochester
Public Library, the Library of Congress, and the National
Archives; for the careful copyediting by Mrs. Mathilde E. Finch;
and for the suggestions and patience of Jean Morrison Parkman,
who critically read and typed various drafts of the manuscript.

I wish to thank the editor of *Rochester History* for permission to
republish material originally printed in that journal, and the
Massachusetts Historical Society for allowing me to cite material
from the Henry Cabot Lodge Papers. I also wish to thank
Doubleday & Company, Inc., for permission to quote from

A.P.

Reading, Massachusetts

David Jayne Hill
and the
Problem of World Peace

1

The "New Lewisburg"

ON MARCH 11, 1879, THE TRUSTEES OF THE UNIVERSITY AT LEWISBURG, Pennsylvania, elected David Jayne Hill the president of their institution. Twenty-eight years old, he had graduated from Lewisburg only five years before. The University was seeing its worst days, and the selection hinted of desperation, but the trustees at least had the distinction of electing the youngest college president in America.[1]

Hill was born in Plainfield, New Jersey, on June 10, 1850, the youngest of the four children of the Reverend Daniel Trembley Hill and Lydia Thompson Hill. He came from English stock which on both sides of his family had migrated to the Massachusetts Bay Colony before 1640. Several of his early American ancestors were Puritan divines, including the Reverend William Jayne, an Oxford scholar and chaplain in Cromwell's army who had fled to the colonies following the Restoration. And both Hills and Jaynes were Revolutionary War patriots. It was a family heritage in which Hill took perhaps excessive pride and which was to color to some degree his political philosophies.

Lydia Hill died when David was four. His sisters looked after

15

him for several years until Daniel married Sarah Jane Merritt, a very religious woman who saw to it that he continued to have a good Baptist upbringing. Because the Reverend Hill was always hearing "calls" to new pastorates, David went to several different schools in small towns of New York and New Jersey. At seventeen, he entered the Connecticut Literary Institution at Suffield to prepare for college, but then hearing of an academy at Cooperstown, New York, and romantically associating it with Leatherstocking's frontier, he persuaded his father to let him go there. Early in 1869 he was dismissed with a half dozen other boys for "conspiring to. break school rules." Returning to Deckertown, New Jersey, where his family was now living, Hill entered the office of a local attorney to read law. That autumn his father moved to another church, in Pawling, New York, where David at first planned to continue with law, but the Reverend, a minister of the old style who had simply obeyed a "call" without the advantages of higher education, wanted him to go to college. Daniel wanted his son to be a scholar and, while he never openly urged it, he hoped that a college education would lead David into the ministry. Daniel selected the University at Lewisburg because of his admiration for the character and learning of George Ripley Bliss, its Professor of Greek and Latin, but it was perhaps not coincidental that most of Lewisburg's graduates became Baptist ministers.

Because he was deficient in Greek, required for entering the Classical course, Hill spent the winter reading the Gospels in the original. At first interested only in linguistic training, he discovered by the time he had finished that he really believed for the first time in the divinity of Jesus and wanted to be baptized, a ceremony his father performed in a nearby creek. To enter the ministry, however, was a decision he was not ready to make. He had found in the Gospels a spiritual truth that appealed to the heart and conscience of man and furnished a guide for a better life. But in books on astronomy he had found a material truth of exact mathematical science relating to force and matter. Unlike his father, who did not trouble himself as to their relationship but rested his faith wholly on personal conviction, Hill struggled with the problem of how the anthropological conceptions of religious literature could be fitted together with the demonstrable facts of the universe about him.[2] As the same question was already challenging the American denominational college, he was soon to be grappling with it on an institutional as well as a personal basis.

Arriving in Lewisburg in August 1870, Hill found an institution much like dozens of others scattered over American hilltops earlier in the century by religious denominations anxious to train their ministers and spread their faiths. Boasting a small college for men, an academy for boys, and a seminary for girls, it looked out over the little central Pennsylvania town with a deceptive air of solidity and permanence. It had been founded a little over two decades before by Baptists determined that their denomination in the state should have its own university, and for a few years, despite meager financial resources and a backwoods location, it had made promising strides. It granted its first handful of college degrees, seven in all, in 1851, "in a period of time," bragged the Lewisburg *Union County Whig,* "when other colleges could exhibit no higher grade than a Freshman class." A year later it had five teachers and eighty-three students in the College and 235 students in all departments. One wing of "Old Main" and an academy building already graced its campus, and in 1857 a third building went up for the Female Institute, which up to then had been housed in the village. In 1859, when a center hall and new wing were added to Old Main, the *Lewisburg Chronicle* asserted: "There is no College in the State with a more solid foundation than the University at Lewisburg—none with better buildings—and none with fairer prospects if its friends (both local and denominational) put forth proper efforts to make its benefits available." But in truth the University had by then already ceased to grow, and, bound by poverty and conservatism, it managed in succeeding years to do little more than survive. When Hill entered its classrooms its program of instruction was virtually unchanged, there had been no permanent increase in the number of students, and the College still had only five professors.[3]

Lewisburg, Hill discovered, was "a school of patience," and had he gone there two years earlier, he later recorded, he would never have stuck it out. But having already trifled away some valuable years, he was determined to stay and work. It was Professor Bliss, by guiding his reading beyond his textbooks, who did the most to shape his education. "When I recall how much was suggested to me by this noble scholar," he reminisced years afterward, "it seems to me that my college course would have been meagre indeed, had it not been for these wide excursions into the fields of literature, history and science, made at the suggestion of Doctor Bliss." The rivalry of Lewisburg's two literary societies, Euepia, to which Hill belonged, and Theta Alpha, also helped to make the regimen of drill and drudgery tolerable. As in most American colleges, their numerous literary activities and weekly debates were probably the students' most valuable educational experiences. Making the most of these opportunities for practice in writing and speaking, Hill edited the *College Herald,* the campus journal managed by the societies, and carried off the "Lung Prize" for oratory at the Annual Junior Exhibition, buying with the prize money a handsome set of *Gibbon's Decline and Fall of the Roman Empire.*

The course to which Hill looked forward the most was, perhaps because of his expectations, the most disappointing. The senior course in Butler's *Analogy of Religion,* taught by the University's president, was a three months' study of the book in which college seniors for generations had been expected to find a reconciliation of religious faith and scientific knowledge. Hill found the *Analogy* an able expression of the religious philosophy of the eighteenth century, but of little help to him in the present. He read widely in science and philosophy, including Darwin's *Origin of Species* and Spencer's *Synthetic Philosophy,* but "the Gospel World of Persons and the Natural World of Things" still remained apart.

Entering the ministry seemed out of the question, yet his background, education, and religious convictions pressed the issue upon him. At the invitation of the deacons of his father's church in Pawling, he filled the pulpit for the Reverend, who was ill, during the midwinter vacation of his sophomore year. Thus, by the custom that then prevailed, he was "licensed" to preach. But to urgings that he study purposely for the ministry, he turned a deaf ear. The summer following his junior year he spent in Madison, Wisconsin, visiting the parents of Anna Amelia Liddell, a student at the Seminary with whom he had fallen in love and was soon to marry. There he was invited to preach several times at the Baptist Church and then asked to become its pastor when he had finished his studies at Lewisburg. This forced some serious soul-searching, but because he still felt no sense of a "call," and knowing that without it he could not teach all the church would expect of him, he left the offer hanging. It was not until he was offered an instructorship at Lewisburg, upon graduating valedictorian of his class the next year, that he felt the question was finally closed. The ministry was given its dignity by the finding and proclaiming of truth, he reasoned, and as a college teacher this could still be his, and in his own way and upon his own responsibility, with a free mind and conscience.

Directly from the graduation ceremonies, Hill went to Milwaukee, where the Liddell family had moved, and there on August 27, 1874, he and Anna were married. For his first year of teaching he received $800, and could not have made ends meet had not his father loaned him the money to buy a house. But he and Anna were happy, and their household grew. Their first child, Walter Liddell, was born in August 1875, and a second son, Arthur Thompson, came in May 1878.[4]

Hill was a fresh breeze in Lewisburg's little faculty, and the *College Herald* repeatedly signified its approbation. "All who are acquainted with his sterling qualities, ripe scholarship and eminent fitness for that department," it rhapsodized upon his appointment to Instructor in Rhetoric after one year of teaching, "will vindicate the wisdom of the choice." Two years later he was elected Crozer Professor of Rhetoric, a chair from which he taught not only rhetoric but also logic, botany, and political economy in the College and Greek and Latin in the Academy. Additionally, he lectured weekly to the junior class on English literature and supervised the college library. The courses in rhetoric had for years been taught with the same ancient and ponderous texts, and suffering students found them not only dull but useless. Hill wrote his own text and tried other new approaches, eliciting from the *College Herald* the encomium that he was rapidly making his department what it ought to be. The course in political economy had been almost as bad. Squeezed by the rigid curriculum into a period of seven weeks, too brief a time to complete a textbook by the customary recitation method, it had been at best a partial survey that was never finished. Hill dispensed with the text and by lectures and diverse readings made it more comprehensive and even interesting. It was another innovation in teaching enthusiastically noted by the student paper, and one that Hill gradually extended to other classes.[5]

In 1877 Sheldon and Company of New York published Hill's textbook, *The Science of Rhetoric,* a small, tightly organized work that pulled together essentials previously found only in several volumes. Its immediate success brought from Sheldon a request for a more elementary text for high schools and academies. Hill responded with *The Elements of Rhetoric,* published the next year. The *Elements* was even more successful than its predecessor, and within two months was being reprinted in London. "Think of a London firm's coming to our own loved Lewisburg," exclaimed Professor Grier, "to find a man to make a proper text book for the English people!" Fifty years later Hill was still receiving royalties from it.[6]

With his rhetorics on Sheldon's best-seller list, Hill began writing biographies. Harper and Brothers had recently struck the public fancy with a series of inexpensive little volumes entitled *English Men of Letters,* and Hill had suggested that Sheldon publish a similar series called *American Authors.* The first two volumes, *Washington Irving* and *William Cullen Bryant,* came out in the spring of 1879. They filled a real need for short, popular works on famous American writers, and reviewers predicted that the series could hardly fail of success. But Hill was forced to set the project aside before it was fairly begun. He had just finished the third chapter on the life of Edgar Allan Poe when he was elected to the presidency of the University.[7]

After more than twenty years of dedicated, if not always imaginative, effort, the University's second president, the Reverend Justin R. Loomis, had resigned. Like the Reverend Howard Malcom, who had resigned in 1857, Loomis was tired and discouraged.

Enrollment in the University had dropped precipitously for several years and by 1878 was down to 135. Hardest hit was the College, supposedly the heart of the institution, which had only forty-four students. The College's academic program had simply become too outdated. In its early years the College had offered only the usual smattering of studies outside Latin, Greek, and mathematics, but it had been no more behind the times than other colleges. Little had changed in higher education for more than two hundred years. Latin, Greek, and mathematics were still the staples of a liberal education, learning was based on authority, and instruction was largely dogmatic. But by the 1870s a revolution was taking place in American higher education as traditional concepts and methods gave way before advances in science and technology, ideas brought in from German universities, and increasing liberalism in all areas of thought. New universities and technological schools were springing up to meet new demands on education, and many older colleges were revising their curricula, adopting new methods of instruction, adding the laboratory to the textbook, and sometimes even admitting women. Lewisburg, however, had changed hardly at all. It had added little to its curriculum except a bit of French and German, a little biology, and some weekly lectures on history and literature; and since these were grafted to a prescribed program, the result was probably only increased superficiality. Elective studies were limited to a single choice between a term of Greek or a term of French. In 1876 when a new Latin Scientific program was established, the College was still looking to the past rather than the present. The old three-year Scientific program had substituted a few terms of mathematics, history, and physiology for the Latin and Greek of the Classical program. But since a college education without Latin had never been considered quite respectable, the new four-year Scientific program included all the Latin required of students in the Classical program.[8]

These educational shortcomings were made no less intolerable by unpopular restrictions on extracurricular activities. Fraternities were under a rigid ban, with every incoming student compelled to sign a pledge not to join one. But only driven underground, they became secret sources of mischief and revolt that vexed Loomis sorely. Baseball, which was then sweeping the country, had also recently been outlawed when players had failed to give apparently needless pledges not to play during study hours. The morale of the students was low, and they showed it by an increasing lack of respect for college rules and college property.[9]

The financial condition of the University was equally depressing. Money had always been hard to come by, pledges made in repeated subscription drives had never been fully met, and by the mid-1860s the endowment fund, pared by yearly operating losses, amounted to less than $58,000. Debts, meanwhile, had accumulated to nearly half that figure. By raising almost $86,000, of which over $59,000 was added to endowment, President Loomis had momentarily eased the strain. But by 1873 finances were again so straitened, and salaries so inadequate, that the faculty was forced to find outside work. The following year the University launched a "grand forward movement," an elaborately organized and well-publicized campaign to raise $300,000 for endowment. Two years later, with less than $10,000 to show for it, the effort came to an end and the University's financial situation continued to worsen.[10]

Failure was laid to "the financial embarrassment of the times," but the fact was that the University's friends and alumni had lost confidence in its administration. They were discontented with the University's educational conservatism and unhappy over their inability to initiate change. Nearly two-thirds of the alumni were Baptist ministers in charge of the very churches to which the University was constantly pleading for more money, yet the trustees had recently twice rejected alumni petitions for reinstating fraternities and had turned down an alumni demand for representatives on the board elected by themselves. By charter provision most of the University's administrative responsibility was in the hands of its twenty trustees, but there was also a board of forty curators who were entrusted with various auditing functions and general supervision over scholarship. The boards had always irritated one another and worked at cross-purposes, but now their relations were becoming more abrasive than ever as the curators, many of them alumni, pressed for charter amendments that would allow them a greater share of governing power.[11]

The last straw was laid in June 1877, when President Loomis charged Charles S. James, Professor of Mathematics and Natural Philosophy since 1851, with neglect of duty and a hostility toward him damaging to the University and asked the trustees to dismiss James. Although Loomis's charges appeared to be unfounded and the outcome of personal differences between the two men, a majority of the trustees voted to let James go. James was an able and respected teacher, practically every alumnus had been his student, and his ouster after twenty-six years at the University raised a tremendous commotion, with Loomis becoming the butt of all the discontent that had long been accumulating. By June 1878, the Philadelphia alumni were demanding his resignation. When it was learned that he had submitted it, to take effect at the end of the next academic year, the Alumni Association and curators asked the trustees to make it effective at once. Although the trustees refused, Loomis was so disheartened by the outburst against him that he arranged to leave office in December.[12]

At their midwinter meeting that month, the trustees elected a new president, the Reverend Poindexter S. Henson, a prominent minister of Philadelphia. They voted him a salary of $3,300 a year, a huge sum for the time and $1,000 more than Loomis had been paid. Presumably his prestige among Baptists of the state would restore confidence in the University and bring it prosperity. But Henson turned the offer down. When the trustees met again on March 11, 1879, their nominating committee suggested Professor Newton L. Andrews of Madison University. Two members of the board then suggested David Hill. Knowing their own professor the better, the trustees elected him by twelve votes to two on the first ballot. Not rating him in the same league with Henson, however, they set his salary at $2,000.

Not only was Hill not a prominent Baptist minister, he was not a minister at all, and some of the trustees thought he should be one. Hill saw no necessity of it, believing that though he had doubts about Christian theology he could still conscientiously represent the University's evangelical interests. But yielding to the trustees' wishes, he was examined for a half-hour in the autumn of 1879 by a conference of brethren not anxious to make him out a heretic and ordained a minister.[13]

The alumni, the students, and the townspeople of Lewisburg responded to Hill's election with enthusiasm, the latter groups each of an evening turning out the town's cornet band and marching to his home in noisy acclaim. Hopes for the University suddenly and irrationally ran high. Yet within months they seemed to be vindicated. "The University at Lewisburg has emerged from the gloom of fogyism and the shadow of precedent," declaimed the *College Herald* in January 1880, "and although weak from a long existence under these evils, nevertheless under the guidance of President Hill it is making rapid progress in those directions which are characteristic of the live Colleges of the present day." Already a few electives were in the curriculum, fraternities were back on the campus, college property was being extensively repaired at the request of the students and with their implied pledge to preserve it, and on some matters, even, the students were being consulted.[14] A "New Lewisburg"—soon to become a current phrase—seemed indeed to be in the making.

Yet, without more money, the University could not survive. Between December 1879, and December 1880, the trustees were forced three times to "loan" from $4,000 to $6,000 from the endowment fund to the operating fund to meet expenses, each time reducing income the more as productive funds were drained away. In June 1880, the treasurer reported the endowment at nearly $122,000; a year later he reported the "invested" endowment nearer to $106,000. Sometime earlier he had informed Hill that the University must increase its endowment or close its doors.[15]

Before taking office, Hill had lectured the guests at a reception given him by the Baptist Social Union of Philadelphia on the needs of the University. The most pressing was to increase endowment, which required convincing the public that the college did not exist merely to educate clergymen. "Lewisburg awaits the coming of some good friend," he also told them, "who will make her past a pedestal for a monument more enduring than brass." To another gathering of Baptists shortly after, he pointed out with less ambiguity that the University was actually unchristened and he hoped that a gift of fifty or one hundred thousand dollars might lead to the prefixing of a name to it. At the commencement exercises in June he appealed in his inaugural address for "a generous friend, among those whom

God has entrusted with wealth, who will place his name on the same illustrious roll with those of Gardner Colby and Asa Packer.... And, while this beautiful valley stands, here on this hill-top, upheaved by the hand of Providence as a fit pedestal, shall tower his everlasting monument."[16] It was not a blindly aimed ploy, for Hill had already singled out a benefactor. William Bucknell was a devout and active Baptist of Philadelphia who had made a fortune in real estate and public utilities and already given over half a million dollars to Baptist religious and educational institutions. He had been a charter trustee of the University and given to it generously in its early years. But despairing of its management, of constant conflicts between its boards, and of hostilities within its faculty, he had resigned his trusteeship in 1863.

Before his election to the presidency, Hill had never met Bucknell. He soon contrived an introduction, and visited the Philadelphian frequently. Bucknell was always hospitable, though he would not at first even speak of the University. But Hill persisted, until finally in April 1881, Bucknell agreed to come to his assistance on specific terms. He would give $50,000 to a new board of trustees if the present trustees would raise an additional $50,000; the present endowment must be converted into $100,000 of secured and permanent investments, approved by the subscribers of the new funds, through the sale of all property belonging to the University except its campus; all claims and suits against the University must be met without impairing these funds; control of the University must be placed in the hands of a single board of twenty members chosen by the new subscribers; and the present trustees must accept his offer within three weeks and fulfill all its provisions by the following November.

Hill presented Bucknell's conditions to both boards, determined to resign if either rejected them. To reorganize under a new, single board of trustees would no doubt cost the University some old friends, but their resentments could be borne better than their quarrels, for he did not intend constantly to be caught between conflicting policies arising from divided responsibility. There was less difficulty, however, than he feared. For the past year the curators had been urging reorganization under a single board, and now if the University were to survive there was no other choice. Meeting in special session on April 21, 1881, the trustees "gratefully accepted" Bucknell's offer and named Hill their special representative in meeting his conditions.[17]

The campaign to raise $50,000 was directed by the Reverend George M. Spratt, Secretary of the Pennsylvania Educational Society and subsequently one of the new trustees. Although by October 12 subscriptions totaled only about $34,000, and on October 27, with less than a week to go, the *National Baptist* of Philadelphia reported that the whole sum was not yet raised, the tough deadline of November 1 was met. The new board of trustees was organized in Philadelphia on March 7, 1882. One by one the old trustees offered their resignations and were replaced or retained according to a list of nominations drawn up by a committee, chaired by Hill, representing the new subscribers. The atmosphere, which would have been tense in any case, was close to explosive until the Reverend James Wheaton Smith, a trustee for twenty-eight years, arose and withdrew his name for membership in the new board, commenting that the success of the University was of far greater importance than his connection with it. Bucknell, as everyone knew, had given notice that, because as he could not work with Dr. Smith, one of them had to go. When the meeting closed, only eight of the old trustees were left, several of the oldest and most devoted had been set aside, and no one could doubt where power lay in the new board. It elected Bucknell its chairman when it met again in June.[18]

Hill was able to get along with Bucknell without lowering his own dignity, and Bucknell's continued generosity benefited the University handsomely. He built or provided for a new chapel, an astronomical observatory, two residence halls, and a chemistry laboratory. He improved existing property through gifts of money and equipment, more than doubled his original subscription to the endowment fund, and established a number of scholarships and prizes. Before his death in 1890 he gave all told more than $268,000 to the University he had once abandoned as hopeless. In 1886 the other trustees, meeting when he was conveniently absent, named the University in his honor.[19]

The University deserved a new name, for Hill was turning it into a new institution. New courses appeared in its catalogue every year as offerings in natural and social sciences and in language and literature steadily broadened. Methods of instruction were improved, and laboratory practice in the sciences was required. An honors program was established. Music was given the place it deserved in a liberal arts college, and so was an improved library, which was opened for at least a part of every day instead of the former hour or two twice a week.[20]

The expansion of the curriculum inevitably meant more elective courses. Hill was critical of the elective system, at least of its indiscriminate use, believing it ignored the skill and experience embodied in an established curriculum and abdicated a faculty responsibility to unprepared students. "The permission of choosing their own studies which is extended to pupils by the elective system," he had written in the *College Herald* in 1875, "is not only almost certain to result in wasting time, crippling scholarship, and blasting all hopes of a round, solid culture, but it practically leads to a gigantic system of fraud and deception where students, whose parents suppose them to be going regularly through college, are actually idling their time at useless or familiar pursuits." Colleges should offer a variety of courses for differing needs, he agreed, but the selection of a student's program should be carefully supervised to strike a proper balance between prescriptive "disciplinarian" and permissive "utilitarian" ideas of education. The collegiate degree at Lewisburg, he announced in his inaugural address, was to be a certificate of attainment that the elective system would not be allowed to cheapen or deprive of definite meaning. Therefore, while by 1888, Hill's last year at Lewisburg, more than a third of the courses offered were electives, choices were restricted to specific alternatives.[21] The elective system was also very expensive, and if the flexibility of the curriculum was still not large, it was all that the College, which with three new professors had enlarged its faculty by half, could afford.

More important than the growth of electives in measuring liberalizing currents at Lewisburg was the changing nature of its required courses. By 1888 the amount of Greek and Latin required in the Classical program had been reduced from twenty three-month terms to nine terms, and the eighteen terms of Latin required in the Scientific program had been cut to eight terms of either Latin or Greek. An equally significant break with the past was revealed in the courses that Hill taught. As a matter of tradition he had inherited the President's Chair of Metaphysics and Moral Philosophy, which meant that he was to teach, in addition to Political Economy and a new course in Constitutional Law, the senior courses of Moral Philosophy, Intellectual Philosophy, and Butler's Analogy. These were all parts of the venerable course in Moral Philosophy that had been taught to seniors by American college presidents ever since it had come from English and Scottish universities to colonial colleges in the seventeenth century. A mixture of philosophy and social sciences with emphasis on religion and ethics, its purpose was to fit one for a virtuous and useful life by discovering his duty to God, his fellow men, and himself. Although heavily dependent upon syllogistic logic and a priori assumptions, invariably arriving at orthodox conclusions, and usually finding universal truth very much the same as the prevailing ideas of the place and time in which it was taught, it had nevertheless generally been the most beneficial course to which the students were exposed and often the first to ask them to think. The advance of scientific knowledge and a freer spirit of inquiry, however, were bringing its long day to a close as it gave way to courses more specialized and less moralistic. A year after Hill took over at Lewisburg, Moral Philosophy, Intellectual Philosophy, and Butler's Analogy disappeared from the curriculum, replaced by Psychology and Ethics. Two years later Hill introduced a course on anthropology, making Lewisburg the first college in America where it was a regularly required subject of study.[22]

Religion was by no means ignored by Hill. The theory of evolution, new archeological discoveries, higher criticism, and new theories about the origin and growth of religions were all at this time calling into question accepted foundations of religious beliefs, and Hill feared that the views of Baptist fundamentalists on these subjects might destroy the denomination's influence among intelligent men. If religious faith were to survive, it had to have a tenable foundation outside these new fields of controversy. He strove, therefore, to impress upon his students that the New Testament was designed only to be a vehicle of religious truth, that a distinction had to be made between the World of Persons treated in the Gospels and the World of Nature that was man's material environment. The growth and influence of Christianity, he also believed, were owing to the personality and teachings of Jesus alone, and not to any legends or dogmas that were later arbitrarily clustered about Him and then declared necessary to salvation. He also saw no reason for special revelation of what man by study and experiment would in time discover anyway. To many Baptists these "liberal" ideas were absolutely heretical, yet Hill discussed them at Lewisburg without encountering any difficulties or unpleasantness.[23] Nothing better illustrated the changing nature of the University.

In his inaugural address, Hill declared that he would make no distinction of sex in regard to choice of study. The new board of trustees that came into office in 1882 was of the same mind and was also seeking ways to economize. Therefore developments in the education of women at Lewisburg followed two lines. By 1883 the Female Institute was offering a full collegiate program under the supervision of the professors of the College, and two years later it began granting a collegiate degree. The trustees had meanwhile instructed Hill to arrange for the joint instruction of the students of the three schools to the extent that was practicable and advantageous. Consequently, in 1883 the psychology and chemistry classes of the Institute and College began meeting together, and with special permission three young women began taking all of their studies with the College's freshman class. This led to the decision in 1885 to admit women to the College in full standing, and in June that year the College awarded its first degree to a woman.[24]

Organized athletics was another innovation in American colleges that Hill encouraged at Lewisburg. No man, he thought, was fully educated in the best sense without the physical health necessary to carry on a useful life. By the end of his administration baseball and football, which had declined on the campus after a brief spurt in the early 1870s, were flourishing sports. Tennis was thriving with four clubs, and bicycling, which was just then coming into vogue, also had its club. Hill was himself an ardent cyclist, who wrote testimonials for Columbia wheels. Sports became such an accepted part of campus life that an Athletic Association was formed to direct them, and the alumni, responding to Hill's appeal, began raising funds to build a gymnasium.[25]

The promotion of athletics no doubt helped to moderate at Lewisburg a rowdyism which then prevailed on most college campuses. Hill in any case had no intentions of tolerating unruly behavior. In his own first days at Lewisburg he had been so outrageously hazed by upper classmen that in cold fury he had bought a pistol with which to shoot their ringleader. The weapon was taken from him by a friend, but it could have been a tragic episode, and it was one he never forgot. He began his presidency by warning the boys that the College had laws and giving each boy a copy of them. "And it seems that this was all that was necessary," piously commented the *College Herald*. "The laws were no sooner known than they were observed." But no college was that tame, and late one night not long afterward, Hill had occasion to lay his cane in a not-unusual prexy fashion on a tipsy youth whose return to the campus had been too noisy for his own good. When the boys gathered in chapel the next morning, he bluntly told them that there would be at least one college in America where there was neither hazing nor drunkenness, or there would be one less college president. There is no record that he ever swung his cane again, for the personal force of his character seems to have been instrument enough. "In his influence over his students," reminisced Dr. William C. Bartol, Professor of Mathematics and Astronomy at Bucknell for nearly fifty years, "President Hill was unusual. He always had his way with them, and it was a kindly, agreeable way.... Always when President Hill gave his orders to the boys, no matter what they chanced to be, they were immediately greeted with consent, sometimes applause, and due obedience followed. Hill was a gifted college president."[26]

College presidents of the nineteenth century were usually masters in the art of public address. Their audiences were always at hand, for the American public had an immense appetite for sermons, oratory, and didactic lectures, and the speeches of college presidents and professors provided both a form of adult education and a way to enjoy an inexpensive evening's entertainment. Happily for the University, Hill thoroughly enjoyed meeting the requirements of this tradition; and in talks by the score to audiences ranging from local Sunday School picnics to the patrons of Point Chautauqua, he provided the school with the best public relations work it had ever had. Lewisburg audiences prized him, and the Baptists in and out of the state regarded him with proprietory pride. In 1883 Madison University, a sister Baptist institution, honored him with the degree of Doctor of Laws.[27]

Several more books by the young president of Bucknell helped further to make the University, and himself, better known. Two new texts, *The Elements of Logic* (1883) and *The Elements of Psychology* (1888), completed what Sheldon and Company called the "Hill's Series." The former was a recasting of W. Stanley Jevons's noted *Elementary Lessons in Logic*, which had been designed for reading under the direction of tutors, to meet the requirements of American students who were expected to recite daily on particular lessons. The work on psychology, however, evolved in Hill's own classroom, the product of both his own need for a satisfactory text and the request of his publishers for a book having the same structural qualities that had made his other texts so successful. Hill's other publications had an entirely different focus. Like many college presidents and religious leaders, he was disturbed by social problems arising in America with the gigantic growth of industrial capitalism, and like them, his attention centered mainly on the strained relations of capital and labor and a presumed growth of socialism within the ranks of labor. Contributing to the current flood of strictures and solutions, he wrote a series of editorials on "The Principles and Fallacies of Socialism" for the Pittsburgh *Commercial Gazette*, which in 1885 reappeared in the popular *Lovell's Library* paperback series. Over 10,000 copies were sold, many to business firms for distribution among their employees. He delivered a paper on "Socialism: False and True" to the national Baptist congress meeting in New York in 1885, and two years later he expounded on the subject again in a series of lectures at the Newton Theological Seminary on current social problems. The lectures, entitled *The Social Influence of Christianity*, were published the next year by Silver, Burdett and Company of Boston.[28]

Hill believed that socialism, though it "assumed chameleon

forms" and wore "as many masks as Proteus himself," amounted to no more than a demand for an equal distribution of wealth by men who were not equal in fact but imagined they were by right. Anarchistic, agrarian, state, and Christian socialism alike were based on the fallacious assumptions that all wealth was produced by the labor of society, was therefore the property of society, and justice could be realized only by dividing equally that which belonged to all. Socialism was thus "a dream of impossible remedies for imaginary wrongs." Defending the status quo, he invoked the era's catalogue of clichés on the moral and divine origins of wealth, the duties of stewardship, and the self-made nature of poverty. For admitted imperfections in the social system, his remedies were platitudes on self-help.[29]

Hill was ready to dispute the dogmas of the church and try the new in education, but on the urgent social and economic questions facing his generation, he never broke free from prevailing conservative thought. In this he was no different from most progressive educators, for the same Darwinian concepts and laissez-faire attitudes that helped so greatly to liberalize American education paradoxically provided as well the intellectual underpinning for American social and political conservatism.

The steady improvement of the University during the nine years of Hill's presidency revealed little of the anguish and later happiness of his private life. Upon taking that office he moved into a big, rambling house next to the campus, which President Loomis had built and the trustees had purchased. Anna enjoyed her new home less than a year. On March 15, 1880, two weeks after giving birth to a third son, David, Jr., she died at the age of twenty-nine. Her parents, now living in Charlotte, North Carolina, took over the care of the children. Six weeks later the baby died.[30]

In a state of despair, Hill turned chiefly to his books for companionship. Obsessed with finding an acceptable intellectual basis for religious faith, he fell for several years into a narrow round of work and study. Fearing at last that his monasticism would encrust him, and suspecting that he was really very much of a small-town provincial, he decided early in 1884 to spend the summer in Europe. Events then took an unexpected turn. One

Sunday when he was invited to preach in the Lewisburg Presbyterian Church he met Juliet Lewis Packer. The daughter of a late Williamsport judge and niece of a former governor of Pennsylvania, Juliet belonged to one of Williamsport's best families. Some weeks later Hill was asked by the Williamsport Presbyterian Church to preach there, and if it was an odd coincidence that he was put up across the street from the Packer residence and invited to the Packers for lunch, he never noticed or cared. Juliet had been intruding constantly into his thoughts, and before the day in Williamsport was over, he was sure he was in love.

Hill traveled through England and Scotland and visited Paris that summer, keeping a meticulous journal in lengthy letters mailed every few days to Anna's sister. Returning to Lewisburg late in the evening on September 29, he was greeted at the railroad station by some four hundred students and townspeople waiting with a carriage, torchlights, and the town band to escort him home. Two days later his sweetening world again turned sour. He received a telegram from Anna's parents telling of the death of his son Arthur, who was only six years old.[31]

Hill visited Williamsport frequently during the next two years, until on June 3, 1886, he and Juliet were married. The wedding was described by the *Williamsport Gazette and Bulletin* as "the society event of the year." Leaving soon for Europe, Hill and his bride toured the British Isles and the Continent until December.

Although Juliet had none of her husband's taste for speculative philosophy or compulsion to find a viable basis for her religion, she was fluent in several languages and well versed in history and literature, and these intellectual interests afforded Hill a welcome relief from his own sober meditations of the past six years. As the lady in the President's House, she made a great hit. She gave parties for the students, who thought her a "royal entertainer," organized college classes in conversational German that were eagerly attended, and helped to direct a reading of Shakespeare that seems to have been the start of dramatics at Bucknell. Hill's son Walter came to live with them, and Hill's household was again happy.[32]

Still, Hill was no longer content at Lewisburg. He had changed the University greatly, but it was still a small college in a small country town, and he felt isolated in an intellectual sense. He wanted to go abroad again for a year of study and travel, even if it meant giving up the presidency. And anyway, he confided to President Donald Coit Gilman of Johns Hopkins University, he would rather be a writer or teacher than an administrator.

In expressing such sentiments, Hill was in some measure no doubt merely bargaining. President Martin B. Anderson of the University of Rochester in western New York was retiring, and Anderson wanted the young president of Bucknell to be his successor. The Rochester trustees, though differing considerably in their expectations, also believed Hill to be the man they wanted, and in June 1888, they unanimously elected him president of their University.

Gilman urged Hill to accept the position, arguing the broad opportunities that Rochester offered for his talents. So did President Elias H. Johnson of Crozer Theological Seminary, a Rochester alumnus who had urged his election at Rochester for fear he would otherwise be lost from Baptist educational institutions. At the behest of Dr. Edward Bright, president of Rochester's board of trustees, Johnson also wrote to Juliet, describing the city's exceptional beauty, cultivated atmosphere, and pleasant social life, into which, he assured her, no one would be more readily welcomed than she. After visiting briefly with Anderson in Rochester and conferring in New York City for forty-five minutes with a committee of the Rochester trustees, Hill accepted when the trustees agreed to grant him an immediate leave of absence at half pay for a year of study and travel in Europe.[33]

Declaring that Hill's resignation would be "the greatest loss that could befall our University," the trustees at Bucknell offered him a year's leave of absence at full pay, pledged to do everything within their power to better the institution, and promised to build a new President's House. This not availing, they voted in mid-July to accept his resignation immediately while continuing his salary to September 1, explaining that it was not fair to keep him working until the day he was scheduled to leave for Europe. They also appreciated that he was going abroad for a year, for it lessened the chances of Bucknell students following him to Rochester.[34]

In Europe, Hill made Berlin his headquarters while he nosed about Germany's leading universities, inspecting their facilities and talking with their professors. Happening upon G. Stanley Hall, who was similarly spending the year in Europe before taking up the presidency of newly established Clark University, he went with the noted psychologist to see Switzerland's universities, and then on to Italy, Crete, and Athens. They visited Smyrna, and intended to take in Constantinople, when Hill had to rush back to Berlin. Juliet, who had remained at the German capital studying several languages and attending lectures on art and literature at the Victoria Lyceum, had suffered a nervous breakdown. Hill took her to winter at Nice, then for a few weeks to Algiers, where she could enjoy more sun. They crossed to Hyeres in southern France in April, intending to stop off at Paris before going home early in June when Hill was to deliver his inaugural address at Rochester. But Juliet's health failed to improve enough for the trip. Dr. Bright suggested that Hill come alone to Rochester at the trustees' expense and return to Europe until September. Unwilling to leave Juliet by herself, Hill mailed home his address, which was read by Professor William C. Morey. After spending the summer in Switzerland, where Juliet recovered, the Hills sailed for home late in August to start their new life in Rochester.[35]

2

The Sectarian Challenge

ROCHESTER WAS AS PLEASANT AND CULTIVATED A CITY AS DR. JOHNSON
had said. Its clubs and literary societies welcomed the Hills. David
became a favorite after-dinner speaker, and Juliet a popular
hostess. They had the pleasure of children, for twins, Catherine J.
Packer and David Jayne, Jr., were born in May 1890. But in their
expectations of finding a less provincial university they were disappointed. Anxious to escape from a small-town environment,
Hill had been too casual in his investigation. The University of
Rochester was almost as untouched by the revolution in higher
education as Lewisburg had been a decade before, and more dis-
couraging still, there were Baptist die-hards who seemed determined
that it stay that way. Ultimately, Hill gave the University the priceless
gift of a new spirit, but at the cost of a sectarian reaction that blighted
seven years of effort.

The University had been founded in 1850 by Baptists of New
York tired of the provincialism, theological quarrels, and financial
troubles wracking Madison University, their only institution of
higher learning in the state, tucked away in the little village of
Hamilton. They first tried to move Madison to Rochester, where

local Baptists had long wanted a college, but when this plan was blocked in the courts by residents of Hamilton, they established an entirely new university, which promptly attracted most of Madison's professors and many of its students. The University's founders promised that while it would be of Christian character and controlled by their denomination, its educational policy would be liberal and nonsectarian, and in neither its charter nor plan of instruction did they make mention of denominational status. When Martin B. Anderson became its first president in 1854, he announced a similar intention to promote liberal Christian education rather than sectarian interests, and during his administration students from all churches attended the University, several of its professors and trustees were men of other denominations, and the principal donors of its campus and buildings were non-Baptists.[1]

Yet people in Rochester generally thought of the University as being exclusively Baptist. According to Dr. Edward M. Moore, a non-Baptist trustee who became president of the board in 1893, pleas for assistance usually met with the reply, "Oh, it's a Baptist institution—let the Baptists take care of it." Anderson continually insisted that the University's ends were not denominational, but his words were largely ignored, for his social relations with the community were slim, and those few he had were almost exclusively with Baptists. More effective in forming local attitudes was the presence in the city of the Rochester Theological Seminary, an institution established at the same time as the University by the exodus from Hamilton, which, never content with furthering only its own properly denominational interests, constantly sought to force a denominational policy on the University as well. Anderson always resisted these attempts as best he could in view of his continued dependence upon Baptist funds, and there was generally a want of good will between the two institutions, but the University nevertheless, in the words of one prominent alumnus, "kept taking on more and more, the character of a Baptist nursery."[2]

On other matters Anderson was less liberal. Although believing that college instruction should be broad and up-to-date, he had an exaggerated conception of the value of classical studies and no patience whatever with the elective system. Consequently, while the curriculum did expand during his long administration, the University did not keep pace with more progressive colleges elsewhere, including newer, competitive colleges in western New York and in states to the west, from which it had originally drawn many students. Anderson also refused to institute a dormitory system, believing that the manners and morals of the students would be better safeguarded if they lived with private families. By thus compelling the boys to find their own accommodations, which they generally did in boarding houses of no greater refinement than dormitories, he unwittingly further discouraged students coming from outside the city.[3]

When Hill took over the University it had eleven professors, several of whom were of unquestioned ability, and it had a pleasant campus with three substantial buildings in an attractive part of the town. But its curriculum was outmoded, its growth had long since stopped at less than 175 students, and it was becoming chiefly a college for candidates for the ministry and for local boys who could not go elsewhere. Baptists were niggardly in their support, alumni and local assistance was weak, and annual income seldom met expenditures. According to William S. Kimball, a wealthy Rochester businessman whom Hill persuaded to become a trustee, "It was fast dying of dry-rot."[4]

President Anderson had ruled the University with a rod of iron, and this too added to Hill's difficulties. At Lewisburg he had himself filled a patriarchal role, personally supervising nearly everything in the life of the college, but, knowing that the patriarchal college belonged to the past, he wanted the trustees, faculty, and alumni at Rochester to share initiative and responsibility with him. But the habits of the three-and-a-half decades were not easily changed; everyone waited for the new president to move, and no one would act until he did. Some faculty members interpreted his policy as "a want of Presidential Enterprise," and one professor resigned for lack of confidence in the new administration.[5]

For several years the only noticeable result of Hill's new approach was the creation by the faculty in 1889 of a committee to

Hill while president of the University of Rochester

revise the curriculum. Although Hill chaired the committee and appointed its other two members, it still seems to have been the first time the faculty assumed responsibility for a question of educational policy. The new curriculum, introduced during the next two years, offered four programs of study. Although the only major difference in them was the amount of classical language required, and most students continued to take the classical program, the revised curriculum marked a revolutionary step at Rochester by permitting the boys to choose about a third of their courses from electives.[6]

Eventually Hill's "cooperative policy" bore greater fruit. The University continued to adopt more courses until by 1896 the number offered had increased from forty-six to ninety-five. A professor was brought in specifically to teach biology, a subject never before named in any University publication, with Hill's assurance that he would not be hampered in teaching the theory of evolution, and provisions were made, for the first time, for teaching physics and geology with laboratory practice. As he had done at Lewisburg, Hill replaced Moral and Intellectual Philosophy, the great old anachronisms he again inherited, with psychology, ethics, and anthropology. Beginnings were also made in University extension and graduate work, which, though of little importance at the moment educationally, further evidenced the University's new vitality. The larger significance of these innovations was only indirectly revealed by the changes appearing in the University catalogue. The new courses and facilities represented, as Professor Joseph H. Gilmore noted in 1894, a great change "in the methods of instruction—the spirit that dominates the new college. Investigation has taken the place of dogmatism."[7]

By this time a new mood was also evident among the students. Anderson had supervised their conduct with the utmost seriousness, but despite all his patient and paternal appeals, the college was pretty rowdy. Hazings, rushes, and scraps went on uninterruptedly, sometimes destroying college property and sometimes erupting in the streets, forcing the local police and courts to take a hand. Indeed, the boys were none too reluctant to start a row just to see

Anderson come into action, charge into them, and scatter them left and right with the two canes upon which he always depended in his later years. Hill was no less patient and certainly no less firm than Anderson, but his appeals hit a more responsive chord. "There is no doubt that a new spirit has entered our university during the last few years," noted the student newspaper, the *Campus*, in March 1894, "not a spirit of sullen obedience generated by strict discipline, but rather a loyal, law-obeying spirit filling the students with deep desires for wellfare [*sic*] of the college." As far as order was concerned, Hill wrote his successor some years later, his last two years at the University were close to ideal. The change had come about very gradually and in a manner he could hardly explain. "One element in it I am sure was a constant appeal to the manliness of the students until at first the best and finally the worst, came to feel ashamed of many things that had formerly been common and which are common in most colleges." The college yearbook, *Interpres*, of 1897 attributed the change "more than all else . . . to the quiet and unostentatious influences of a perfect gentleman, whose genial sympathies have aroused the loyalty, and whose courteous bearing has excited the emulation of the whole student body."[8]

A new interest in competitive sports, which Anderson had never encouraged, helped. A gymnasium and an athletic association, Hill said in his inaugural address, were "a hundred times more effective against rowdyism and barbarism than proctors and informers," and because he also believed that intellectual and physical fitness went together, he assisted the boys in organizing interclass and then intercollegiate football, baseball, track, and other sports. He failed, however, in repeated attempts to stir the alumni into providing a gymnasium, "the most imperative need of the University." Indeed, on one occasion, the alumni dinner of 1895, he, a trustee, and a guest offered among them to give more than two-thirds of the money needed, yet the old grads just sat on their hands as they had all through his administration.[9]

One development of the modern university that Hill did not encourage at Rochester was coeducation. A movement to open the University to women was already on foot in the city when he arrived; with Susan B. Anthony in town it could hardly have been otherwise. Hill had promoted coeducation at Bucknell, but the whole force of the movement here, he thought, lay with parents who wished to give their daughters a college education and could not afford to send them elsewhere, and with a coterie of people who adulated Miss Anthony and saw an opportunity to further their propaganda efforts. It was not a movement likely to benefit the University, whose faculty and resources were already much too inadequate. Several women's clubs in the city insisted that if the college were opened to women they could easily meet the additional costs by raising $300,000 or more, but Hill and some of the trustees knew better from hard experience, and during his administration no action was taken. Women were finally admitted to the University in 1900 after the club ladies had spent two years scraping together $50,000, which the trustees accepted in lieu of $100,000 they had originally stipulated. To complete even that sum Miss Anthony had to pledge her life insurance.[10]

When he came to Rochester, Hill had hoped to raise $500,000 for the University in short order. With that sum, he wrote to Anderson, "we can have and hold the educational leadership of our denomination in this country," and it could be done, he thought, if he could get $300,000 from trustees, alumni, and friends in New York City. He visited New York several times during the next year, but the attitude of Baptists there, he found, was that the University was filling its mission quite well enough. "With the University as it was and the Theological Seminary at Rochester, ministerial education appeared to be pretty well provided for, and that was a sufficient effort for a denominational college!"[11]

If youth were to be educated in a Christian atmosphere, colleges ought to be under denominational control, Hill believed. Universities, whose function was to provide specialized education, should not be. Since the University of Rochester was for the present suited only to be a liberal arts college, it should be so administered and remain denominational. But a narrow and outdated ecclesiastical purpose had no place in his thinking. For more than two decades sectarian colleges had been de-emphasizing ministerial training, liberalizing their curricula, broadening their appeals for financial assistance beyond their denominations, and looking to merchants, bankers, and industrialists rather than to clergymen to fill their boards of trustees. At Lewisburg, Hill had guided the University along these lines without opposition, in part, perhaps, because Baptist control was ensured by its charter and so the question was never raised. But Baptist control of the University of Rochester rested only on moral right, and a number of conservative Baptists, some of whom had inexplicably expected Hill to make the University more sectarian than ever, were soon alarmed by his religious liberalism, his enthusiasm for the sciences, and his appeals to the city, rather than exclusively to Baptists, for financial support.[12]

The first open indication of this apprehension appeared in a report on the commencement week of 1891 in the Philadelphia *National Baptist.* Its author, under the pseudonym, "Rochesterian," commented that President Hill in his baccalaureate sermon, by paying no respect to theological systems or traditional orthodoxy, and representing Christ as having recognized nothing authoritative in the Old Testament, had certainly placed himself in the "advanced wing of religious teachers." In his speech at the alumni dinner, the unidentified reporter also noted, the president had indicated that his policy would be "to appeal, not so much to the Baptist denomination for the support of the University, but rather to the citizens of Rochester and of Western New York." Since liberal Baptists had congratulated Hill for the "courage" and "plain words" of his sermon, no doubt to conservative ears it was unorthodox; and at the alumni dinner he had appealed to the city for support—"for our chief support," one newspaper quoted him. Yet there was an element of misrepresentation in the *National Baptist* report, and, apparently already irked by sectarian criticism, Hill believed that it had been intentionally designed to portray him as a heretic trying to alienate the University from Baptists. Replying in the *National Baptist,* he scathingly said so. From the Reverend J. W. A. Stewart, pastor of the First Baptist Church and member of the Theological Seminary's executive committee, he received a private reply. Stewart protested that he had not written in the spirit Hill supposed, explained why he had written under a pseudonym, and regretted that he had written the account at all.[13] Still, however innocent his intentions, Stewart's report sharpened the fears of conservative Baptists that Hill was out to snatch the University away from them.

These fears dominated a committee of trustees meeting in New York City the following May to consider ways of getting the University out of the red. A Mr. Gates, who was not a trustee but took an active part in the meeting, was certain that Baptists would not give money to the University unless it were absolutely and undeniably under their control and confined itself to Christian education; and he urged that the University and the Seminary be united under the presidency of Dr. Augustus H. Strong, the president of the Seminary. Both he and the Reverend Dr. Robert S. MacArthur, pastor of the Calvary Church of New York City, favored amending the University's charter to require that at least two-thirds of the trustees be members of regular Baptist churches. Protestations by John P. Townsend of New York City that this was probably illegal and surely unnecessary, for no one wanted to take the University away from the denomination, could not dissuade the two conservatives, for their suspicions had been honed the more by an earlier suggestion that the board solve its financial problem by co-opting wealthy men like Chauncey Depew and J. Pierpont Morgan.[14]

At the annual meeting of the trustees the next month, MacArthur moved that at least two-thirds of the board should be members of regular Baptist churches. Several trustees questioned the propriety or necessity of the resolution, but when a motion to table it lost by a vote of six to seven, the board adopted it unanimously. He had proposed the resolution, MacArthur explained in the New York *Christian Inquirer,* to clarify the denominational standing of the University, which was being injured by fears and rumors. It was said that Rochesterians would not give freely to it because it was so strictly denominational, and that many Baptists were afraid to give lest it someday slip from denominational control. Now all doubts could cease; the Baptist churches could heartily support Dr. Hill, and the non-Baptist people of Rochester could take advantage of the generous recognition given them on the board of trustees. However, according to the later testimony of John H. Deane, another trustee of New York City who had attended the meeting there the month before, MacArthur had revealed that his real purpose was to get rid of Hill and elect Dr. Strong. If this was so, the resolution failed to weaken Hill's backing on the board. There were sixteen Baptist members, four non-Baptist, and four vacancies when it was adopted. The board thereupon elected four new members from the Rochester business community, all non-Baptists and all partisans of Hill's effort to bring the city and the University into closer union.[15]

Consequently, rumors about the University continued unabated. "From many different sources we hear the statement made that our college is becoming irreligious, skeptical, heterodox, heretical, and several other dreadful things," commented the *Campus* in March 1893. "The alumni are heard to bewail our low spiritual condition. The people of the city frequently ask us with doubtful accent 'how the battle is going.' Over at the seminary we are sometimes set down as a 'hot-bed of heresy.'" Some professors, the *Campus* explained, were being shamelessly misrepresented by oversensitive students, "trembling for their notions of faith, and ready to take offense at everything not exactly in harmony with it," who simply failed to understand what their instructors were saying. A few professors, it conceded, held unorthodox views and perhaps at times overemphasized them, "but never have we heard anything . . . at variance with our notions that need move a jot the simple, living faith of the most sincere follower of Christ. On the contrary, these very things, that some find so disturbing to their peace of mind, have been to us a means of clarifying our vision, and broadening, deepening, testing and strengthening the foundations of our faith in the essentials of Christianity."[16]

But it was precisely this attitude of religious liberalism, which smacked of Hill's teaching of the sole essentiality of Christ, that Baptist die-hards found upsetting. And Hill soon set them on edge the more. To show that the University was not merely a stronghold of Baptist interests, he preached the baccalaureate sermon that June in the Central Presbyterian Church instead of in the First Baptist Church where the service had previously been held, and then followed this at the alumni dinner with a new plea for community support. "Let us arise as one man and say that we will build for our city and in the cause of honest education," he exhorted. "The day has gone by for any small number to build an institution for a small purpose. Humanity is larger than any creed or sect. Let us say, one and all, we will build here on this campus a university whose foundations shall be laid upon truth and righteousness. That is a sufficient creed for union in a great work like this, although every man's personal creed will probably exceed it."[17]

The reaction came thundering in two weeks later in a letter to the New York *Examiner* excoriating both events as implementations of Hill's scheme to hand the University over to whoever would furnish the money to build it up. "Rochester," for the letter was again pseudonymous, was dismayed that Baptists should surrender without a struggle the advantage that possession of the University gave the denomination "for the moral defense of its distinguishing principles." Insisting that this did not require the University to be sectarian in any narrow sense, "Rochester" in the same breath spoke of "the narrow range of aims in which it has hitherto been held" and of surrender "to alien control with reference to alien interests." "There are, indeed, those who think and say," he commented, "that a man who was elected as a Baptist to administer a college under Baptist control is not true to his trust if he seeks to place it upon foundations other than those laid for him by those who established the institution."

Editorially, the *Examiner* disputed that anyone wanted to make the University anything but a Baptist institution in the only sense it ever was one and deplored the tone of the letter, but as this was the first time anyone had ventured to say in public what many had been whispering in private, it thought it better for all concerned if the matter were discussed openly rather than by "winks and shrugs and innuendos." The *Examiner*'s editor was Henry C. Vedder, a Rochester alumnus and later a trustee, who privately implored Hill to answer the letter promptly. He was astonished by the industry and success with which an anti-Hill

faction had been propagating their views, Vedder wrote. Hill
had once hinted that he might be hounded out of the University
by their underhanded work, Vedder recalled, and he was afraid
that this would happen unless Hill answered and silenced those
who were traducing him. Trustees Myron G. Peck and Martin
W. Cooke were of the same opinion. They thought the letter
was inspired by the Seminary, and Cooke suspected it was written
by the Reverend Dr. Henry E. Robins, its Professor of Christian
Ethics.[18]

Hill already believed that the Seminary was behind the campaign against him, and several recent communications from Dr.
Strong had hardened his convictions. When calling for community
support at the alumni commencement dinner, he had also spoken
of the need for still more courses at the University, whereupon
Strong, who was also at the speakers' table, had handed him a
note and left. "I unfortunately got ready a speech which would
advocate the fixed curriculum and discourage the proper
University idea," Strong had written. "It would seem to cut into
your views and would be all out of place. So let me off, I insist."
He saw now that it would not have been best in any case for him
to advise, Strong wrote a week or so later. He thought he understood Hill's plans better than at first and his mind had been
relieved of fears about Baptist control of the college. "I wish
we could some day have a frank and full conference with regard
to matters of management as well as matters of doctrine," he
added, "but time and work do not seem just now to favor,—that
is, unless you will come down to this resting place of the Saints
and see me." Since Strong had intended to propose at a University
function a policy that he already knew conflicted with Hill's,
and was now suggesting that Hill come to the Seminary to discuss
the University's management and *doctrine,* his words were less
placatory than intended. He was glad to hear that Strong's mind
was relieved about Baptist control of the college, Hill lashed back.
Now an anonymous correspondent was charging him with
denominational treason. He would not imply that this misguided
zeal had the official sanction of the Seminary, but he intended to
state in the *Examiner* that the hostility toward him arose from

the same desire on the part of a few to hold the University merely tributary to the Seminary against which Dr. Anderson had struggled all his life, and that now, in order to unite the two institutions, a secret movement was afoot to force him out. Strong protested that he knew of no such plotting and would oppose it if he did. The old ill-feeling between the University and the Seminary had been a purely personal affair, he explained. The present trouble had another origin. Hill had sometimes said things susceptible of two interpretations, and his own friends had reported him as saying it would be better to make the University undenominational in order to secure greater support. All future difficulty might be prevented, Strong suggested, if Hill would show more interest in the Baptist churches of Rochester, and his own church in particular, for he had not identified himself with his own denomination as his predecessor had.[19] Since Strong was obviously referring to Hill's sometime attendance at a Presbyterian church with Juliet, his words were again less than mollifying.

There was no new policy at the University, Hill wrote in the *Examiner*. Every step he had taken was in the spirit of President Anderson's counsels to him. It was those who wanted the University controlled by the Seminary for strictly denominational purposes, and were determined that it should have Baptist money on no other terms, who were trying to force a new course. Let his critics give a bill of particulars over a genuine signature, he challenged, and then he would compare records with them.

To no one's surprise, it was Dr. Robins who replied. With a lengthy list of particulars, including Hill's recent appeal to the community, his appeal of two years before, and even the surprising argument that Dr. Anderson's "broad-minded and sagacious policy" had necessarily died with the man and Hill as another person had to be following a new policy, Robins sought to prove that a new policy did indeed exist at the University that would inevitably put it under alien control. It was also incontestible evidence of something, Robins said, that in order to allay fears for the control of the University the trustees had resolved that two-thirds of their number should be Baptists. But only by counting as Baptists men who did not attend Baptist churches could the two-thirds be made out, and only fourteen of the trustees "ought to be reckoned as Baptists." The character of the four recently elected trustees made this danger to Baptist control immediate, Robins warned, for of the eleven trustees who now resided in Rochester, where actual control of the college necessarily lay, only three could "fairly be classed as Baptists," and of the six members of the executive committee, only two could "be classed as Baptists." The president of the board, Robins went on, was the noble and wise Dr. E. M. Moore, a man to whom the University owed a debt of gratitude it could never repay and who had always acknowledged the moral right of Baptists to control the University. But Dr. Moore was not a Baptist and could not have "a Baptist's instincts" to guide him. He would "naturally and inevitably act along purely secular lines." In making him the head of the board, "a vast step was taken in putting the college under undenominational control." Finally Robins came to Hill's preaching of the baccalaureate sermon in the church of another denomination. It was not merely to express interdenominational goodwill, it was to further Hill's purpose of basing the University's administration upon a creed of "truth and righteousness"—"a creed, without further explanation, altogether too narrow for Baptists to stand upon." It was an event that marked "a period of decline in Baptist prestige and power in Rochester."[20]

Sending Hill a passage from Dr. Anderson's inaugural address in which the late president had appealed for community support on the same basis as had Hill at the recent alumni dinner, Professor William C. Morey, who had been with the University for twenty-nine years, remonstrated: "To those who knew Dr. Anderson it seems a species of puerile folly to use his name as a shield behind which to advocate any sectarian views of a liberal education. . . . Your friends regard your position that there is 'no new policy at Rochester' as solid. The only novelty that the situation presents is the indiscreet and unprecedented effrontery on the part of the disaffected few in publicly announcing that the University should be more of a Baptist institution than it has ever been before." To Professor Henry E. Burton, who had spent twelve years at the University with Anderson, Robins's contentions were "absurdities"; the policy of the University was no different than before, it was simply that non-Baptists were responding more heartily to appeals for their interest and sympathy.[21]

Rebutting in the *Examiner*, Hill point by point reduced Robins's particulars to a collection of fears and misrepresentations arising from the Reverend's own strictly sectarian ideal for the University. So little remained of them, commented Vedder in an accompanying editorial, that until somebody was ready to name the Baptist trustees who would betray their denomination and the non-Baptists who would violate their honor, further discussion of the subject would be a waste of good white paper and printers' ink.[22]

But if Baptist control of the University was as firm as Vedder seemed to think, conservative Baptists might still wonder to what end. In an address to the national Baptist Congress in Philadelphia the year before, Hill had extolled higher criticism and practically thrown everything but Christ out of Christianity.[23] If there were still any lingering doubts about his heresy, he removed them in the fall of 1893 with the publication of a book on philosophy that denied any room at all to orthodox theology.

A broadly ambitious work, *Genetic Philosophy* was Hill's reconciliation of science and religion for which he had been groping since youth. Claiming to be completely scientific and inductive of method in extending real order of phenomena ideally in time and space beyond the perception of the senses, Hill explored the genesis of matter, life, consciousness, feeling, thought, will, art, morality, religion, and science in order to form a consistent picture of the world. His investigations, however, invariably led him into metaphysical rather than scientific problems. With hardly the pretense of scientific demonstration, the universe became a monistic entity, an expression of "will" or "force" or "Dynamic Reason," of which mind and matter were two aspects held together in dynamic unity. Where dualism left a "chasm" between phenomena, to be filled in by faith, the "unknowable," or left vacant, Hill explained, scientific monism placed "Dynamic Reason, with all the possibilities of hope and faith grounded upon reality." The Supreme Being, as known to science, was both reason and energy, "infinite to our understanding, but not altogether 'unknowable.'" "The elemental concomitance of the psychic and the physical in being as known to us," he reasoned analogically, "indicates the existence of a psychic unity above our own which may be called cosmic; and if this is not personal, it is because it is more than personal, surpassing the limits within which we are accustomed to circumscribe personality as manifested in ourselves."[24]

Scholarly reviews, unable to find the scientific basis that Hill claimed for his conclusions, saw little in *Genetic Philosophy* that threatened to turn the world of philosophy on end. "Suggestive as the book is," *Oxford Magazine* commented typically, "it is rather useful as a well-written popular sketch of the recent work in various sciences than as a philosophy. Those who can make nothing of the results will be able to find much satisfaction in some of the studies preparatory to the result." Many Baptist journals were critical for quite another reason. The Indianapolis *Baptist*, distressed because Hill's system led to pantheism, worried about students in the University of Rochester's classroom of systematic theology. The Boston *Watchman*, while conceding that the book showed candor and courage, took pains to identify its author for parents who were deliberating where to send their children to college. Several Baptist reviews found Hill's interpretation of the universe materialistic, and almost all took a dim view of his monism. Henry C. Vedder of the *Examiner,* who thought the book's logic irrefutable, balanced praise with misgivings, for it seemed "to have its end in a materialistic pantheism, of all the philosophies the most dreary and the least reconcilable with Christianity."[25]

Philosophy by itself was necessarily inadequate to the needs of Christian theology, and he had written as a philosopher rather than a theologian, Hill explained to Vedder. Suppose, however, that he write an article for the *Examiner* showing that genetic philosophy was entirely in harmony with religious conscience? Nothing would be more welcome, Vedder replied, for it would close the mouths of people who were as busy as ever circulating reports of irreligion at the University. Unfortunately, the article was scarcely conducive to that end. Although ably arguing that his doctrines were not pantheistic, that his conclusions were theistic rather than materialistic, and that monism was supported by both reason and the Scriptures, Hill gave short shrift to orthodox theology. It was historically a patchwork creation of revelation and pagan speculation, lacked inner coherence, and needed to be thoroughly rehabilitated in the light of scholarship and science. When theologians themselves could agree as to what it was, he would undertake to see how far his own doctrines could be reconciled with it. This undisguised scorn took even the *Examiner* aback.[26]

In March 1894, while Baptist journals were still clucking over *Genetic Philosophy*, Hill delivered the Levering Lectures at Johns Hopkins University. Speaking on "Religion in the Light of Science," he outlined the struggle waged throughout history by science, conscience, and scholarship against theological oppression; called for untrammeled scientific investigation, confident that the authority of the Bible would remain unimpaired; rejected the elaboration of creeds; and, as always, emphasized the prepotent role of Christ in Christianity. The Levering Lectures were annual discourses devoted to the defense and promotion of Christianity, and owing to the recent publication of Hill's book, reported the *National Baptist* and the *Examiner,* particular attention was attracted to them that year.[27]

Sales of *Genetic Philosophy* were disappointingly small, but it received enough publicity in Baptist journals, along with Hill's addresses at Philadelphia and Baltimore, to satisfy conservative Baptists beyond doubt that modernism had taken over the University of Rochester. The last straw for some die-hards was laid in January 1895, when Hill decided to make an unmistakable declaration of policy. In order to draw support from the whole of western New York, as it should, he told a meeting of the local alumni, the University must enter upon a new course of development. In every college the transitional point to public usefulness and greatness had been the abandonment of the purely ecclesiastical aim of replenishing the ministry, an aim that subordinated knowledge to dogma. The University of Rochester had started right in this regard; its founders had wanted to educate men in general rather than ministers in particular, and to join with non-Baptists in this work, and no honest man had ever doubted the institution's Christian character. Later, a retrogressive spirit had appeared. Although this spirit had not triumphed or shown much strength, the plain course of the University was to maintain the purpose of its founders.[28]

On March 4 the Genesee Baptist Ministerial Association, meeting at the Theological Seminary, responded with a formal set of resolutions declaring that the University had been founded in the interests of the Baptist denomination, had been held true to that end throughout the administration of Dr. Anderson, and should continue to be held true to that end. This did not involve a narrow sectarianism, the ministers said, but it did require "that in the weight and ability of its teaching force, its governing officers and executive agents, the denomination which it represents shall be easily foremost; . . . that the influence of every classroom shall be unequivocally Christian in the sense which Baptists put upon that term; and . . . that in order that the education given in the University may be Christian in this sense, it must be held close to the heart of the churches of the denomination which gave it life."[29]

Special invitations to the meeting had been sent out, an alumnus of the University of Rochester, one of the very few present, had been selected to present the resolutions, and they were immediately released to local and denominational newspapers. But who wrote and promoted them was never disclosed. Direct questioning by Hill and Cooke of several of the clergymen as to why they had taken this action brought only vague replies about injured Bapist sensibilities and "current tendencies." The Reverend Frederick L. Anderson, pastor of the Second Baptist Church and member of the Seminary executive committee, was no less vague from the height of his pulpit. "Current tendencies," he explained, had persuaded the ministers that the University was in real danger of being taken from the denomination's control, and they felt it their duty to declare that if origination, money, labor, and possession counted for anything, it was a Baptist institution. "To take it out of Baptist hands, either formally or virtually, is simply stealing. It is easy to be liberal with other people's institutions and other people's money. We do not propose to look on and see our property stolen without protest. It strikes us as a question of common honesty." It was at best an ill-tempered tirade, yet Dr. Strong stated for the newspapers that he endorsed every word of Dr. Anderson's address, just as he had endorsed the resolutions. The Reverend C. A. Barbour, president of the Ministerial Association, however, later publicly declared that he had been misled into voting for the resolutions by statements that he afterwards learned were untrue.[30]

The resolutions had to be answered, Hill told the executive committee of the trustees, for they were an attack on the University designed to convert it to purely ecclesiastical ends, and they brought into question the fidelity of every member of the corporation. For the full board, meeting in June, he historically documented that the University's purpose as interpreted by its founders and by Dr. Anderson had always been educational, not ecclesiastical, and he called upon the trustees to reaffirm that purpose in order to remove all doubts about the institution's future policy. The committee charged with considering his report then endorsed it, in language no one could misunderstand, with an emphatic declaration of the University's independence from ecclesiastical interference. The trustees approved both reports without a dissenting vote, though perhaps with one or two unwilling ones.[31] There was never again any question as to what the intellectual stance of the University would be.

Hill had broken the University away from an outdated patriarchal mold and equally outdated ecclesiastical meddling. He had modernized its instruction and infused its students, faculty, and trustees with new enthusiasm. Equally significant, his whole administration had been one of a new appeal to the community on a credo of expanded usefulness; and he did arouse in the city an interest that would ultimately help make the University the institution he envisaged. But the translation of this interest into financial support to the measure needed was just beginning. Between 1888 and 1895, gifts to the University amounted to over $357,000, virtually a third as much as had been raised in the previous thirty-seven years of its existence, and over sixty percent of it came from non-Baptists. Yet because of its considerably enlarged program, the University still had a small annual deficit. To sustain its work at the level it had reached required at least $100,000 additional endowment, Hill reported to the trustees in June 1895, and unless this were obtained the work that should go on expanding would have to be reduced.[32] Before the year was out, an unprecedented expression of community interest in the University promised, briefly, to provide this sum.

The day after the trustee meeting, Hill handed Dr. Moore his resignation, to take effect any time in the coming year convenient for the University. He had intended to present it at the meeting but had deferred to advice that it would be best for the University if it were not made public until shortly before he was to leave. Despite the board's emphatic endorsement of his policy, he knew that his work at the University could never be wholly congenial, and it was a step he had long been considering. The past unpleasantness had not affected him alone; Juliet, as one of the "aliens," had been made the subject of whispered scandal for having led him so far astray as to be married, take communion, and have their children christened in her church. Hill also had new ambitions. Like not a few college presidents of those years, he looked longingly to a diplomatic post abroad, an aspiration probably kindled by his friendship with Andrew D. White, president of Cornell University and former United States Ambassador to Russia. He also wanted to write a history of the diplomacy of Europe, an idea inspired by Professor Morey, for which a diplomatic mission in Europe would ideally offer leisure and opportunity for research. The inadequacy of diplomatic salaries at attractive posts presented no great problem, for Juliet's mother had recently bequeathed them an estate of $200,000.[33]

That autumn Hill prevailed on the trustees to make his resignation known, and on November 20 the local papers announced that he would leave the University in June. The next day every student in the college joined in petitioning him to stay. The faculty published an open letter, signed by every member, defending his administration and urging him to remain. In the next few weeks various educational, religious, professional, and business organizations in the city similarly petitioned him not to leave. The Chamber of Commerce appointed a special committee to confer with the trustees on how he could be induced to stay, and the trustees appointed a special committee to request him to reconsider.[34]

On December 10 Hill promised the trustee committee he would give them a definite answer on January 1. Meantime, a member of the Chamber of Commerce committee suggested that Rochesterians give him the auditorium and gymnasium he had asked for at the last commencement, an inducement to remain which the Rochester *Herald* promptly raised to a quarter of a million dollars and the other dailies took up. On December 20 the Chamber of Commerce announced it would raise $100,000 by popular subscription—the $250,000 figure was discarded as beyond reach and not necessary—which on Hill's advice would be used to support free scholarships for local boys, which had been causing annual deficits. On January 1, though the Chamber had secured pledges for only $20,000, it assured Hill the whole sum could soon be raised and asked for a chance to find out exactly how much the people of Rochester thought of their university. Although he apparently never contemplated withdrawing his resignation, Hill was reluctant to discourage this unique civic effort and agreed to postpone his final answer. In the next few weeks, however, the Chamber was able to raise only $10,000 more, and finally on March 7 Hill informed the trustees that he could not withdraw his resignation without sacrificing personal plans he greatly desired to carry out. He hoped the scholarship endowment drive would continue, but the Chamber dropped it, blaming the financial stringency of the times.[35]

Without added endowment, the University was left with hard days still ahead. Yet the fact that the city's business community had sponsored a fund-raising drive at all was witness to a new relationship developing between the college and the city. Though an unpleasant personal experience, Hill's clash with Baptists determined to hold the institution to sectarian ends had finally brought about acceptance in Rochester of the idea that the University existed, as Hill said, for purposes "larger than any creed or sect."

3

Assistant Secretary of State

IN 1896 ALMOST THE ONLY WAY TO GET INTO THE FOREIGN SERVICE of the United States was to be rewarded for political services..Wholly lacking in career provisions whereby trained and experienced men, selected and promoted on a basis of merit, would represent the United States abroad, the diplomatic and consular services were for the most part filled with spoilsmen, ranging from millionaire industrialists to ordinary political hacks, appointed solely for their assistance in getting somebody else into political office. The pressure for place, intensified at least in the lower positions by the extension of the civil service system in other departments, was almost indescribable. Hill would certainly never have thought of himself as a scrambling spoilsman, but wanting a place in the diplomatic corps, he set out by the only means available to get it.

Hill already had some claim as a deserving petitioner. He had often delivered addresses and presided at local Republican party meetings, and there was no question of his fidelity to party doctrine. Back in 1891, for example, when former Representative William McKinley had come to town to debate the tariff issue with Representative Roger Q. Mills of Texas, he was selected to do the after-dinner speaking honors at the inevitable party banquet. Directing his remarks to the occasion, he delivered a spread-eagle attack on professors of political economy because they generally favored tariff reduction: they were misguided, metaphysical dreamers trying to apply the insular, free-trade ideas of the Manchester School—doctrines that were not only unsound but un-American as well—to a continental people. "I affirm that when a man claims there is no difference between the people of this nation and those of any other he has no American spirit," he orated. "I affirm that he is no patriot." Not to be outdone in equating party principles with Americanism, McKinley congratulated Rochester on having such a president for its university: "If we had more like him in the colleges of the country we would have fewer free traders and more Americans."[1]

Later that year Hill published a statement, "Why I Am a Protectionist," in the *American Economist*. He repeated the customary arguments about industrial independence, higher wages, lower prices, and the needs of a continental nation, but the deepest root of his adherence to a protective policy, he said, was a moral one. In order to work out the great political problem of mankind, the nation had been divinely endowed with great material advantages for building up a free, intelligent and happy people, and it must not impoverish itself and deny its destiny by sharing its birthright with others. Free trade would give to every other country all the advantages that belonged to America by putting its labor into open competition with the labor of Europe and Asia. Free immigration at least obliged the participant in American prosperity to come to America, but free trade would send him the fruits of American industry without the trouble of crossing the ocean. "Whether it be against foreign goods, ideas or men, I would raise a protecting barrier that would secure this God-given continent to the preservation and development of the institutions of our fathers. The article in our political creed that most needs emphasis is 'America for Americans.'"[2]

Hill often voiced the nativist reaction building up in the nineties as a swelling tide of immigration from Southern and Eastern Europe filled American cities with strange people too unlike the descendents of earlier immigrants to be trusted. In 1895, for example, he warned the New England Society at its annual dinner in New York City that the nation had no greater peril than the importation of men and ideas hostile to its native civilization. Patriotism could not be generated by an ocean voyage or taught by the pictorial symbols of a blanket ballot. "To place the supreme right of sovereignty in the hands of men who have no part in the nation, either by education or ancestry," he pontificated to the society's applause, "is to expose our splendid heritage of law and liberty to the devastation of Goths and Vandals, and to offer our cities as booty and pillage to the merciless Alarics of municipal corruption."[3]

American nationality represented the widest extension of the purest political principles on the face of the earth, Hill declared to the Rochester G.A.R. in April 1896, and for the nation not to protect its markets, its prosperity, and its destiny as a commercial and industrial agent in the world was to deny the principle of nationality. By this time the money issue was overshadowing all others, and Hill's views on it were equally congenial to most Republicans. The highest function of a sovereign state was to maintain the standard by which all values were measured, he told the old veterans. The money of a country was the medium through which equity and justice were secured, and to debase it, or make it equivocal, was as criminal as to poison men's food or water. "Curses and the brand of infamy," he fulminated, "are the penalty of the politician or the party that ventures in the hope of gain to sully the national honor, or defraud the laborer of his hire, by corrupting the money of the people."[4]

A few months earlier, Hill had begun writing editorials for the Rochester *Post Express*, which under new management had recently switched from an independent to a Republican position. At first he devoted himself mainly to censuring President Cleveland's policies in Hawaii and Venezuela, but as the Republican National Convention at St. Louis in June drew near, he turned his attention to it. The local Republican organization, obeying the dictate of Thomas C. Platt, the state's party boss, supported the favorite son candidacy of Governor Levi P. Morton. The *Post Express,* however, was one of the first papers in the state to come out for McKinley, with Hill urging that Morton withdraw and the New York delegation unite behind the Ohioan on the first ballot. Cautiously, though, Hill avoided aligning himself with an attack that was being made on the local party machine in the name of McKinley's candidacy. Part of a Good-Government reform movement begun two years before, its real purpose was to overthrow George W. Aldridge, the well-entrenched Republican boss of Monroe County. Seizing the opportunity it offered to write to McKinley, Hill informed the heavily favored candidate that the city's Republican businessmen were almost unanimously of the opinion that the attack was a mistake and they could best serve his interests by not revolting against the party organization. Many Rochester Republicans merely wished to see a complimentary vote given to Governor Morton, he explained, after which they wanted their delegates to vote for their real choice. Asking how he could best promote the Ohioan's candidacy, Hill hoped that he might also be allowed to speak in the campaign once the nomination was won. McKinley, always circumspect about what he committed to paper, replied that surely Hill could understand that he could not interfere with the endeavors of electors in the various states to give expression to their sentiments.[5]

Following McKinley's nomination at St. Louis on the first ballot, Rochester's Republicans, hoping to get the jump on the rest of the country, hastened to open his campaign with a huge ratification rally. They wanted Hill to deliver the main address, and since he had already gone to his summer home in Cohasset, Massachusetts, the rally was held on July 2, the earliest date on which he could return. With all the hoopla of old-time campaigns, the evening's speakers were escorted in an open carriage by a regimental band and the Republican marching clubs of the city from the home of their paramount orator on University Avenue to spacious Fitzhugh Hall. Hill's speech was of course a partisan one at a partisan affair, filled with the magic of protectionism and gold, but in its animadversions of the Democracy and waving of the bloody shirt it was, for a "scholar in politics," clap-trap beyond belief. Perhaps Hill affronted his own intellect. The next day, as one who had "much to learn in practical politics," he asked George Aldridge for his opinion of the political wisdom of it.[6]

Still, more than ambition had stoked Hill's words. Like many men that year, he believed the nation stood at Armageddon. "We seem to me to be at present in the most critical state since the breaking out of the rebellion," he wrote to Andrew D. White the next week. "Another revolution is upon us, and the American people are once more before the judgement-seat of history." The more he studied it, the more the proposition to coin silver without limit at 16 to 1 grew in stupidity and infamy until it seemed almost diabolical. "The Republican party now goes forth to battle against hell let loose." Dr. White agreed. The crisis the nation faced was in some respects even greater than that of 1861, he thought. That had involved merely wreck; this involved wreck and dishonor.[7]

The rally, nevertheless, marked a rise in Hill's political stock, especially when Lewis P. Ross, president of the Rochester Republican Businessmen's Association and chairman of the meeting, proposed sending him to the United States Senate. Not surprised, for he had known for months that his friends were likely to spring a senatorial boom, he did not take it seriously, knowing the office was beyond his reach. Not sure, either, of a diplomatic appointment, he cast a more hopeful if momentary eye on the Monroe County seat in the House of Representatives, which usually went to whomever the Republicans nominated. A number of Rochester Republicans, dissatisfied with Congressman Henry C. Brewster, favored his candidacy when it was suggested by Francis P. Mitchell, owner of the *Post Express*. The idea died aborning, however, since George Aldridge, with whom the nomination really rested, felt that Brewster had "paid for two terms."[8]

Hill was more interested, in any event, in having Aldridge's backing for a diplomatic position, and Aldridge, for his part, wanted a favor. The county boss, then State Superintendent of Public Works aspired to the governor's chair. He had the blessings of Tom Platt, and through patronage and corruption on the New York State Canal had lined up more delegates to the convention at Saratoga in August than any of the dozen other hopefuls that the strength of gold sentiment in New York had brought out.[9] Completing his preparations, Aldridge chose Hill to head the Rochester delegation and place his name in nomination. The former president of the city's university would not be just another politician presenting a candidate to other politicians; his recommendation supposedly would be personal and carry more force because of his freedom from political obligations.

But Aldridge was not without handicaps. Beset by a Good-Government movement in his own city, he was also under attack by a state Civil Service Reform Association for corruption on the canal. And while Hill was slow to appreciate the risk of taking his first step into statewide politics tied to an arraigned boss, some of his friends were not. For his own good, Charles E. Bostwick and Martin J. Calihan, who were charged with making out the list of Rochester delegates, ignored the understanding that had been reached and omitted his name from the slate altogether. Learning of it indirectly at Cohasset, failing to understand the reason for it, and thoroughly incensed, Hill phoned Aldridge and arranged to make the nomination anyway. A few days later he received an explanation from Bostwick and advice from four other politically experienced people not to compromise himself. Thereupon, with only a week left before the convention opened, he begged off, lamely explaining to Aldridge that he was being falsely accused in the press of making the nomination solely for his own political advancement—a charge that had in fact appeared in the Brooklyn *Eagle*—and he could not be put before the public in that light.[10]

From Saratoga, Aldridge peremptorily wired that it was his earnest wish that Hill come there as early as possible. Hill came, but not until the evening before the convention opened, and he still refused to make the nomination the next day. Desperate for a last-minute substitute of suitable reputation, Aldridge was forced to turn to Rochester Judge William A. Sutherland, whose personal feelings toward him were not friendly. Perhaps intentionally, Sutherland's speech was of the kind to kill a candidate. It was overly eulogistic, too long, and smacked of defiance of Tom Platt and all other party leaders.[11]

After three ballots with Aldridge leading, Platt pulled the rug out from under him by switching his support to Frank S. Black of

Troy. Aldridge was being so fiercely attacked by the independent press that McKinley's political manager, Marcus Hanna, had warned that he would weaken the national ticket in New York. But Platt's sudden switch was perhaps for another reason. Aldridge was using his patronage on the canal to build up a state-wide organization,[12] and the defiant tone of Sutherland's nominating speech may have jolted the state boss into perceiving a threat to his own machine. Whether or not Aldridge read the events this way, he was furious with Hill and ready to even the score.

This was Hill's only blunder in gathering political negotiables. Reputed to be one of the best orators in the state, and having made it known that he was anxious to take the stump for McKinley, he was asked to campaign by the Republican State Committee. His first assignment, magnificent in opportunity for a newcomer, was to share the stage with former President Harrison and eminent party strategist Chauncey Depew at the formal opening of the Republican national campaign at Carnegie Hall on August 27. His speech, which dealt with the money question as a great moral issue, was brief, restrained, and effective. The next day, General Powell Clayton, chairman of the speakers bureau of the National Committee, invited him to work with the higher organization. In constant demand for sound-money speeches in New York and Massachusetts, Hill also spoke at his own request in northern Ohio.[13] Speeches there were more likely to come to the attention of McKinley, ensconced on his front porch at Canton.

More important than his work on the stump, for the party had hundreds of orators, was Hill's authorship of a little pamphlet entitled *A Primer of Finance: An Honest Dollar the Basis of Prosperity*. With seemingly irrefutable facts and figures it presented the muddled money question with convincing logic and clarity from the gold point of view. It was the armory of sound-money arguments used by the party's army of campaign speakers, and it was so heavily demanded for general distribution that the National Committee was compelled to print two editions of over 100,000 copies each. General William M. Osborne, the committee's secretary, rated it among the best things the committee published, while the Brooklyn *Daily Times,* describing Hill as "one of the picturesque figures" of the campaign, pronounced it the "simple truth to say that the doctor has probably done as much to convert the voters of this country to sound money and McKinley as any other one man."[14]

The election over, Hill set out to collect his reward. He day-dreamed about the embassy at Berlin, but realistically bid for the less highly prized legation at Brussels. Although plans for a delegation from Rochester to deliver a sheaf of endorsements from prominent politicians, businessmen, educators, lawyers, and writers to McKinley personally at Canton went awry, and although George Aldridge managed for a short time to stay Congressman Brewster and Boss Platt, who had been elected to the Senate by an obedient legislature, from helping him, Hill marshaled enough influence to win the President's assurance, when Brewster brought him to the White House in March 1897, that he would not be overlooked.[15]

Later that month, however, hopes for the Belgian mission vanished when McKinley appointed Andrew D. White to Berlin. General Horace Porter, the leading fund-raiser for the party in the recent campaign, had already been given the French embassy, and with two ambassadorships going to New York, the Belgian legation was not likely to be added to the state's quota of diplomatic appointments. It went to Bellamy Storer of Ohio, a lieutenant of Secretary of State John Sherman. Although skeptical of success, Senator Platt pressed McKinley to give Hill the next post in importance still vacant, the legation at Madrid, arguing that since the appointments of Porter and White were the personal ones of the President, they should not be charged against the state organization, which was entitled to at least one diplomatic mission. Unimpressed, McKinley appointed Stewart L. Woodford of Brooklyn. With prospects of a legation dimming, Hill hoped the President might make him consul general at Berlin if White suggested it—or even consul at Dresden if nothing else were practicable, Juliet soon urged—but White advised them against striking for a consular position, warning that it was not likely to give much satisfaction.[16]

Early in May, Hill had another audience at the White House, this time in company with John Van Voorhis of Rochester, who had sat with McKinley in Congress. If William R. Day had not accepted the assistant secretaryship of state, the President confided, he would have given the post to Hill. He still had Hill constantly in mind, he assured them, and would some day send his name to the Senate without consulting him. Since the possibility of Day's succeeding the aging Sherman was perceived even then, Hill came away buoyed by the hope that the assistant secretaryship might still be offered to him.[17]

Two months later, acting on the advice of Andrew D. White, Hill sailed for Europe to study international law and the history of diplomacy at the Ecole Libre des Sciences Politiques in Paris. He was one of the first Americans to study at this school, the only one in the world that at that time provided scholastic preparation for a career in diplomacy. All his work there was grounding, too, for writing a history of the diplomacy of Europe, for which he compiled a bibliography and did some research in the archives of Paris and London. He and Juliet together attended other lecture courses at the Sorbonne, and enjoyed with the American colony in Paris the winter's social season. "Taking it all together," he wrote to White, "it was a festival year for me, an epoch in my life."[18]

In the spring of 1898, John Van Voorhis and Lewis Ross urged Hill to come home and run for Congress. It would be simply a stepping-stone to the Senate, and his chances were excellent, they assured him. Brewster was out of the race, the other likely aspirants for the Republican nomination were machine men, and as the defeat of Aldridge's candidate for mayor by an insurgent Republican vote in the last city elections had shown, machine men were not running well in Rochester that season. Mitchell would put the *Post Express* behind him, and would even start a morning paper if he would come home to take the chief editorship.[19]

Replying that his ambitions lay in another direction, Hill killed the proposal, though at that moment his prospects for a diplomatic career looked exceptionally bleak. Sherman had just resigned and McKinley had made Judge Day Secretary of State, but he had given the assistant secretaryship to John Basset Moore, a former Assistant Secretary of State and professor of law at Columbia University. He could not conceal a feeling of chagrin over failing to receive the appointment, Hill wrote to Van Voorhis. Carefully constructed, his letter reviewed much that Van Voorhis already knew: their conversation with the President the year before, Hill's unique preparation for diplomatic service, and even the use the party had made of his pamphlet in the recent campaign. Not missing the point, Van Voorhis sent the letter to McKinley. The First Executive had not forgotten Dr. Hill, the President's secretary assured the Rochesterian. But perfunctory to the extreme, the reply seems to have dashed whatever hope Hill had left.[20]

Renting a villa in the seaside town of Scheveningen near The Hague, Hill spent the summer researching in the Dutch archives. He planned to spend the winter back in Paris, working in the Bibliothèque National and the Archives, and had already leased a house, when the news broke that both Day and Moore were resigning in order to go to the coming peace conference with Spain in Paris. By the time Hill learned of it, Van Voorhis had already dashed off letters to McKinley and his new Secretary of State, John Hay, who was still at the American Embassy in London, telling them whom to choose for Assistant Secretary. General William Osborne, now Consul General in London, urged both men to the same decision, and from Paris, Ambassador Porter also contacted Hay. The new Secretary, however, not knowing how things stood in the State Department or what he would have to say about appointing his assistant, left London early in September without committing himself.[21]

On October 2, 1898, Hill received a cable from Hay reading, "Will you accept place assistant secretary and come immediately." Two years of waiting were now climaxed by insistence on haste. Asking if November 1 would be soon enough to be in Washington, because he had to pack and close up in both Scheveningen and Paris, he was requested to start home as early as possible, for he was urgently needed. Since all business in Holland and France took a course of leisurely dignity, it was difficult to get anything done in a hurry. But by dividing their forces, Juliet going to Paris while Hill closed up at Scheveningen, they managed to sail from Liverpool on October 15. Ten days later Hill was sworn into office at Washington as First Assistant Secretary of State.[22]

Ironically, while Hill would have preferred a diplomatic post in Europe, he was to remain in Washington as Assistant Secretary for over four years, longer than all except one of his twenty-four predecessors. Hay relied on him heavily, giving him general oversight of numerous special matters, and because of the Secretary's frequent illnesses, he served exceptionally often as Acting Secretary. "He was a fine Acting Secretary, just as he was a fine Assistant Secretary," wrote the Washington correspondent of the *Saturday Evening Post* some years later. "He was a diplomatist in every way. It was a beautiful experience to wander into Mr. Hill's room and see him at his desk, solemn, dignified, learned, impressive, exuding diplomacy at every pore." Colonel William Henry Michael, Chief Clerk of the Department, felt the same way. "Somehow I feel better when you are here," he wrote to Hill, on vacation in September 1899. "I feel that the *poise* is more complete—if that conveys to you any meaning at all." Thomas Morrison, Chief of the Bureau of Accounts, who had been with the Department since 1867, thought that Hill was probably the ablest Assistant Secretary ever to hold the office.[23]

However highly regarded by intimates and contemporaries, Assistant Secretaries, because of the mostly anonymous nature of their office, seldom loom large in history. References to Assistant Secretary Hill in studies of American diplomacy are few, brief, and usually erroneous. The most significant references, moreover, are mistakenly derogatory. They stem from a disingenuous letter written by Secretary Hay, the background of which was not readily apparent.

On February 2, 1900, Hay signed a treaty with Sir Julian Pauncefote, the British ambassador at Washington, releasing the United States from the restrictions of the Clayton-Bulwer Treaty of 1850, which had debarred either nation from exclusive control of an isthmian canal. When the treaty was submitted to the Senate three days later, it was immediately attacked for not conceding to the United States sufficient power over the canal. Although the United States was given the exclusive right to construct and manage the passage, it was to be free and open, in wartime as well as peacetime, to all nations on terms of entire equality; the United States was prohibited from fortifying it; and all other powers were to be invited to adhere to the treaty. After several days, however, the opposition appeared to be subsiding, when suddenly it was given new force by a statement penned by Governor Theodore Roosevelt and published in the New York *Sun* on February 12 criticizing the treaty for its disregard of the nation's military security and the Monroe Doctrine.[24] Naturally provoked by this turn of events, Hay was particularly incensed when he learned that Hill had been present when Roosevelt's statement was prepared.

Hill had been invited to spend Sunday, February 11, at the Yonkers home of Frederick W. Holls, an aggressive young lawyer who fancied himself influential in domestic and international politics. "Governor Roosevelt is to spend the day with me in Yonkers," Holls had written on January 31, "and I would like to have not more than four choice and selected spirits meet him. These four are N. Murray Butler, Albert Shaw, Senator Horace White, of Syracuse, and last but not least, our distinguished Assistant Secretary of State." The gathering was intended to be social, but by February 11 the Hay-Pauncefote Treaty was under consideration by the Senate, and the conversation that Sunday turned to it and to the political and economic implications of an isthmian canal generally. Finally someone, probably Holls, urged Roosevelt to issue a public statement opposing the treaty. With the assent of the others, Roosevelt wrote out the statement, which Butler, a teacher and administrator at Columbia University, took back with him to the city to give to the *Sun*. "Poor Doctor Hill was ... perfectly innocent in the matter," Butler relates in his memoirs, "for in accepting Holls's invitation he could never have dreamed of what was going to take place."[25] Yet however much Hill personally disapproved of the treaty, he need not have stayed and abetted in public criticism of his chief's policy once the idea emerged, nor should his companions have expected him to. Hay had good reason for anger.

The rift between Hill and Hay became a choice item of newspaper gossip and rumor. By May 15 the New York *World* was carrying the headline, "EXTRA! DR. HILL A POSSIBLE SUCCESSOR TO HAY: Rupture In the State Department May Lead to the Advancement of the Rochester Man." Hill aspired to the Secretary's chair, the *World* reported, and some powerful Republican senators who were dissatisfied with Hay's policies were urging McKinley to give it to him. There was also a coolness between the wives of the two secretaries, the *World* gossiped, for Mrs. Hay was jealous of Mrs. Hill's brilliant social successes and the open admiration the diplomatic corps had shown for her.[26]

There is no evidence that Hill ever allowed his ambitions to soar into aspirations for Hay's place. Juliet, it is true, was indeed a social success; some years later the Philadelphia *Press* described her drawing rooms at 1313 K Street as "the nearest approach to the famous gatherings of Paris which the capital city has seen since the brilliant Kate Chase presided over the home of the Chief Justice." But the gossip of rivalry with Mrs. Hay was more fiction than fact: "a strange mingling of truth and falsehood—largely falsehood," Hill described one such press story.[27]

Although the press misrepresented the rupture, Secretary Hay, always sensitive to criticism and smarting under senatorial and press attacks on his treaty, was for some months out of sorts with his first assistant and not always candid. Early in August 1900, "a filthy little fever" and unusually torrid Washington heat forced him to take refuge at his summer home in Newbury, New Hampshire, where he was compelled for the next several weeks to spend most of his time in bed, "not ill enough to be interesting, but too ill to do or enjoy anything." Hill had left the capital shortly before for a vacation at Nantasket, Massachusetts, where he was busy writing campaign literature when he learned of the Secretary's illness. With the Boxer crisis in China at its height and the legations in Peking still beleaguered, he immediately wrote to Hay on August 8 offering to return to Washington. Hay replied on August 17 that he had sent the letter to Second Assistant Secretary Alvey A. Adee, who had answered, with many thanks, that he thought he could manage. "So, also with many thanks," wrote Hay, "nothing is left me but to say you would better 'loaf and invite your soul' without fear & with a manly heart."[28] Yet two weeks later Hay wrote to Adee: "It is incomprehensible to me that Hill should not long ago have cut his leave to go back to Washington, to divide with you the work and the Kudos you are gaining. It is the biggest job the State Department has been engaged on in our time and insures you already a bright page in our history. Only I dread every day to hear the news of your breaking down from overwork."[29]

This passage, quoted in Tyler Dennett's biography of Hay, was hardly fair to Hill. Read together with other letters in which Hay consciously catered to the Cinderella complex of the dedicated and long-serving Adee, it also seems to be the basis for Graham H. Stuart's assumption in his history of the State Department that Hill was of little use there and Hay at times became incensed because he did not share in the work more fully. Overlooking the almost unique length of Hill's service as first assistant, Stuart dismisses him from any role of influence because of his unfamiliarity with departmental organization and procedure and states that Hay was forced to depend for advice almost entirely on Adee.[30]

Without hearing anything further from Hay, Hill cut short his vacation anyhow and returned to the capital. "I am glad to know you are again in Washington for many reasons," Hay wrote upon learning of it, "and yet I cannot help regretting you should have so truncated your well-earned holiday." Newspapers critical of recent steps in the administration's China policy had no such regrets. The *New York Times* and the *Washington Times* both breathed a sigh of relief on September 4 that Hill was back at his desk. The *Washington Times,* ever hostile to Hay, went on to suggest that McKinley should take the opportunity to give the Secretary the permanent rest from official responsibility to which his isthmian and Alaskan policies entitled him and let Hill, who had "the best diplomatic brains of the Department," handle foreign relations for the remaining months of the administration.[31]

Hay returned to the State Department on October 1. A week before, he had written to Hill: "You gave up your well-earned vacation & have spent this month—which was destined to better uses—in Washington. If you care to recoup yourself by taking a better month, you can do what you like with October. I write this instead of waiting to suggest it orally, so that you may have a week to enjoy it in anticipation." Hill needed the month off the Secretary was offering. He had been stricken with malaria on his return to Washington, yet had stuck to his post throughout September, far more

ill than Hay seems to have been. To regain his health he retreated
to Nantasket as soon as Hay returned.[32]

When Hay wrote to Adee in the summer of 1900 he was a hurt
and sick man. Two years later, to President Roosevelt, he wrote
very differently about his first secretary. He knew of no one more competent and trustworthy for high diplomatic appointment, he told
the President. "He is thoroughly versed in international law and
history; an elegant and correct writer, and morally, has all the
qualities that can be wished for, truthfulness, courage, and unshak-
able integrity."[33] He was not quite candid in telling the President
of the advantages to the government in giving him a high diplomatic position, Hay at the same time wrote to Hill, "for I do not know
a place where you could do the Government such valuable services
as you are dong now. I doubt if there is an Ambassador anywhere
who does half the work which you and Adee are daily rendering
the country."[34]

How Hill felt about Hay is revealed in a letter written to Andrew
Carnegie many years later: "I loved the man and was happy to
serve him, which in the last three of the five years I was with him
I think I *really* did."[35]

4

International Arbitration

TWO YEARS BEFORE ENTERING THE STATE DEPARTMENT, HILL HAD read a paper, his first in the field of international relations, before a meeting of the American Social Science Association at Saratoga, New York. Entitled "International Justice; With a Plan for its Permanent Organization," the paper had sketched out the history of international law and presented a blueprint for the establishment of a permanent court of international arbitration.

Hill proposed bringing an international court into existence by a treaty which, while open to all states, would require only the signature of the United States and England to give it effect. The court would resemble national courts in that its judges would be appointed for life and it would apply its own law, codified by an expert commission of its members. It would have jurisdiction over all disputes between members except those involving sovereignty and independence, and any state that refused to submit to it a case within its jurisdiction, or comply with its decision, would be permanently excluded from its privileges and protection. Hill saw this last provision as the only means by which international law could be enforced, but he believed it would be fully effective. "If the most powerful nations were united under the jurisdiction of the court," he contended, "it would become a moral impossibility to refuse or violate its requirements."[1]

The paper hit a responsive chord. Resort to arbitration for the settlement of international disputes, revived after a long era of isolated and insignificant application by the Jay Treaty of 1794 between the United States and England, had been growing throughout the nineteenth century. This development was registered not only in numbers of cases, but also in their importance. Leading the way in the movement, the United States and England had made a particularly notable record of resorting to arbitral tribunals. By 1896, therefore, there was considerable interest in both countries in establishing some regular and permanent system of arbitration, and a bilateral treaty to this end was in the process of negotiation.

Hill was invited to deliver his paper again before the Brooklyn Institute of Arts and Sciences and to have it published in the October 1896 issue of the *Yale Law Journal*.[2] Two years later it figured in America's preparation for the first International Peace Conference at The Hague in 1899.

The conference was proposed by Czar Nicholas II of Russia in a circular note handed to the diplomatic corps at St. Petersburg in August 1898. Suggesting that the nations discuss means of insuring peace, the proposal in its specifics centered its concern solely on checking increases of armaments. Lofty humanitarian considerations had lesser place in Russian motivation than did fear that huge new expenditures necessary to reequip Russia's artillery to match new German and Austrian arms would bankrupt the nation's treasury, and the Russian officials responsible for the appeal did not really expect anything positive to come from it. The foreign offices of Europe, although feeling obliged to accept the proposal, received it with as much skepticism as it was offered, a reaction that their representatives at St. Petersburg felt was fully justified. "The general consensus of opinion among the members of the diplomatic corps now present," the American chargé at the Russian capital reported early in November, "appears to be that the proposition is visionary and utopian, if not partaking of quixotism." In Washington the proposal was greeted with the same lack of enthusiasm. Because its peace-time military force was so conspicuously smaller than those of the armed powers to whom the Czar's appeal was especially addressed, President McKinley told the Congress, the proposal was of no practical importance to the United States save as marking an auspicious step toward the betterment of world conditions, but it was in this view that it behooved the nation to support the project.[3]

One of few government officials not inclined to write off the conference completely was Sir Julian Pauncefote, the British ambassador to the United States, who shortly after Hill became Assistant Secretary called at the State Department to discuss it. Ushering the ambassador directly into Hill's office, Secretary Hay explained that Sir Julian had brought with him Hill's little pamphlet on *International Justice*. Pauncefote was an equally great champion of international arbitration, and in conversations together he and Hill agreed that while there was no hope for limiting armaments at the conference, it might be possible to give the world a push toward settling disputes by judicial methods. They were encouraged in this idea when the Russian foreign office proposed in January a specific program for the conference, the eighth and last point of which provided for the discussion of pacific methods of solving international differences. They thereupon agreed that the delegates of the United States and Great Britain should be instructed to work toward the establishment of an international system of arbitration.[4]

This decision influenced the form and content of Hill's entire instruction to the American commission, which the President and Secretary of State approved almost without change. In respect to the first seven articles of the Russian program, Hill was very brief. On the first proposal, which called for limiting the size of armed forces, the delegates were to leave the initiative to the heavily armed powers where it properly belonged. They were to skirt clear also of three proposals for outlawing certain new weapons and limiting the power of explosives because the articles were "lacking in practicality" and unrealizable. They were to support implementation of the next three proposals, which sought the revision and extension of rules of war relating to the care of wounded and the protection of noncombatants. "Not knowing till day before yesterday who the delegates would be," Hill wrote to Andrew D. White on April 7, 1899, "I have been specially anxious to cut off all chances for 'flapdoodle' and to open the way for our representatives to do the one thing that the nation will approve and which will, if adopted, as I think, help the administration and the world at large." It was the eighth article of the program, relating to the use of good offices, mediation, and arbitration, Hill enjoined the delegates, that opened the most fruitful field for discussion and offered an opportunity unparalleled in history for promoting a rule of law among nations. They were to propose a plan for an international court, which was appended to the instruction, and were to use all their influence to secure its substance.[5]

The plan called for a court to which member states would agree to submit all disputes not settled by ordinary diplomacy, except those involving political independence and territorial integrity, and which would be open to the use of all states. It would consist of a continuously sitting bench of judges, learned in international law, one from each participating state. The full bench by unanimous agreement would appoint judges for each particular case, excluding members from states whose interests were in litigation. Keeping details of organization and operation to a minimum, Hill phrased the entire plan in little more than six hundred words. "I feel, my dear Holls, that all small details will look after themselves if the great principles are right," he explained to the secretary of the American commission. "It would have been very easy to concoct a plan which would anticipate in an omniscient way every difficulty and contingency that might possibly arise with its corrective, but the result would be a scheme so complicated with its many wheels within wheels, and such a buzz and whirr of machinery when it once got going as to make everybody afraid of it, lest in its unintelligible complication it might contain some vicious intention."[6]

The plan, Frederick Holls wrote in his history of the peace conference published in 1900, was almost identical with one elaborated by a committee of the New York State Bar Association and distributed to all members of the conference. John W. Foster, former

Secretary of State and president of the National Arbitration Conference, similarly wrote a few years later in his study *Arbitration and The Hague Court* that the Bar Association plan, which had been presented to the President in 1896, became the basis of the instructions to the American delegates and that the essential features of the Hague Court were in accordance with it. Historians of the peace movement have repeated this version of how the Court got its structure. In fact, however, although Hill did draw on the Bar Association plan for certain details of organization and procedure—in an appended résumé of America's traditional interest in arbitration he acknowledged incorporating features from earlier plans—the court he proposed was distinctly different in its basic concept. The Bar Association's plan provided for a voluntary court to which cases would be submitted by special treaties between the disputants; Hill's plan provided for an obligatory court to which disputes would be referred without special treaties. Inherent in one was the assumption that the court's authority would be defined in each case by a *compromis;* inherent in the other was the assumption that the court would determine its authority from a code of law adapted to its use.[7] Foster was right in that the essential nature of the Permanent Court that emerged from the conference was in accordance with the plan of the New York State Bar Association, but it was a far different tribunal from that contemplated in the American instructions, and far less substantial.

Who would carry out the instructions was a question that remained very much up in the air until almost the last minute. Even whether the United States would be represented by a delegation or a single commissioner remained undecided. Hill was convinced that only a distinguished commission, preferably headed by Andrew D. White, could do justice to the occasion and bring about the establishment of an international court; but neither his faith in the possibilities of the conference nor his concern over the selection of the delegates was widely shared in official Washington. Concluding that the way to influence his superiors was "to magnify the proposition of the Czar from the political point of view," he pressed Hay to consider the popular credit the administration would garner from a conspicuous success at the conference by an American delegation.

But it was ultimately the President who must be convinced, and here Hill was aided by Frederick W. Holls. That ambitious young attorney, whose main interest was in making a place for himself, had already been urging McKinley to appoint an elaborate commission when he came to Washington to see Hill late in January 1899. To bring more influence on the President, they enlisted the help of Nicholas Murray Butler, already the intimate of many prominent public figures, who went to see McKinley personally. Butler also contacted Senator Henry Cabot Lodge and Representative Robert R. Hitt, members of the Senate Committee on Foreign Relations and the House Committee on Foreign Affairs. Butler agreed that Hill's political argument was the most impressive one to stress, and since Hill had already urged it strongly upon Hay, he thought it would prevail if Mark Hanna, as the party's political strategist, backed it up with McKinley. It was decided that the opportune moment for this move would be immediately after Congress adjourned on March 4, and Holls arranged with Hanna to go with him to the White House at that time. But the President hurriedly left Washington on vacation without making any decision, and two weeks later Hanna wrote that McKinley was still undecided even about whether to send more than a single commissioner. At Hanna's suggestion, Holls drew up a bill of arguments for a high-caliber commission and sent it to McKinley with a request for another opportunity to see him on his return to Washington.[8]

How much Holls influenced McKinley beyond securing a place for himself is difficult to say. Hill probably had more influence through his daily contacts with Secretary Hay. In any event, he could write to Andrew D. White early in April that he was much relieved by the happy issue of the efforts of Holls and himself to have the American commission do justice to the country and the occasion. "When he sees you," he informed the ambassador, "Mr. Holls will tell you much, and I could tell you still more of the perils which we have fortunately passed of having the wrong men appointed. The ecclesiastics have been rampant for places, but I felt and those in higher places have seen that sectarian appointments for personal or denominational glorification would not only be fatal to the dignity of the Commission, but injurious from every point of view."[9]

Since the newspapers had been prophesying that he would be one of the delegates, White was also relieved. Nothing he had seen during his embassy in Russia encouraged him to believe that the lethargic Nicholas II would actually lead a peace movement against the powerful military party of his empire, and he was decidedly skeptical about the whole matter. He had even drafted a letter declining an appointment, he wrote Hill, but when he saw who his colleagues were to be, he felt it was an honor too great to be refused. Headed by White, the commission also included Seth Low, president of Columbia University; Stanford Newel, United States Minister to the Netherlands; Captain Alfred T. Mahan, United States Navy; and Captain William Crozier, United States Army. Much to the disgust of Secretary Hay, who thought him an overweening ass, Holls was named secretary to the commission.[10]

White was scarcely more optimistic than before, however, about the outcome of the conference. Nothing could be done about disarmament, he wrote, unless the Czar disbanded a considerable fraction of his own great army, but no one expected him to do it, and even the Russian ambassador at Berlin was profoundly skeptical of any beneficial results. The same attitude prevailed at The Hague, Stanford Newel reported. None of his colleagues believed that anything significant would come out of the conference. "The Italian Minister confessed that if the U.S. had proposed it, everybody would have laughed and called it 'Yankee humbug,' but the Czar of all the Russias must be very respectfully treated." About the only people in Europe who expected anything to be gained, Newel observed, were the Dutch hotel-keepers, who stated frankly that this was their opportunity to make a little something and had doubled their prices. It was in this atmosphere of indifference, distrust of Russian intentions, and even resentment on the part of some at having been sent on a mission doomed to fail, that delegates from nineteen nations of Europe, five of Asia, and two of the New World assembled at The Hague on May 18, 1899.[11]

Limiting armaments, the original purpose of the Czar's proposal, was an idea that had died at birth. The conference buried it by remitting it to the nations for further study. Since none of the great powers, and very few of the lesser ones, were any more willing to risk restrictions on the use of weapons they already possessed, Russian proposals in this direction resulted meagerly in the interdiction of gas projectiles, expanding bullets, and projectiles launched from balloons—weapons that were nevertheless perfected and later used. Security not being at stake, the powers extended the Red Cross rules of the Geneva Conventions of 1864 and 1868 to naval warfare and revised and broadened the Laws and Customs of Warfare adopted by the Brussels Conference of 1874 but never ratified. Fortunately for the fate of the conference, the delegates were from the beginning more interested in finding ways of avoiding war than in making it slightly less destructive or slightly more humane, and as they worked toward something that seemed practicable in this area, their gloom and pessimism began to lift. The result, the one notable achievement of the conference, was the Convention for the Pacific Settlement of International Disputes. This treaty established procedures for the use of good offices, mediation, and commissions of inquiry, and, more important, it established a Permanent Court of Arbitration.[12]

The creation of the Court owed much to Anglo-American efforts. Russia, while it wished to establish some regular method of arbitration, was at first decidedly equivocal about establishing any permanent organization for it. Germany was hostile to the whole idea of permanent arbitration machinery, and for a time her opposition threatened to break up the conference. "There can be no doubt whatever that the position of the American and English delegates unitedly standing for a permanent International Tribunal has brought about the change of feelings in Russia and many other Powers," Holls wrote to Hill early in the conference. "Without it we should probably have adjourned, after passing a few platonic resolutions declaring Arbitration in general to be a very desirable thing."[13]

The Permanent Court was actually merely a panel of jurists to which each signatory power might appoint up to four members and from which parties to a dispute might select arbitrators of their own choice. An Administrative Council, consisting of the diplomatic representatives of the signatories accredited to The Hague, was entrusted with the supervision of an International Bureau, or records office, and all administrative detail. Resort to the Court was entirely voluntary. Proposals for obligatory arbitration of certain classes of disputes had encountered varying degrees of opposition and had been dropped without much reluctance on the part of any delegation. The American delegation, seeing the temper of the conference, and doubting that the compulsory feature of their own plan would in the end be acceptable to their government, had secured permission from Washington to make the scheme wholly voluntary before presenting it.[14]

While this radically different court was being formed, Holls and White assured Hill from The Hague that the fundamental features of his plan were being preserved. Presumably, what they regarded as fundamental was that for the first time in history an international judicial organization with a permanent administrative apparatus and body of judges was being established—and to this everything else was indeed secondary. But no one in a position of responsibility deceived himself as to what had been accomplished. It was a beginning and nothing more. "We believe that, though it will doubtless be found imperfect and will require modification as times goes on [sic]," the American commission reported, "it will form a thoroughly practical beginning, it will produce results from the outset, and it will be the germ out of which a better and better system will be gradually evolved."[15]

Though the Court was a far cry from his plan, Hill was not at all disappointed. "Personally, I know too well the necessity of generous compromise in order to obtain the general consent of a body composed of antithetical elements to expect that any good plan, having for its object so difficult an enterprise as an international tribunal, can hope to succeed without considerable modification," he had written to Holls while the conference was in progress. "The Conference, itself, realized all that I, personally, expected from it and I think fully met the expectations of the President and Secretary of State," he later wrote to Dr. White. "Its results, it is true, constitute only a beginning but I think there is great force in Mr. de Beaufort's metaphor of the growing child. It remains to be seen after the Convention is ratified, what the permanent tribunal can accomplish. But if it does its first work wisely and well, I am inclined to think that gradually more and more important questions will be submitted to its decisions."[16]

Essential to the success of the Court was the cooperation of the great powers, and the power most likely to be uncooperative was Germany. To cement that state's reluctant acceptance of the Court and overcome her hostility toward organized arbitration, Hill hoped that a case might arise in which Germany had good grounds and would taste the satisfaction of success. Almost immediately an ideal case arose over an imbroglio in the enchanting but politically stormy islands of Samoa. But unfortunately for Hill's objective, it came much too soon to await ratification of the Hague Convention. The condominium through which Germany, Great Britain, and the United States had governed Samoa since 1890 had never pleased any of the powers, and Germany had already suggested a partition, when, in January 1899, civil war broke out between rival native factions over the kingship of the islands. Arbitrary and illegal action by a German official in support of one of the parties was followed by a bombardment of that faction's forces by American and British warships on March 16, 1899, in the course of which the German consulate at Apia was damaged and a number of native houses were destroyed. In the negotiations that followed, resulting in a treaty of partition signed at Washington in December, Germany raised the question of indemnity for losses sustained by her subjects during the American and British bombardment, which she considered unwarranted. Great Britain came to an agreement with her to refer all claims for indemnity to the arbitration of the King of Sweden and Norway, an engagement to which the two powers then invited the United States to adhere.[17]

Ordered by the President to accept the invitation, Hay, who was then at his summer home in New Hampshire, was disposed to do so merely by an exchange of notes. Hill thought this of doubtful expediency. Unlike situations that might be cited as precedents, it appeared that in this case the United States would have the most to pay, and if the executive branch assumed the responsibility alone, the door would be wide open for a partisan tempest when Congress came to appropriate the money. It would be prudent at least, he advised Hay, to have a specific opinion from the Attorney General on the legality of effecting this arrangement by an exchange of notes, and it would be better still to draw up a special convention to be ratified by the Senate. Hay, to whom the Senate was at best an unnecessary and troublesome institution, thought the less sent to it the better. "An appropriation requires only a majority," he complained, "while a treaty requires two thirds and involves an ocean of talk." He thought the suggestion to consult the Attorney General judicious, however, and then added: "If you and Adee see any way of altering the agreement in our interest, before we adhere, do it by all means. I am sure whatever you do will be right."[18]

It was Hill's counsel that prevailed, and on November 7, 1899, the United States signed a claims treaty at Washington with Great Britain and Germany. Ratifications were exchanged the next March. On October 14, 1902, the King of Sweden and Norway found the United States and Great Britain responsible for the losses caused by the military action of their naval vessels. The United States and Great Britain then agreed that each should pay half the sums found due to the subjects of other governments.[19]

In the meantime, Hill had handled the State Department's preparations for another major international conference that was dominated by the subject of arbitration—the Second International Conference of American States, which met in Mexico City on October 22, 1901. In his annual message to Congress in December 1899, President McKinley had suggested that the time was ripe for calling a second conference to pick up the work begun in Washington a decade before. With the exception of Chile, the Latin American republics had responded favorably, Mexico had offered to host the conference, and at her suggestion the executive committee of the International Union of American Republics had recommended a program. Drawn up in Washington on May 23, 1900, by the diplomatic representatives of Costa Rica, Guatemala, and Argentina, and sent to all the republics for comment, the program, a model at least of brevity, stated:

   I. Points studied by the previous conference which the new con-
       ference may decide to reconsider.
  II. Arbitration.
 III. International Court of Claims.
  IV. Means of protection to industry, agriculture and commerce.
       Development of communications between the countries of the
       Union. Consular regulations of ports and Custom Houses.
       Statistics.
   V. Reorganization of the International Bureau of the American
       Republics.

Before it was even put on paper, the program was headed for
trouble. The Chilean foreign office on May 21 had informed the
American minister at Santiago that it was opposed to any discussion at the conference of arbitration relating to pending questions.
For years Chile had shied away from any commitment to the
principle of arbitration, fearing that it might be applied to her dispute with Peru over the provinces of Tacna and Arica. By the
Treaty of Ancón, which had ended the War of the Pacific in 1883,
Chile was to hold the conquered Peruvian provinces for ten years,
after which their ownership was to be determined by plebiscite.
But Chile had repeatedly refused to arrange for the plebiscite, and
she suspected that the conference was a trap to bring up the question. This suspicion hardened when Mexico sent out invitations
to the conference in August, enclosing the tentative program and
referring to it as having been generally approved.[20]

The program was too vague, Carlos Morla Vicuña, Chilean
minister to the United States, protested to the State Department
on November 25, 1900. Instead of facilitating agreements, it would
strain relations among the nations invited to the conference.
"There are some among them," his note pointedly observed, "that
have been, as Chile was, dragged to war, and that have had to annex considerable American territories as adequate indemnities."
The executive committee should define precisely some of the subjects of its program. Moreover, the note continued, Chile would
never accept an invitation to the conference without the inclusion
of "a decisive and unequivocal proviso establishing that no subjects can be brought under discussion, no resolutions can be adopted,

and no agreements can be concluded against which a delegate of any of the republics may have raised an objection."[21]

From this demand for a broad and absolute veto Chile refused to budge until the next April when Vicuña was finally persuaded, after considerable personal effort by Hill, who was then Acting Secretary of State, that any Chilean suggestions about the program would be earnestly considered. The executive committee must define precisely the meaning of the first three articles, Vicuña stipulated. Only then could his government give a definite answer to Mexico's invitation. The Secretary of State being chairman ex officio of the committee, Hill called it together on May 6. Affirming that unanimity was essential if the conference were to achieve any practical results, Joaquín Bernardo Calvo of Costa Rica, the only current member of the committee who had participated in drawing up the program, presented definitions that met Chile's requirement that discussion of arbitration would relate only to future questions. In the ensuing debate, Hill agreed with Calvo. If the committee refused to make the definitions demanded by Chile, he argued, she would not attend the conference, and any resolutions it might pass could not be enforced against her. The obvious logic of this overcame the opposition of Carlos Martínez Silva of Colombia and Luis Felipe Carbo of Ecuador, who had advocated consideration of pending questions, and the definitions offered by Calvo were unanimously approved. A week later Chile said it would come to the conference.[22]

Three days before the Chilean cable was received, however, Fernando E. Guachalla of Bolivia, the fifth member of the executive committee, had returned to Washington from the Pan-American Exposition at Buffalo demanding that the committee reconsider the resolution it had adopted while he was away. When the committee met again on May 16, Guachalla, whose nation with Peru had suffered defeat by Chile in the War of the Pacific, insisted that it formally declare whether its program, including the modifications of May 6, were binding on the conference or if the conference could establish its own program. To head off an even more disruptive situation certain to result from a flat declaration either way, Hill moved that "the tentative programme will be regarded as indicating the range and character of the subjects discussed by the Congress except as may be modified by the further agreement of all the members composing the Congress." Since this verbal contortion would still permit Chile to block discussion of the Tacna-Arica dispute, Guachalla would have none of it. Unanimity was impossible, because everyone knew the situation, he retorted; the resolution would "close the doors of the Conference." On being put to a vote, the motion was supported by Calvo and Carbo and opposed by Silva and Guachalla. Cautiously, for the stage was set for resentments to be turned northward, Hill asked whether they wanted him to cast a deciding vote or adjourn. When there was no agreement on this, he recessed the meeting, suggesting that they try to arrive at a solution in a confidential manner.[23]

Hill continued to meet with the Latin American diplomats, trying to break the deadlock, but refusing to take sides. The issue had arisen from a purely Latin American quarrel, and the success of the conference appeared to depend upon the southern republics' reaching a solution among themselves. But the resentments and suspicions bred by the War of the Pacific were too strong, and it became questionable if there would be a conference at all. Chile and Peru closed out the events of May with each nation pleading its version of the Tacna-Arica dispute in the Washington *Evening Star*. Hitherto the issue of the conference program had been treated as if it were one of principle, and specific mention of that quarrel avoided. Throwing it into the arena of newspaper debate could do nothing but embitter it further. Chile continued to refuse to attend the conference unless discussion of arbitration were restricted to future questions. Peru and Argentina announced that they would not attend unless discussion were without restriction, and Brazil, Bolivia, Uruguay, and Paraguay were reported ready to follow their example.[24]

While not a few of the southern republics seemed more determined to exacerbate the issue than solve it, they were inclined to blame the United States for the impasse. The Latin American diplomats in Washington insisting upon unrestricted consideration of arbitration were reported as condemning Hill's motion of May 16 for being contrary to the historic advocacy by the United

States of arbitration in its broadest sense. All that Secretary Blaine had done for Pan-American unification, they charged, according to the New York *Herald,* had been spoiled by the attitude of Chile encouraged by the State Department. Most of the Argentine press was outspokenly critical of the United States and approved a resolution of the Argentine government not to take part in the conference unless unrestricted discussion of arbitration were permitted. Brazilian newspapers were equally quick to pull Uncle Sam's beard. In Chile, both the press and government misrepresented the situation to create the impression that a diplomatic victory had been scored on the United States.[25]

Yet in the end, the republics came to the conference with the issue of the program still unsettled. The modifications of the program adopted by the executive committee on May 6 were never formally communicated by Mexico to the other republics. It was not that Mexico was opposed to their circulation, her foreign office explained. It was simply that as host of the conference she had already issued invitations with a certain program, and she wished to remain neutral in disputes between her sister republics and allow the conference to modify its program as it saw fit. The explanation had just enough equivocation in it to allow Chile to accept Mexico's invitation, which she did in September, with the statement that she did so to deal with the matters indicated in the program adopted by the executive committee on May 6. Peru and Bolivia, on the other hand, came to the conference claiming that they had been assured by Mexico that the original program would be maintained.[26]

Irrespective of the dispute over the program, the suggestion from Washington to hold a conference had inspired a large section of the Latin American press to display its endemic distrust and suspicion of the United States. Although some newspapers defended the United States, many warned that the Colossus of the North was promoting the conference for selfish and imperialistic reasons and that a "Yankee Peril" was plainly evident. That Hill was keenly appreciative of these fears is manifest in every paragraph of the instructions he was charged with writing for the American delegation to the conference. The delegates were admonished again and again to avoid doing anything that could possibly wound Latin American sensibilities, stimulate greater prejudice against the United States, or raise suspicions that it was acting from selfish motives. They were not to assume the part of leadership in the conference or involve themselves in political differences between the other republics. If a question arose over the program, they were to hold that it was for the conference itself to determine the limits of its discussions. On the touchy subject of arbitration, they were to be guided by the principle that it should be wholly voluntary. If the dispute between Chile and Peru were brought before the conference, they were to do all they could to preserve general harmony while maintaining strict neutrality. On questions of commerce, they were to stress mutuality of interest and avoid even the semblance of an attempt to gain unfair advantages. In developing closer relations with the southern republics, the instructions finally cautioned, the United States must be most careful of their autonomy. "The most beneficent form of Pan-Americanism for ourselves, as well as for our sister Republics, will be found in a free local development over the entire continent. If the influence of the United States spreads southward, it will be a pacific and not a hostile influence."[27]

The delegates chosen to carry out these instructions were Henry G. Davis, former senator from West Virginia and delegate to the First Pan-American Conference; William I. Buchanan of Iowa, former United States Minister to Argentina and Director-General of the Pan-American Exposition at Buffalo; Charles M. Pepper of Washington, D.C., journalist and editor; Volney W. Foster of Wisconsin, lumberman and industrialist; and John Barrett of Oregon, journalist and former United States Minister to Siam.

These men discovered that while Latin America might distrust the intentions of the United States, it was still no easy task to avoid a role of leadership. The delegates from Latin American countries who traveled with them by special train from Washington to Mexico City were unanimous in their desire that the American commission be given the first vice-presidency of the conference. The commision resolved not to accept any vice-presidency. Upon the organization of the conference the permanent presidency, instead of being proffered to the head of the host delegation as was usual at international congresses, was first offered to Henry Davis. Perhaps these gestures were intended only as elaborate compliments to the nation that had first suggested the congress, but journalists covering the conference later noted that the American commissioners were constantly being urged to put themselves more to the front and were at times criticized for lack of decision and not assuming the leadership they were expected to wield.[28]

The danger to Latin America present at the conference was not the Colossus of the North, but the wrangle over arbitration. "It is very evident that we are over a powder-mine in the attitude of Peru and Chile . . . ," John Barrett wrote to Hill eight days after the conference opened. "We are all hoping that we can guide the consideration of the subject of Arbitration in such a way as to prevent a clash which might prove disastrous." Every delegation supported arbitration in principle, and many demanded compulsory arbitration, but beyond that there was little agreement. Among the delegations demanding compulsory arbitration, some wanted it to cover all questions, pending or future, except those involving independence or national honor, while others wanted it to cover only future questions, with those to be exempted specifically defined. To keep the lid on acrimonious debate, an attempt was made to confine discussion of arbitration to a committee composed of one member from each delegation. But the committee was too large and its proceedings too public, and after three meetings it confessed its failure by turning its work over to a seven-man subcommittee. After six futile sessions the subcommittee tacitly agreed that it was useless to continue until somebody came up with a plan likely to be accepted by most of the delegations.[29]

It was John Barrett, according to the account he gave Hill, who first conceived the solution of adhering to the Hague Court. As signatories to the Hague Convention, the United States and Mexico could sponsor the admission of the other republics. Turning to an already established and entirely voluntary plan seemed the only way out of a hopeless snarl, and it had the additional merit, Barrett thought, of likelihood of approval by the United States Senate. The Senate had taken no action on the obligatory treaty of arbitration fashioned at the First Pan-American Congress—it was not ratified by any of its eleven signatories—but having approved the

Hague Convention, the Senate would not be likely to reject a new treaty consistent with it. Barrett broached his plan to William Buchanan, the commission's representative on the arbitration committee, and each man cautiously sounded out delegates from other countries and got an impression of approval. Buchanan telegraphed the proposal to the State Department, asking for instructions, while Barrett unofficially sent an outline of the protocol he had in mind to Hill.[30]

Receiving approval from Washington, Buchanan proposed that the conference request Mexico and the United States to negotiate with the other signatories of the Hague Convention for the adherence of the American republics. He further proposed that it also request the President of Mexico to sound out the other governments and prepare the most advanced general arbitration convention that would be approved by them all. Despite this provision, the American plan was at first opposed by the advocates of compulsory arbitration, but forced to recognize that they were hopelessly at odds even among themselves, they finally accepted a compromise offered by Mexico. Acting outside the conference, all the delegations would sign the protocol proposed by the United States. Those delegations choosing to could sign a second treaty promising to arbitrate all questions in existence or arising among them that did not affect their independence or national honor. Both treaties would then be accepted by the conference and incorporated into its minutes without debate. Thus angry discussion and a direct vote on the principle of compulsory arbitration, which might break up the congress, would be avoided. After much negotiation and an insignificant modification, this plan was carried out. All of the republics ultimately adhered to the Hague Convention. Nine states signed the treaty of compulsory arbitration, and six ratified it.[31]

With a historic enthusiasm for compulsory arbitration greater than their record of ratification or use of treaties warranted, all the republics by another treaty obligated themselves for five years to arbitrate all monetary claims that could not be adjusted through regular diplomacy. Hill had advised the American commission that any general claims convention was more likely to be ratified if it were not compulsory, and would in the end have better results. "Every successful effort to accomplish its purpose would then strengthen its support and gradually commend it to public confidence." Acting on later specific instructions in the same vein, John Barrett was the only member of the Committee on International Courts of Claims who did not favor recommending a compulsory treaty to the conference. Yet Hill's caution was justified. Only seven of the republics ultimately joined the United States in ratifying the convention.[32]

The Second Pan-American Congress produced a number of treaties, resolutions, and recommendations relating to political, economic, and cultural matters, none of which was of earth-shaking significance, but all of which offered more real possibility for better inter-American relations than did the treaties of arbitration. Yet the fate of the conference had hinged on that explosive issue. If Hill failed to bring the Latin American states to some prior agreement on it, without his efforts the conference would probably have labored under even greater difficulty by the absence of Chile and possibly some other states. If his policy drew criticism, the outcome of any other course would undoubtedly have drawn more. His instructions to the American delegation also showed understanding and realism. In terms of specific directives, the ideal of the Good Neighbor has never been better expressed.

5

The Extension of Civilization

URGING THE PRESIDENT IN THE FALL OF 1898 TO APPOINT HILL ASSISTANT
Secretary of State, John Van Voorhis had suggested that McKinley
give him the office, bring him home, and use him on the stump in
the Roosevelt campaign in New York. The President brought Hill
home, but it was Senator Platt and Chairman Benjamin Odell of
the New York Republican State Committee, telegraphing four days
after his arrival late in October, who pressed him to campaign, stress-
ing the importance of his making last-minute speeches at important points. Explaining that he had come to the State Department,
worn out from a sea voyage, to find two weeks work piled in front
of him, Hill begged off. Much as he regretted not being able to lift
his voice for the hero candidate, he bantered, for he had earlier told
Platt that he thought military heroes ought to stick to their trade,
he felt that duty bound him to his desk in Washington unless the
situation in New York became desperate.[1]

Hill was much more interested in any case in the greater national
debate initiated earlier in the year by the roar of Dewey's guns at
Manila. That the United States should retain possession of the
Philippines was to him a proposition beyond doubt; and until the

91

question was finally put to rest with the election of 1900, he directed his not inconsiderable rhetorical talents almost exclusively toward ensuring that the nation accept that responsibility.

The United States had not gone to war to conquer territory overseas, he explained to the Rochester Chamber of Commerce six weeks after taking up his duties at the State Department, but having liberated twelve million people from oppression and misrule, it had no alternative to governing them. It could not restore the territories to the vengeance of the vanquished, nor leave them to the occupation and partition of other powers, nor abandon them to their own inexperience and internal discords, but must establish within them the conditions of peace and ultimate self-government. Territorial expansion had marked every period of the nation's history, he reminded his listeners, and no one in all the vast area that had been incorporated into the United States regretted for a moment the historic necessities that had given to the united Republic a common law and a common liberty. Was America's expansion now to be bounded by the oceans? A burgeoning trade with Asia and Oceanica had made the Far East the land of promise for the merchant. Should the nation forget that it was now a Pacific as well as an Atlantic power, that the people of the West must also have their maritime cities and their share of international trade, or that the political subdivision and commercial occupation of Asia by foreign powers involved the perpetual isolation of this continent? But the destiny of nations was not in any event determined by the individual will, nor could national duties be measured by private standards, Hill declared, capping his arguments with the reigning authority of teutonic history: nations grew by obeying the instinct of development planted in them by God, and America's mission was to scatter the seeds of self-government prepared by her New England Puritans.[2]

A week later, before the Baptist Social Union of Washington, speaking on "The Expansion of Civilization," Hill developed the theme of America's mission more fully, extravagantly wrapping it in current concepts of Darwinian inevitabilities and duties of stewardship. "Since the advent of man upon the earth, inferior races have either receded before the advance of their superiors, or have been transformed by assimilating a higher type of civilization," he declaimed. An inexorable law of development had prepared the earth for man and had led, or would yet lead him, from savagery to barbarism, from barbarism to civilization, and on toward the perfection of society and the fuller life of the individual. "Races, indeed," he continued, "may suffer an arrest of development, linger, deteriorate, and ultimately fall; but mankind moves on toward the goal of its destiny, and of every race is exacted an account of its stewardship to humanity." A great era of human expansion was at the very moment underway. Europe, congested, was seeking new fields for the development of its industrial and commercial forces in Africa, Asia, and islands of the Pacific; if the course of history remained unbroken, there would not be an acre of the globe over which some flag would not float as the symbol of a civilized sovereignty. And if civilization were destined to expand until the earth was covered, which of its types was to become dominant? Hill asked. Were free institutions and self-government to remain the luxury of a few? Were republics alone to renounce commerce and shut themselves away to nurse the traditions of their fathers? "The struggle for existence cannot be suddenly arrested . . .," he asserted. "The question cannot be suppressed, if civilization is destined to unlimited expansion, what is there inexpansible in the form of it peculiar to the American people? Does it not savor of arrogance for us to assume that we alone are worthy of American liberties and American institutions?"

But, Hill went on, he would perhaps be asked what would become of the idea of self-government if America were to govern territories without the consent of their inhabitants? And what would become of its government if it were to admit to full citizenship twelve million aliens ignorant of its institutions and perhaps incapable of comprehending them? These were serious questions, he admitted, but it could not be forgotten that there was a period of minority in the development of nations as well as in the development of individual men, and it had never been assumed that political capacity could be developed without a certain tutelage and maturity. The natural rights of man were life, liberty, and pursuit of happiness, and these the sovereignty of the United States would protect wherever its flag flew and its laws prevailed. "Could we ever again call our flag 'Old Glory' if by withdrawing its protection for fear of encountering new responsibilities, twelve millions of human beings were hurled back into discord and anarchy?" he asked, prefacing a last burst of hyperbole.

But what more glorious consummation could be imagined than the slow development of a civic consciousness reaching out after liberty secured by law? When at last this nation is brought before the judgment seat of history, to render an account of its solemn trust, what will its answer be? Shall it say to the Lord of Nations, here is that which is thine, I have hid it in a napkin and buried it in the earth, behold thy treasure undiminished? Or shall it say, with thy talent I have gathered increase, behold the wilderness now populous with thriving cities, behold the sea made the highway of human intercourse, behold its islands blossoming with plenty and smiling in the security of peace? The true glory of a nation is not the spoils of conquest, but the harvest of the faithful husbandman. . . . In the name, therefore, of all that has made our Country great, let us go forward to the completion of our task, not to perpetuate the system we have demolished, but to extend the blessings of our civilization to those who are ready to accept the gift.[3]

Six weeks after delivering this address in Washington, Hill published a revised version of it in *Forum* magazine. He changed the title from "The Expansion of Civilization" to what he thought was a more fitting term—"The Extension of Civilization." His rhetoric for the printed page was more restrained. And his message was subtly altered. The civilizing mission of America was not diminished, but to a greater extent than before he emphasized the lack of any alternative to American rule. The real problem of the moment, he explained, was how best to secure the permanent peace for which the war had been fought, and in the midst of the questions agitating the public mind there was one clear certainty, namely, that the presence of the Stars and Stripes was "the best security against international intrigue, chronic revolution, and every form of violence to the inalienable rights of man." What America ought ultimately to do with its new possessions was a question to be determined by the future, but for the present it surely should not give them up: "To withdraw the protection of our flag and to recall our fleets and armies, would be to act upon an impulse and to render impossible that patient examination of the subject which its importance clearly demands. There is, therefore, no reasonable alternative to our temporary government of the ceded territories pending the settlement of ulterior questions."[4]

Throughout the nation, newspapers quoted the new Assistant Secretary with approval. Perhaps the arguments were not unique, but the phrases were always ringing and the State Department source was impressive. Even such an articulate advocate of expansionism as Senator Henry Cabot Lodge asked Hill to send a copy of his Washington address to a friend who wanted to discuss the subject.[5]

If Hill's magniloquence seems a bit excessive today, he was, by then prevailing canons of taste, a gifted and much sought-after public speaker. He was also an ingenious one, with a talent for making his topics vehicles of the new expansionist creed. Thus, lecturing under the auspices of the National Geographic Society of Washington on "The Original Territory of the United States," he extensively, if quite extraneously, commented on the universality of the federal Constitution and its capacity for indefinite growth and future expansion. At a commemoration of the one-hundredth anniversary of the death of George Washington by the patriotic societies of the capital, he neatly transfigured the Father of his Country into the Father of Expansionism, invoking his sanction for current territorial acquisitiveness. At the University of Chicago, in a convocation address on "The Place of America in World Politics," he placed the nation squarely in the forefront of advancing civilization, liberty, law, and commerce, especially in the region of the Pacific, which was to become the most magnificent meeting-place of nations known to history.[6]

In June 1900, Hill spoke at another Chamber of Commerce dinner in Rochester, given in honor of General Elwell S. Otis, commander of the American Army in the Philippines suppressing Aguinaldo's insurgents. Defending the American presence in the Islands, made embarrassing by Filipino resistance to it, Hill invoked a new argument of legality for that presence and blamed the insurrection on American critics of expansion. The Peace of Paris, he observed, was concluded in full harmony with international law, the examples of the past, and the principle of self-government. But the charge of "imperialism" brought against this extension of the nation's sovereignty had excited the suspicions of a people accustomed to oppression and deception, giving ambitious young men in the Philippines an occasion for armed revolt against the American liberating army. The American government was then faced with the choice of being driven from the Islands by force, leaving them to the mercy of a self-constituted dictator of a single tribe, or suppressing the insurrection and creating the conditions of civic existence. Whatever criticism theorists might raise, the Assistant Secretary maintained, it was a legal and material fact that the Philippine Archipelago was under the sovereignty of the United States, and the indisposition to recognize this fact, whether by Americans or Filipinos, had cost much precious blood and delayed for months the establishment of self-government so far as the people of the Islands were prepared to enjoy it.[7]

Four days after Hill delivered this address, the Republican party opened its national convention at Philadelphia. The convention drew up a platform in which it defended American authority over the Philippines as an inevasible responsibility. It also opened a vacancy at the governor's mansion in Albany by naming Theodore Roosevelt its vice-presidential candidate. Shortly thereafter Hill was sounded out, he reported to Holls, as an eminently available candidate to succeed the earlier Assistant Secretary from Washington—he was from western New York, was acceptable to the state organization and especially to the national administration, was not too deeply soaked in the native juices of local politics or in a position to be regarded as a tool of the organization, and was a man of scholarly attainments and allegedly honorable life, tempered by party loyalty but not corrupted by personal party obligations. "I really do not take the matter seriously," Hill added, "except at one point—I think the party might go further and fare worse, which it is very likely to do." To Lewis Ross he wrote that his replies may have closed the matter.[8] Apparently they did, and while Hill played a significant part in the campaign of 1900, it was a publicist rather than a candidate.

His electioneering work had begun in April when General Charles Dick, the Washington secretary of the National Committee, asked John Hay to prepare a brief review of the McKinley administration. Hay turned the task over to Hill. Some weeks later, the Committee began to put together a campaign "Text Book," and at President McKinley's suggestion, General Dick asked Hay to prepare a chapter on the Nicaraguan canal and treaty matters relating to it. In view of the Senate's handling of the treaty that Hay had negotiated with Pauncefote earlier in the year, it was not one of McKinley's better ideas. "Can you do anything with this? I can't," Hay scratched on a note pad and again turned the request over to Hill. Hill also wrote another chapter for the text covering the administration's policy in China, again at Hay's instruction.[9]

Early in June, before the parties held their conventions, Hill proposed to C.R. Buckland, publicity editor for the National Committee, and to General Perry S. Heath, secretary of the Committee's western headquarters at Chicago, that he write some pamphlets, their topics depending upon the concrete form in which the issues were joined by the parties in their platforms. If the Democrats adopted a sixteen-to-one plank, he thought it would be useful to bring up to date the sound-money pamphlet he had written for the last campaign. He had, in fact, already received a request from a Pennsylvania state senator for twenty thousand copies of a revised edition of it.[10]

Meeting at Kansas City the first week in July, the Democrats reaffirmed their demand of 1896 for the free and unlimited coinage of silver at a ratio of sixteen to one with gold. The Republican National Committee thereupon accepted Hill's offer, and the Assistant Secretary spent the first part of his August vacation at Nantasket revising his sound-money pamphlet. Renaming it *The Vital Issue,* he accused the Democrats of raising a fictitious cry of "imperialism" in order to obscure the only real issue between the parties: the same and by now discredited one that had divided them in 1896. The Committee published 1,500,000 copies in English and 500,000 copies in German condensed to half-length—according to the party's campaign managers, a sixteen-page pamphlet was the utmost a German voter would digest on any one subject.[11]

Hill spent the rest of his vacation writing a second pamphlet entitled *The Fiction of "Imperialism." The Sovereignty of the Nation the Safeguard of Self-Government*. Drawing together the arguments he had been developing for a year and a half, he defended the administration's Philippine policy in terms of national propriety, duty, and responsibility. And believing that the best defense was a good offense, he flayed Bryan and the Democratic party for vicious calumny and base deception. If the word "Imperialism" had any meaning, he asserted, it signified the substitution of arbitrary force for law. But the cession of the Philippines by the Treaty of Paris had been concluded in harmony with the law of nations and the Constitution of the United States; and the ratification of the treaty had made it the constitutional obligation of the President to execute its provisions, suppress the insurrection, and enforce law and order. In placing this legal duty upon the Chief Executive, Hill noted, Mr. Bryan and his friends had joined in full share, for without Bryan's urgings the Senate votes necessary for approval would not have been secured. There would then have been no question of "Imperialism." But showing a strange conception of political and moral obligation, Bryan had said: "With the treaty ratified, a clean-cut issue is presented between a government by consent and a government by force, and imperialists must bear the responsibility for all that happens until the question is settled." "He was quite willing," Hill acidly commented, "to fasten upon his friends, the Filipinos, 'a government by force,' in order to create a political issue in his own country and to be able to represent his party as the defender of the idea of 'government by consent.' What do the people of the United States think of such motives in a candidate for the chief magistracy of a great republic?"

Despite clear assurances by the President of the benevolent intentions of the United States, Hill went on, explaining the persistence of the insurrection originally directed against Spain, political partisans and sensational writers had raised the cry of "Imperialism." Although these people had received little sympathy and support at home, they had given Filipinos the impression that the United States was divided in its purpose toward them and that the prevailing party intended to crush them under a heel of despotism similar to that from which they had just been liberated. Had it not been for these assurances of support from a great political party, the leaders of the insurrection would never have held out against a united country or dreamed of establishing their supremacy over the entire archipelago. These insurrectionists, Hill sought to show from testimony presented by Filipinos themselves to the Philippine Commission sent by the United States to investigate conditions in the islands, did not represent the aspirations of the eighty-two tribes scattered over 1200 islands but the ambitions of a single dictator of a single tribe on a single island whose oppression exceeded the worst days of Spanish misrule. American sovereignty would be welcomed by all but these military adventurers, Hill contended, and nothing short of American sovereignty could safeguard self-government to those who wished to enjoy it against the rapacity of local despots. Although perhaps most Filipinos were fitted for a degree of local self-government, they had no unity of race, tradition, religion, or aspiration, and no political experience. Having broken the sovereignty of Spain in the islands, the United States had no choice but to extend its own sovereignty over them to prevent domestic anarchy, the certain intervention of other powers that anarchy would invite, and the eventual division of the islands. "Only through American occupation, therefore," Hill concluded, "is the idea of a free, self-governing and united Philippine commonwealth at all conceivable."[12]

Whatever questions *The Fiction of "Imperialism"* may have left begging, it was unquestionably an effective campaign document. Like *The Vital Issue,* it was translated into German and given a total publication of 2,000,000 copies. The two pamphlets were sent out by the National Committee in nearly 2,000 packages to county committees throughout the country. The American electorate was thus saturated with the argument that comprised the main strategy of the Republican campaign. Although the Democratic platform stated that imperialism was the "burning" and "paramount" issue, the Democrats could not make it so. By seizing upon the free-silver plank, which Bryan had forced on the Democratic convention, and insisting that the paramount issue was again the old free-silver question, the Republicans escaped from the defensive position into which they had been driven by the embarrassing Philippine insurrection.[13] As much as to anyone else, the strategy owed its formulation to Hill. The titles and subtitles of his pamphlets bannered it: *The Vital Issue* was *An Honest Dollar the Basis of Prosperity.* The Democrats had created *The Fiction of "Imperialism,"* but in reality *The Sovereignty of the Nation* was for the Filipinos the *Safeguard of Self-Government.*

On September 4 Hill cut short his vacation and returned to Washington because of the Boxer crisis. Although busy and ill, he prepared another article on the administration's policy in China, which the National Committee sent out in October through newspaper services. After having become so involved in the campaign, to be attacked by malaria and forced into inactivity as soon as Hay returned to Washington was for a man who so thoroughly enjoyed a speaker's platform a most unhappy turn of events. "The month of September was simply awful," he wrote to Andrew D. White from Nantasket on October 14. "It brought me down and made it necessary to run up here for recuperation. I have been chafing under my restraint for I am burning to go into the campaign on the stump. I have not been thrown out wholly, however, as my pamphlets have been printed in editions of 2 millions and reprinted in many newspapers. I am still hoping to put in my voice before the month closes."[14] But Hill's campaigning for that year was over.

If America were to play the broader role in world affairs that its new expansionist policy foretold, it occurred to some people that it was time to reorganize the diplomatic and consular corps to ensure that the nation was represented abroad by qualified men. In the Senate, Henry Cabot Lodge introduced a bill to improve the foreign services, and in the House, William F. Aldrich of Alabama submitted a more far-reaching measure to establish a service college under the control of the State Department. Both bills came to nothing, as did all other suggestions for upgrading the foreign services. To Hill this was a matter of direct concern, for as Assistant Secretary of State he was the official head of the consular service.

He was constantly being importuned by post-seekers for assistance, but as he replied to one solicitor, he could not place the best-qualified person in the country in the most humble consular office unless the applicant could come to Washington loaded down with political endorsements, and even then he would probably have to wait until appointments were made wholesale at a change of administration. Just as Andrew D. White had earlier advised him, Hill advised others to stay away from the consular service. "Unless circumstances combine to open the way for a young man to enter this branch of Government Service in some unusual manner," he answered another aspirant, "I hardly think it is worth his while when there are so many attractive avenues in life to waste his time in a long struggle to secure a consular position, which when attained, may have to be abandoned in a few years and almost invariably leads to nothing else."[15]

Several times when speaking before academic groups, Hill tried to stir up support for the development of career services.[16] More important, at least in providing qualified young men who might perhaps break into the present services, was the assistance he gave to the newly established School of Comparative Jurisprudence and Diplomacy of Columbian University. Opened in November 1898 to give graduate training to young men interested in careers in public administration, the foreign services, or international law, the school was unique in the United States and almost in the world. The only other institution of its kind was the Ecole Libre des Sciences Politiques in Paris. Since Hill was one of the few Americans to have studied at the Paris school, the dean of its new Washington counterpart, Charles W. Needham, called on him for advice in developing courses of study. Needham also asked Hill to give a course himself on the history of European diplomacy. "Probably no course in the school," the *Washington Post* noted in November 1899, shortly after Hill began to teach it, ". . . is attracting wider notice or more favorable criticism."[17]

Despite the anomaly of preparing young men for positions for which there was neither any direct demand nor any sure career, the school was a successful educational, though not financial, venture. And because of new interest in foreign affairs stirred by the war with Spain and its expansionist fruits, there soon appeared innumerable plans for similar schools of diplomacy all over the country. But neither the Columbian school nor the others being proposed—none of which materialized—seemed to Hill adequate to the needs of the time. A school that would put political science on a "really scientific plane" should not be a department of a university, but an independent institution designed to crown the work done in political science throughout the country. Furnishing uniquely high and broad instruction, it should bring together for short periods the best teaching talent of the United States and abroad and the most advanced students, with the study done there being credited in the universities from which the students temporarily came. With the best teachers and the best students examining special problems together, and preserving the best results in publications, the study of political science throughout the country would be stimulated, directed, and unified. The school should be located in Washington, where government in operation could be directly observed, and where, Hill believed, it would ultimately help to improve international relations by bringing national and international problems continually under study.[18]

Drawing up specifics for such a school, Hill sent them to Andrew D. White, who was at that time corresponding with Andrew Carnegie about the educational institution the ironmaster had decided to found in Washington. Having no fixed ideas as to the type it should be, Carnegie had asked advice from White, whom he held in high esteem and sometimes probed for suggestions on how to use his wealth. White included Hill's plan in a broad educational scheme he sketched out for Carnegie's consideration, but when the plans for the Carnegie Institution were announced, they did not include provisions for university type of instruction.[19]

Hill also proposed his plan to Frederick T. Gates, an associate of John D. Rockefeller who watched over the educational foundations established by the famous oilman. Gates and John D. Rockefeller, Jr., were sufficiently interested to call in Starr J. Murphy, a New York attorney employed to assist them in evaluating such schemes. For almost a year, exploring every facet of the proposal, Gates and Murphy corresponded with Hill, and Murphy made several trips to Washington to see him personally. But finally in November 1902 Hill received a brief note from Gates informing him that Mr. Rockefeller had concluded that it would not be best for him at the present time to establish the institution Hill had so earnestly and ably advocated.[20]

Several weeks later, on the eve of sailing from New York for what was to be a decade of residence in Europe, Hill made the acquaintance of Andrew Carnegie through his friend Holls. Hoping that Carnegie might still be persuaded to support his plan, Hill took the opportunity to send him another statement of it. Although the two men later developed a close association through Carnegie's interest in promoting international arbitration, and Hill several times visited Skibo Castle, Carnegie's princely retreat in northern Scotland, the ironmaster never expressed any interest in the plan, and Hill never mentioned it again.[21]

In 1907 Hill's plan received a somewhat odd form of recognition. The George Washington University, reorganized from the old Columbian University in 1904, published it on the occasion of a major endowment drive in order to promote its own College of the Political Sciences, stating that Hill now favored the development of this school instead of the creation of the new and separate institution he had contemplated five years before. It is doubtful whether Hill really did, for two years later, upon being sounded out for the presidency of the University of Michigan, he wrote to Andrew D. White that the one opportunity he would not hesitate to accept would be the chance to carry out the plan he had long been elaborating for an independent college of political science. Hill nursed this hope for a very long time, until he was finally ready to confess in 1925 to a would-be promoter of a somewhat different kind of school that the obstacles he had encountered in trying to establish this unprecedented type of college had diminished his interest in the subject.[22]

6

Switzerland and the Netherlands

LIFE IN WASHINGTON WAS PLEASANT FOR THE HILLS. INCOME FROM INVEST-
ments enabled them to live more affluently and entertain more
generously than David's salary alone would have permitted; he once
remarked that it cost him to live, in the manner expected of him,
more than twice what he was able to earn. Their home became
known for its hospitality. David was reputed by *Harper's Weekly*
to be one of the most accomplished conversationalists in the capital, while Juliet was regarded as the finest linguist in Washington
society and the favorite hostess of the continental diplomats. Her
weekly afternoon receptions, for which no invitations were ever
issued, were always so packed that they became known as "Mrs.
Hill's crushes." After the work and social preoccupation of the
winter, David and Juliet enjoyed the relaxation of summers at
Nantasket Beach on the Massachusetts coast, but because Juliet
would remain with the children well into October, there were long
absences from David, who had to spend at least half the summer
months in Washington's enervating heat. This was a lesser discon-
certion, however, than the fact that although Hill was elected
president of the Washington Literary Society, his work at the

State Department left him little opportunity for writing.[1] The materials he had collected for his history of diplomacy lay gathering dust, and he longed for a diplomatic post in Europe where he would have the leisure to begin work on them.

In the summer of 1901 rumors began to circulate that Andrew D. White would resign from Berlin. Since the German capital was not now the overly ambitious goal it would have been in 1896, Hill asked Secretary Hay and Senator Platt to urge his appointment on the President. At this same time, he was asked by David R. Francis, president of the Louisiana Purchase Centennial Exposition, if he would accept a commission to tour Europe to enlist foreign participation in the great fair to be held in St. Louis in 1904. When Hay spoke of both matters to McKinley, the President agreed that Hill was fitted for the highest diplomatic work, but he did not think White would resign. In any event, he protested, he could not permanently keep the country's three principal embassies in the hands of New York men. As for the Exposition offer, he would be sorry to have Hill leave the Department, McKinley said, but it was for Hill himself to decide. "He is as much at loss as I am in regard to supplying your place, if you should go," Hay reported back to Hill. "In all my large acquaintance, and in his, which is ten times as large, we do not know a man whom we should think capable of replacing you. If we fell back on the *semper paratus* Adee, the difficulty would be equal, of filling *his* place. So you see my perplexity about advising you. If I followed my own selfish and tortuous inclinations I would in the usual diplomatic fashion say 'Stay with us, and we will give you the first Embassy we find floating up the river on a brick-bat.' But I can only say, as Garibaldi said to his volunteers, 'Come with me. I offer you privation, hunger, wounds and death—and the service of your country.' It amounts to something like that. If you stay, we shall be glad and grateful. If you go, you will go with our blessing." The next day Hill declined Governor Francis's offer.[2]

Hill apparently knew for certain that White would retire, and he was not discouraged by McKinley's initial reaction to the suggestion that he succeed him. He did not believe that the President, after having sanctioned a New York representation to Berlin for so long, would really think it improper to appoint another man from the same state.[3] A few weeks later, however, McKinley's tragic death and the elevation of Theodore Roosevelt to the presidency left Washington with a new pattern of political obligations and uncertainties.

Early the next year, Roosevelt appointed Hill to head a delegation charged with the reception and entertainment of Prince Henry of Prussia when the brother of the Kaiser visited the United States in February and March. It was the first time the hospitality of the nation had been formally extended to a foreign prince. The earlier visits of the Prince of Wales and the Grand Duke Alexis of Russia had been of unofficial and informal character, and Hill had no precedents to turn to in arranging all the details of the Prince's itinerary and activities. Yet, if anything went wrong, he knew where the blame would fall. But everything went without a hitch, the Prince appeared pleased with his visit, and Hill could hope that he had bettered his prospects for the Berlin mission.[4]

In mid-March, immediately after the Prince's tour was over, Hill began writing to friends who might help influence the President.[5] A few weeks later, the newspapers reported that White would retire on November 7, his seventieth birthday, and speculated that his successor would be either Hill or Bellamy Storer, who was now minister to Spain. Calling on Roosevelt as old friends, Nicholas Murray Butler and Frederick Holls urged him to name Hill. Roosevelt told them he was committed to give the first vacant embassy to Storer and was also reluctant to allow Charlemagne Tower to drop out of the diplomatic service. Tower was a Philadelphia public utilities multi-millionaire and lavish contributor of Republican campaign funds who was presently at St. Petersburg but wanted to be transferred to Berlin, a request backed by Pennsylvania's powerful senators, Matthew Quay and Boise Penrose. Other friends of the President were working for other candidates, and, as Holls wrote to White, there was "a lot of 'pulling, hauling and intriguing' in Washington."[6]

White's letter of resignation arrived at the State Department on August 1. It came to the attention of Chief Clerk Michael late in the day when he was there alone, and Michael immediately sent a copy to Hill, who had left that morning for his vacation at Nantasket.[7]

Consequently, almost as soon as Roosevelt and Hay learned officially of White's resignation, Hill was organizing a barrage of political
endorsements upon the President, and former Congressmen John
Van Voorhis and James M. E. O'Grady were getting together a
Rochester delegation to go to Oyster Bay.[8]

Prominent among the endorsements were those from the Secretary of Agriculture, mid-western congressmen, the meat packers
of Chicago, and politically influential German-Americans, for it
was part of Hill's strategy to be presented to the President as the
candidate of the country's agricultural interests and its German-
American people. Commercial relations with Germany were
strained. Its manufactures shut out of the American market by
high tariffs, Germany had retaliated with import restrictions on
American fruit, meat, and other provisions, and was threatening
by pending legislation to exclude these goods entirely. Having
handled the diplomatic correspondence with Germany at the State
Department and being well versed in the subject, Hill offered a
good case that he was the logical person to improve relations and
revise the mutually unsatisfactory commercial treaties. He also
claimed that because of his knowledge and appreciation of the German language, culture, and character, he would be eminently satisfactory to the country's large German-American population. For
this second prong of his strategy he had begun laying the groundwork a full two years before by sending copies of the German editions of his campaign pamphlets to German-Americans suggested
by Holls and by Professor M. D. Learned of the University of
Pennsylvania.[9]

Writing to Secretary Hay, Hill noted that he had been with the
Department longer than all but one of his twenty-four predecessors, the last four of whom had been promoted to other important
duties after much shorter periods. Because he should by now be
capable of greater usefulness in the foreign service, he hoped that
the President would assign him to a post to which he was fitted.
"I hardly know what to say of your chances," Hay wrote back,
saying that he had sent Hill's letter with a strong endorsement of
his own to Roosevelt. "You have been more optimistic than I have
been. I have pretty well despaired of ever seeing an important appointment go to a man in whom neither the President nor Senators

are vitally interested. Not a man in the service owes his place to me—after four years' service as Secretary of State." Hay's score remained clean. The German embassy, Roosevelt replied, would have to go either to Tower or to Storer.[10]

Until the appointment was actually made, Hill felt he still had a chance. Late in August, Congressman Henry S. Boutell of Chicago instigated more telegrams to Washington from mid-western politicians, Chicago meat packers, and spokesmen of German-Americans. And early in September, Frederick Holls arranged with "Holland," a political commentator featured in newspapers throughout the Middle West, for a plug for Hill's appointment in his column.[11] But when on September 26 a shuffling of diplomatic posts was announced, Hill was left out. Charlemagne Tower was transferred from Russia to Germany, Robert S. McCormick from Austria-Hungary to Russia, Bellamy Storer from Spain to Austria-Hungary, Arthur S. Hardy from Switzerland to Spain, Charles P. Bryan from Brazil to Switzerland, and David Thompson of Nebraska was appointed to Brazil.[12]

Three weeks later, on October 16, Juliet departed for Switzerland, where she rented a villa in Lausanne and placed David, Jr., and Catherine in school. Shortly afterwards, Hill gave up his house at 1313 K Street and took up residence in a club. Nothing indicates that these moves had previously been planned. Apparently, seeing that Switzerland was to be involved in the chain of diplomatic transfers about to take place, Hill had persuaded the President to give the post to him. Before any announcement was made, the American ambassador to Japan died, and Roosevelt offered Hill this higher mission. But anxious to start on his history, Hill declined, pleading that his children were at an age when they required Europe rather than Cathay. Roosevelt also considered sending Hill to The Hague, the seat of the new international tribunal whose development the President wanted to encourage. Although Stanford Newel, who was still the American minister there, had been a delegate to the Peace Conference, he thought that its work had been utterly unimportant. This annoyed Roosevelt, but Newel did not want to leave The Hague, and wary of offending his political backers from the Northwest, Roosevelt hesitated to remove him.

Therefore, on January 5, 1903, when a further shuffling of diplomatic positions was announced, Charles Bryan was sent to Portugal, Francis B. Loomis was brought home from there to be the new Assistant Secretary, and Hill was given the legation in Switzerland.[13]

For the time being, Hill was content with this assignment. After more than four busy years at the State Department, a quiet post where he could rest and write was exceedingly attractive.[14] And a more important mission in the future seemed assured. "I am sorry to have you leave the Department of State where you have been so useful and done so well," Roosevelt had said to him before he sailed. "I would rather have you in Japan where your knowledge of diplomacy and capacity for it would be so useful, or at The Hague on account of your extensive knowledge of international law and interest in The Hague Tribunal, but I am content for the present, since you wish it, to have you in Switzerland."[15]

Hill arrived at the Swiss capital city of Berne in mid-February 1903, and immediately learned his first impressive lesson as an American diplomat abroad. Unlike many governments, the United States did not provide its representatives with residences; they lived wherever their good fortune, financial or otherwise, allowed them. And a suitable house in the Swiss capital, Hill quickly discovered, was simply not to be found. His two predecessors had been forced to live outside the capital; Mr. Leishman near Lucerne, and Mr. Hardy at Rolle. Because of better train service to Berne, and excellent schools for his children nearby, Hill decided to try Geneva. After some searching, he finally found a satisfactory house, with American comforts, in the pleasant quarter of that city known as Les Franchées.[16]

The undemanding diplomatic routine at Berne, broken only by occasional negotiations on a commercial treaty, allowed Hill to work steadily on his diplomatic history of Europe. "I am more deeply interested in it," he wrote to Dr. White, "than I have been in anything for many years." In the summer of 1905, Longmans, Green and Company published the first volume, *The Struggle for Universal Empire*, of a projected multi-volumed work bearing the general title, *A History of Diplomacy in the International Development of*

Europe. Structured around the theme of the imperial idea and the long contest for possession of the universal authority that the idea represented, the volume surveyed the history of Europe from its organization under the Roman Empire through the disruption of the barbarian invasions, the revival of the Empire in the West by Charlemagne, and the rise and conflict of the Papacy and the Holy Roman Empire to the rise of the national monarchies in the thirteenth and fourteenth centuries. "No English writer, with the possible exception of James Bryce," wrote William C. Morey, "has grasped so completely the conception of the continuity of the imperial idea as the key to the international history of Europe from the fall of Rome to the rise of modern nations." Other equally laudatory reviews spoke of the volume's thoroughness of research, ripeness of reflections, judicial tone, and rare felicity of style.[17]

The second volume, *The Establishment of Territorial Sovereignty,* appeared in the autumn of 1906. Beginning with the Hundred Years' War and ending with the Peace of Westphalia, it recounted the formation of the modern states, their schemes of expansion, and their rivalry for primacy. Reviewers were again favorably impressed. Four more volumes were to follow, treating of the Age of Absolutism, the Revolutionary Era, the Constitutional Movement, and Commercial Imperialism, bringing the history of Europe's international development down to Hill's own time. It was a monumental project that promised to rank with the best histories of Europe. The scholarly Albert Shaw, owner and editor of the *American Monthly Review of Reviews,* was already disposed without further waiting to wrap Hill in the great tradition of Motley, Prescott, and Bancroft.[18]

Hill, meantime, had been transferred to The Hague. The President had intimated to Frederick Holls before Hill left Washingtin that this promotion was in store as soon as it was politically practicable, and he had later twice assured Holls that he was keeping the matter in mind. But Hill had been in Switzerland less than half a year when Holls died, and nothing more seems to have been said by anyone about a change of posts. In September 1904, Hill returned to the United States to read a paper before an International Congress of Arts and Sciences convened at the Louisiana

Exposition in St. Louis. Taking the opportunity to visit Rochester, he learned that a revolt was developing throughout New York against the Republican state party organization. Since its effects could easily transcend state lines in a presidential election year, he immediately informed Roosevelt. The President had already received other reports, and began to fear that if a large number of voters tried to cut the Republican state ticket, a good many would vote against the national ticket as well. Since his minister to Switzerland would be of more use to him at the moment campaigning in western New York than he would be at Berne, Roosevelt ordered Hill's leave of absence extended until after the election. In addition to local electioneering, Hill wrote an article for national circulation describing America's recent role in promoting world peace, its purpose being to repudiate the idea that Roosevelt and a Republican administration might plunge the country into dangerous foreign adventures. That he should write it was suggested to the President by Albert Shaw, who with Robert Patterson, owner of the *Chicago Tribune*, was arranging a series of articles that Roosevelt was personally reviewing.[19] The influence of these limited campaign activities on Hill's diplomatic career was probably not large; more important, no doubt, was the fact that the election freed the President from old political pressures. Still, it was not an ill moment to come once again to the President's attention. In the diplomatic reassignments that followed Roosevelt's inauguration the next March, Hill was sent to The Hague.

Although pleased by the promotion, David and Juliet regretted leaving Switzerland. "Our life there was ideal," Juliet wrote to Dr. White. "My husband says the two and a half years we spent there were the best of his life."[20]

Upon arriving at The Hague, Hill again had difficulty finding a suitable residence. He rented a country house at Bloemendaal, where he could stay only until October, then for several months his family squeezed themselves into a tiny villa at Scheveningen. It was not until almost a year after coming to the Netherlands, and after awaiting the installation of central heating, electric lighting, and other improvements, that they moved into a pleasant villa that was close to ideal. Conveniently located midway between The

Hague and Scheveningen on the stately, tree-lined Old Scheveningen Way, the "Banchory" graced what Juliet thought one of the most beautiful spots in Europe.[21]

Such difficulties were not unusual for American diplomats, but Hill also encountered another that was quite unexpected. While still at the State Department, he had been asked by Wu Ting-fang, then Chinese minister to Washington, if he would accept a nomination to the Hague Court from China. China delayed ratification of the Hague Convention for several years, and when it finally inquired if the State Department would object if it appointed Hill to the Court, Hill was about to be reassigned to the seat of that tribunal. Secretary Hay replied that although there might have been no serious obstacle while Hill was minister to Switzerland, there might be a certain embarrassment in having the United States minister to The Hague act as an arbitrator. Wu Ting-fang, who now headed his country's foreign office, thought Hay was too cautious and his objection groundless. Although a diplomatic representive to The Hague from a state signatory to the Convention became a member of the Court's Administrative Council, Wu pointed out that he had no judicial functions or authority and was thus no different in that respect from a diplomatic representative to any other country. But neither Wu's arguments nor similar ones by Hill overcame the Secretary's objection, and Hill had to inform Wu that he could not accept the honor while he was minister to The Hague. This disqualification, he added, would be only temporary and might be quite brief, and if China later had a place on the Court at its disposal he would be happy to accept it. Wu assured him that in such case he would be pleased to recommend him again; but the offer was never repeated.[22]

Residence at The Hague did permit Hill to serve the Court in another way. The day before he had sailed to take up his post in Switzerland, he was present with Frederick Holls when Andrew Carnegie agreed to issue a statement that he would give $1,500,000 for a building and library for the use of the Court. Holls, who with Andrew D. White had been urging Carnegie to make this gift, was under the impression that the ironmaster wanted to set up a corporation to administer it, consisting of Holls and White and Hill,

whose membership would be useful when Roosevelt transferred
him to The Hague. Instead, Carnegie stipulated that his gift was
to be held in trust by the Netherlands government. The Dutch established an administrative foundation, which acquired a site and
selected plans for the courthouse by international competition.
The winning architect, it was announced in May 1906, was L. M.
Cordonnier of Lille, France. But the jury charged with making the
decision found none of the plans submitted really suitable, and
Cordonnier's plans had faults. The most serious was that by housing the library in a separate building attached to the courthouse,
they would push costs far beyond what Carnegie had given. The
foundation's directors, however, decided not to hold a second competition, but to ask Carnegie for more money. Since Hill was by
this time at The Hague, they turned to him as their intermediary.[23]

At the request of Jonkeer Van Karnebeek, the foundation's president, Hill relayed their entreaty to Carnegie, who was spending
the summer at Skibo Castle. The directors asked for an additional
endowment for the special support of the library. But whereas
Carnegie had intended a library for the use of the Court, the
directors were contemplating a library that would be the world's
leading center for the study and promotion of international law, at
a cost of at least another half-million dollars. Carnegie was hardly
enthusiastic, and two days later, when he received drawings of the
winning plans, he was downright irate. The elaborate and showy
building they depicted was a far cry from the simple, dignified
structure of chaste beauty that he had in mind. But it was still
the inflated scheme for the library that annoyed Carnegie the most.
The library seemed to be more important to the directors than the
Court itself, and the ironmaster was "positively wounded." "To
speak of 'The Library and Court of Arbitration' is as if a bereaved
husband were to ask plans for a sacred shrine to 'My nephew and
my dear wife,'" he wrote to Hill. If all the architects had been asked
to submit plans for both a Temple and a library, it was no wonder
that the jury had been unable to find any that satisfied them. "Architects, or the one hereafter chosen, should be asked for plans for a
Temple of Peace, pure and simple."[24]

The directors' reply was stuffy and stubborn. Carnegie's complaint, they said, was not at all in accord with his original intentions, which called for the establishment of a library, and they must carry out the task originally imposed on them. "The only library Mr. Holls ever suggested to me was one for the Court of Arbitration," Carnegie retorted. That was what the trust deed provided for, not for a world library, and the directors would have to reconsider their plan and manage according to their means. "Naturally this matter touches me deeply," he wrote to Hill personally. "If necessary a small committee could come over and see me here, in which case I should have to beg you to accompany them. . . . It seems clear to me that they must make a fresh start. . . . Not a dollar more will I ever give. . . . To me the building proposed is no Temple of Peace, but shouts all over of 'the pomp, pride and circumstances of *in*glorious war.'" To this Carnegie postscribed, "You play the Rooseveltian part of 'The Peacemaker.'"[25]

He had suggested the visit to Skibo, Hill answered. But since the directors, having gone so far afield, would probably feel sensitive about repudiating what they had done, he thought it would be best to wait a little to give them time to see that eventually they would have to execute their trust as Carnegie intended. The directors, however, retreated with haste, for three days later Hill informed Carnegie that in another long talk with Van Karnebeek the president had agreed that the Temple of Peace should be planned and constructed as its donor desired. It would still be well to have a friendly conference, Hill advised. It might help reassure both sides.[26]

At Carnegie's renewed request that he play "Roosevelt the Peace Maker," Hill accompanied Van Karnebeek to Skibo in August 1906. There it was agreed that the Temple itself must first be entirely completed; after that any remaining funds might be devoted to the books, maps, and other materials the directors thought most important to a library for the use of the Court. When the directors later decided, nevertheless, to proceed with Cordonnier's plans, even though they would require considerable modification, Carnegie was again displeased. But he made no further protest. "Like you I am disappointed but we must hope for the best," he wrote to Hill. "We may yet be saved a Bazar instead of a Temple.

I hope you will watch the new plan submitted and express your views again and again."[27] But hoping for the best did little good. Although the separate library building, one of three originally planned towers, and some ornamentation were eliminated, the Temple of Peace when finally completed in 1913 still closely resembled the original drawings that Carnegie had found so offensive.

While Hill was making peace between Carnegie and the directors of the Dutch Carnegie Foundation, preparations were under way for a second conference at The Hague to further the maintenance of the larger peace among nations. Expecting the conference to meet a year before it did, President Roosevelt early in 1906 designated Joseph H. Choate, former ambassador to England, General Horace Porter, former ambassador to France, and Uriah M. Rose, former president of the American Bar Association, to represent the United States. In view of Roosevelt's explanation of only a few years before for wanting him at The Hague, Hill wondered why he had not been named, and spoke of this to Albert Shaw, who visited him at the Dutch capital. Upon his return to the United States Shaw saw the President, who, speaking as if it had not occurred to him before, agreed that Hill should be appointed. Meanwhile, Secretary of State Elihu Root, who had taken office when John Hay died in 1905, had already acted on the matter. Root did not want to make the commission any larger than he thought those of the leading European powers would be, but was willing to add Hill to the delegation in a manner suggested by Alvey Adee. "We do not feel that we can appoint more than three delegates to the Second Hague Conference, all of whom have been selected," the Secretary wrote to Hill, "but it is proposed to send also a military man and a naval expert, and we should be glad to add you to the Commission as an expert in international law."[28]

Accepting the appointment, but not wholly pleased with it, Hill questioned the Secretary about his status with patent indirection. "As the rank of a diplomatic representative is of some importance to his country," he wrote, "I am led to inquire if the naval and military experts in the Second Commission will enjoy the same relative position as Captain Mahan and Captain Crozier did in the first? In placing them directly after the Minister of the United States to the Netherlands it was intended to give them the influence in the Conference which such rank alone could secure to them. To have made them 'attaches' would have deprived them of the greater part of their value. I am probably not wrong in supposing that my Government does not intend to place its experts on a lower level than in the first Conference." The experts, Root answered, would be attached to the commission as advisers and would have no representative character or voice in the conference.[29]

Hill could not properly press the matter further, but Adee and Shaw were not so debarred. Seven months later, in January 1907, Adee wrote encouragingly that Root no longer appeared to regard it important that the delegation be sharply restricted in number. Early in March, Shaw wrote that the matter was settled: he had seen the President and Root about it several times, Roosevelt had said emphatically that he wanted Hill on the commission, and Root had consented. "The Pres. would do the whole thing different if he were making the appointments now," Shaw added. "He wants you on, and Mr. Root's good-will in the matter is perfect. So don't give it any further worry."[30]

The commission as finally constituted was three times the size of the original. In addition to Choate, Porter, and Rose, who were each given the rank of ambassador, the delegates plenipotentiary were Hill, Brigadier General George B. Davis, Judge Advocate General of the Army, Rear Admiral Charles S. Sperry, former president of the Naval War College, and William I. Buchanan, former minister to Argentina, each with the rank of minister. Holding the rank of technical delegates were James Brown Scott, solicitor for the Department of State, as expert in international law, and Charles H. Butler, reporter of the Supreme Court, as expert attaché.[31]

"We are suffering somewhat from unwieldy numbers," Hill wrote to Andrew D. White about a month after the conference opened on June 15, 1907. "Our own delegation, on the whole, is strong but it seems to me unnecessarily large." James Brown Scott in his history of the Peace Conferences also implied that a smaller commission would have been more efficient. The inclusion of three delegates with the rank of ambassador, which was probably more the result of the way the commission was patched together than of intention to give it greater prominence, served no useful purpose. It only inconvenienced hosts in the seating of dinner parties. Other leading powers designated only their heads of delegations as ambassadors, and thirty of the forty-four nations represented sent no delegates at all of ambassadorial status, and all were on the same footing in the sessions.[32] Within the American commission, James Brown Scott, a technical delegate, played a part in the formal sessions second only to Ambassador Joseph Choate, the head of the delegation.

Hill spoke only twice in the formal sessions, making brief technical reservations for the American delegation. As the American member of the drafting committee, and off-scenes, however, he worked hard. Edwin D. Mead, a prominent American pacifist who was present at The Hague, thought that few men were more useful. Ironically, in view of his earlier housing problem and exclusion from the commission, much of Hill's usefulness was related to the fact that he was the American minister resident at The Hague in surroundings creditable to his government. "I have not been away from The Hague one day," Hill wrote to Carnegie in October, after the conference had dragged on nearly four months, "neither have Mr. Choate or Mr. Porter, although our colleagues have been more indulgent to themselves." "We have all worked very diligently and put in peril our digestion," he commented ruefully. "I have personally assisted at about ninety dinners during the Conference. The most profitable of these so far as our work is concerned have been the small ones, of ten to sixteen people, where we have really been able to sound one another and talk familiarly regarding questions in hand. In this way we have brought together in our own house all the leading personalities in the Conference, have made their acquaintance and have ascertained their views from their own lips. Mrs. Hill's Tuesdays have also been exceedingly useful in this respect, so that we have gathered an immense amount of information—some of it important—regarding the attitude of the different Governments on a host of subjects."[33]

The American delegation had again been instructed to propose a continuously sitting Court of Arbitral Justice, and Hill's plan of 1899 had been appended for their guidance. The conference agreed in principle on the draft of a treaty for a new court, entirely voluntary in its jurisdiction, but could proceed no further because of disagreement between the large and small powers over the method of electing its judges. A second major objective of the American commission was to secure the adoption of a general treaty of obligatory arbitration that would expand the usefulness of the existing court. The conference constructed such a treaty, which omitted all questions of "vital interests, independence, or honor" and embraced only a meager list of mainly unimportant subjects, but failed in the end to adopt it because of the opposition of Germany. The conference did adopt over a dozen conventions, but most of them were merely efforts to make less horrible the wars it could reach no agreement on how to prevent.[34]

In a long letter to Carnegie written over a period of several days, Hill described the subtle play of politics in which nations professed to support projects yet conspired to thwart them, and the growing success of Germany in blocking any action toward effective arbitration. "Against it," he wrote, "is the solid German *bloc*, composed of eight powers that have rallied round the German opposition to obligatory arbitration in the form of a general treaty."

> There is no doubt that, at the present moment, Germany is the obstructive element. No other great power stands in the way. But Germany cannot be forced to change her attitude. Her government is founded upon militarism, is strong and believes in itself. . . . It is evident that the great task for our American diplomacy on the continent of Europe is to win Germany, if possible, to our way of thinking, by taking her at her word in her efforts to go forward in the right direction, as she professes the wish to do. She openly accepts the *principle* of obligatory arbitration. She says she is willing to negotiate separate and special treaties. Let us help her to do this, and try to meet her half way in this ourselves. . . . It seems to me a peculiarly pyschological moment in our relations with Germany. Her delegates here feel that the American leadership in arbitration has exposed Germany to the charge of being "reactionary." The word, even, has been

uttered. She entered the conference reluctantly, but with a strong wish and effort to form an *entente* with America. Baron Marschall has done everything in his power to carry out his instructions, but he has found it impossible to meet our wishes on arbitration. When he goes to Berlin he will tell all that he thinks and all that he feels and the result will be that Americanism will not be at a premium at the German capital, for the twenty-one American votes have made possible the majorities that give him disquietude. There will be a disposition there to curb our influence, to divide our friends, and to check our future action in Europe. The proof of it is that it has already begun here.[35]

Whether American diplomacy could bring Germany to sign even the most innocuous treaty of obligatory arbitration was something Hill was to find out for himself. Sailing for America in November to take a leave of absence in the United States, he learned en route by wireless that President Roosevelt had appointed him ambassador to Berlin.[36]

7

Germany

WRITING TO PRESIDENT ROOSEVELT ON OTHER MATTERS IN SEPTEMBER 1907, Ambassador Tower at Berlin mentioned that he would probably ask to be excused from the diplomatic service sometime during the coming summer. Apparently eager to unload a political obligation, Roosevelt, without waiting for Tower's formal resignation, apprised Berlin that his new ambassador would be David Jayne Hill. The German Foreign Office expressed its approval on November 6, and two days later the State Department announced the appointment.[1]

Charlemagne Tower had riches to match the grandeur of his name. His residence in Berlin required a minimum force of twenty servants and an annual expenditure more than double his salary as ambassador. He entertained magnificently. Hill could not live in such princely fashion and so told the President. To Roosevelt it did not matter, but to Berlin society it mattered very much. "The members of the Imperial Court fluttered about the flame the American dollars made," commented the *New York Times.* "American multimillionaires . . . were exceedingly agreeable to the German Kaiser," said Prince von Bülow, Chancellor of the German Empire. "Wilhelm II resembled his uncle, King Edward, in that great wealth made a strong impression on him." The new ambassador, Berlin society was soon gossiping, could never discharge his social duties with the same generous hand of the Towers.[2]

Attempts of a somewhat mysterious nature were made to dissuade Hill from accepting the post, but unaware of the gossip in the German capital, he attached no importance to them. Early in March 1908, he visited Berlin for the State Department to scout for an embassy building in the event that a bill before Congress for purchasing one were passed. He lunched with Consul General and Mrs. Alexander Thackara and dined with the Towers, and did not sense anything disagreeable in the air. But on the evening of March 25, upon arriving in Paris to consult with Consul General Frank H. Mason about residences in Berlin, he learned from a reporter of the Associated Press that the Kaiser had refused to receive him at the German court.[3]

Knowing nothing except that the Kaiser had repented his earlier acceptance of Hill, the press of two continents trouped headlong into the field of conjectural scandal so enticingly thrown open: The new ambassador had offended Prince Henry when the pompous brother of the Kaiser had visited the United States in 1902. He had displeased Germany at the recent Hague Conference. He had somewhere in his writings criticized the German Empire. He was a Catholic. He had shown unforgivably bad manners while Assistant Secretary of State by serving beer to German high officials at an evening entertainment. His wife went marketing at The Hague on a bicycle. "He habitchully disgraces himsilf be thryin' to live within his means," said Mr. Dooley. "He looks like a profissor. He lives in a flat. Well, ye cud go on tellin' about his deficiencies f'r a year."[4]

But the explanation the press took most seriously was that Hill was not wealthy enough to maintain the American embassy's present social brilliance. And that was indeed the fact of the matter. According to the memoirs of Lloyd Griscom, American ambassador at Rome, who had been invited to a dinner given for the Kaiser by Ambassador Tower on March 13, Wilhelm II had deprecated the fact that Hill, *"einer ganz kleiner Mann,"* had been selected as Tower's successor. The next evening at the opera, Griscom further recounts, the Kaiser drew him aside to give him a message for the President. For the past few years he had devoted every effort to build up the most friendly relations between Germany and the United States, Wilhelm confided. Mr. Tower had cooperated splendidly and had created for the American embassy a position never before equaled. Germans were now clamoring to be received there. He had been asked about Mr. Hill informally and had indicated somewhat hastily that the appointment was acceptable. Since then he had obtained other information. His brother said that Hill was utterly unsuited. "We have now a little rosebud of friendship which is sprouting, but which requires the most careful nursing. It would really be a most serious thing for me, and I believe for the United States, if we should allow it to die. I am convinced it will wither if a man of the type of Mr. Hill is sent here." Let the President choose a more distinguished and influential person, the Kaiser suggested. Mr. Meyer (the American ambassador at St. Petersburg) would do splendidly. So would the Griscoms, which he knew two minutes after seeing them. "But in any event, the President should know what a great position your Embassy has here in Berlin. I am determined that it shall not be lost if I can help it." Wilhelm then directed Tower to bring Griscom to the Palace on Monday to continue the conversation.

Griscom records that he was at a loss as to what to do and fearful of harming his own diplomatic career. The Kaiser had made a direct request, which he could not evade, but it would be difficult to persuade Roosevelt that he had not gone to Berlin expressly to intrigue for the German post. The Monday interview proved worse than he had anticipated. The Emperor asked him outright to be the next ambassador to Germany. When he said that it would be a mistake to reject Hill and he could not in any case leave Italy, all the Kaiser would reply was, "If you cannot come, you must send somebody else." Taking long enough to record the conversation and without completing his visit in Berlin, Griscom departed for Rome.[5]

According to Charlemagne Tower, he too was an innocent and embarrassed victim of the Kaiser's about-face. But his version of

what took place differs from Griscom's account. At the dinner of
March 13 the Kaiser freely expressed an unfavorable opinion of
Hill, Tower wrote to President Roosevelt personally and to the
State Department officially. On Sunday, March 15, he lunched
with the Kaiser, Tower went on. When Wilhelm said that
Roosevelt ought to know he did not want Hill at Berlin, Tower
offered to make it the subject of an official communication. The
Kaiser preferred that he communicate it to the President personally. This Tower asked to be excused from doing, since it concerned
his own post and his successor. Understanding Tower's feelings of
propriety, the Kaiser decided to communicate with Roosevelt
through Griscom, who could better act in a private capacity.
Whereupon the Emperor had a long conversation with Griscom at
the opera on Monday evening.[6] According to Griscom, however,
the conversation at the opera had already taken place on Saturday;
and nowhere in his communications did Tower mention the interview that Griscom said took place at the Palace on Monday.

A third account is found in the memoirs of Foreign Secretary
Baron von Schoen. At the dinner given by Tower for the Kaiser,
wrote the Baron, it was Tower who spoke of the difficulty Hill
would have in living like other ambassadors of great powers and
suggested that Roosevelt would be willing to send someone
specially suited for Berlin if he heard the Kaiser wished it. He recommended Griscom as just the right man, and volunteered to suggest this to the President confidentially. Wilhelm inquired of von
Schoen how matters stood on the acceptance of Hill, and being
told that the Foreign Office considered Roosevelt's inquiry as
merely a feeler and there had been so formal agréments, he accepted Tower's proposal.[7]

When the Baron's memoirs appeared in 1921, Tower denied
that this conversation had taken place or that he had ever heard
anyone connected with the German government propose sending an "official" request to Roosevelt to appoint someone other
than Hill. "Neither did I ever hear the subject discussed by anybody in Germany as to whether Dr. Hill was a rich or a poor man,"[8]
Tower added, straining further the credibility of his statement.

According to Tower's own account, he had asked to be excused from communicating the Kaiser's message personally to the President, yet he wrote to Roosevelt the next day. On March 21 he cabled the State Department that the Kaiser preferred someone other than Hill and that a letter forwarding this personal communication to the President was on the way. Secretary of State Root cabled back on the twenty-fifth that he and the President did not see now how Hill's appointment could be changed, but they would await Tower's letter. Before anything further was known in Washington, the story was leaked to the press. Published on March 25 in Berlin,[9] it was carried in American newspapers the next day.

The President and Secretary Root were furious at the affront to their dignity and reflection on their judgment, Hill's former secretary at the Department informed him. Angered they were, but apparently less by the Kaiser than by the suspicion that someone in Berlin had improperly influenced His Majesty.[10]

The German Foreign Office, on its part, was placed by the news leak in an embarrassing position. Off the record, von Schoen admitted to Elmer Roberts, chief of the Associated Press Bureau in Berlin, that the Kaiser had sent an objection to Roosevelt, but said he had to deny that his government had protested. The official denial was telegraphed immediately to Ambassador von Sternburg in Washington and released to the press. On March 28 the Foreign Office issued a second statement. In expressing his regret at Tower's departure, His Majesty may have spoken to the ambassador about his successor, and possibly other Americans were mentioned as suitable candidates, the new statement conceded, but that the Emperor had spoken unfavorably of Hill in no way corresponded to the facts. The next day von Schoen called Tower to the Foreign Office, where it was decided in view of continued newspaper criticism to telegraph another statement to von Sternburg, for release to the press, admitting that Hill's appointment had been more extensively discussed. The German government had never contemplated recalling its approval of Hill's appointment, said this third statement. It was true that doubts had arisen as to whether he "would feel himself comfortable in the post," but these had been removed and nothing stood in the way of his nomination to the embassy.[11]

Hill while ambassador to Germany

THE LESSON OF THE HILL MUDDLE

ALTHO the press of two continents have exhausted their inge-
nuity in trying to throw light on the piquant diplomatic episode of David Jayne Hill and the Kaiser, all that the public now
positively knows of the case may be summed up as follows : Last
November the President was formally notified that Dr. Hill would
be *persona grata* as Charlemagne Tower's successor to the American ambassadorship at Berlin. On March 19 Mr. Tower cabled

UP THE HILL AND DOWN AGAIN.
The old adage of the " King of France ". brought up-to-date in
Germany.
—Doyle in the Philadelphia *Press*.

Relating to the "Hill Incident"
From *The Literary Digest* 36 (April 11, 1908): 508.

On the evening of March 30, von Sternburg saw the President and Secretary Root at the White House. The official press release stated that he conveyed to the American government the Emperor's assurance that his favorable opinion of Mr. Hill, communicated to the Washington administration last November, had never changed. "Apparently some remarks in a casual conversation," the communiqué explained, had "been distorted by gossip and exaggerated by rumor so as to give a totally erroneous impression of the whole matter." To close the "Hill Incident," as the press had dubbed it, without further ado, Roosevelt had earlier in the day requested Tower to resign as of June 1, and the next day he sent Hill's name to the Senate for approval.[12]

The "Incident" could easily have wrecked Hill's career in diplomacy, but fate now seemed bent on making amends. Editors in Germany and America instructed their readers on the new ambassador's intimate acquaintance with German life, his scholarly record, and eminent fitness for the post. German newspapers carried eulogistic reviews of his history of diplomacy, placing him among the most profound scholars contemporary America had produced, and Berlin publishers were reported as planning to bring out German editions. It was also announced that he would address the International Congress of Historical Sciences meeting in Berlin in August. Altogether, when Hill arrived in Berlin on June 12, 1908, he was one of the best-advertised ambassadors ever to set foot on German soil. He was received that afternoon by Foreign Secretary von Schoen, the next day by the Chancellor of the Empire, Prince von Bülow, and the day after that, with unprecedented promptness, by the Kaiser, who came in from Potsdam specially for that purpose. Hitherto new chiefs of foreign missions had waited a week to ten days for presentation to His Majesty.[13]

A few weeks later Hill published in the Berlin *Neue Revue* the address on diplomacy he had delivered at the Louisiana Purchase Exposition four years before. It had attracted little notice then, but now everything the new ambassador did was news. "It was probably commented upon by practically all the important German newspapers and did as much as anything else to give me a good start in my mission here," he wrote to James Brown Scott. A week or so later *Persönlichkeiten,* a serial of biographies published in Berlin, devoted its twenty-second number to "David Jayne Hill und die amerikanische Diplomatie." Since its recent issues had featured Chancellor von Bülow, Graf Zeppelin, Clemenceau, Tolstoy, Thomas Edison, the Emperor of Austria, and Kaiser Wilhelm, Hill was in rather stellar company. "If things keep on with our Ambassador to Germany," commented the *Nation,* "every future newly accredited diplomat to a foreign court will be wishing that the monarch might begin by calling him a liar, or at least that the Minister for Foreign Affairs run over him in an automobile."[14]

The "Hill Incident" had similarly remarkable effects in the United States. Political pundits immediately began jotting Hill down as presidential candidate Taft's Secretary of State or the new senator from New York. More than speculation, however, was an attempt at the New York state Republican convention in September to nominate him for the governorship. The national party organization had said that Charles Evans Hughes must be renominated. "A situation had been created in which there was nothing to do but to nominate Hughes," Elihu Root later wrote to Hill. "Anything else after our delegation had taken his name to Chicago as New York's candidate for the Presidency would have been regarded throughout the country as a turning down of Hughes, and we should have been terribly punished for it at the polls." And opening the Saratoga convention as temporary chairman, Root laid it on the line that Hughes must be renominated if the party did not want to go down in defeat. But New York's Republican machine bosses, many of them ignored or offended by the Governor, were hostile, and responded by pushing through a motion to adjourn until the next afternoon. Twenty or more of them met that evening in the cottage of State Chairman Timothy L. Woodruff, hoping to find an alternative candidate who would be equally attractive nationally. They offered the nomination to Root, who refused it. They listened to several other suggestions without much interest. Then, at the proposal of George Aldridge, who cast old resentments aside, they jubilantly fastened on Ambassador Hill, the impeccable and well-publicized scholar-diplomat whom even the Kaiser had not been permitted to decry. Although Root reminded them that as a member of the Roosevelt administration Hill, like himself, would have to support Hughes, the fractious bosses planned to meet again the next morning to get general agreement on the Ambassador. Root's remarks, nevertheless, had sobered them somewhat, and the next day, when word came from Oyster Bay that while the President had no intention of dictating, he had said in the strongest possible terms that he favored the renomination of Governor Hughes, their rebellion collapsed completely and they did as they were bid.[15]

The office-fillers had never bothered to consider what Hill wanted. "What I should like best would be to be let alone and given a chance to do my work here provided I am considered adapted to it," he wrote to Carnegie. Following customary practice, however, he submitted his resignation to President-elect Taft after the November elections. This led to a number of anxious weeks, for newspapers reported on the strength of rumors coming out of Washington that he wanted to be recalled from Berlin, or would be dropped altogether from the diplomatic service, and Hill suspected that somewhere in the capital influences were being brought to bear against him. Whatever was behind the reports, Taft took the advice of Elihu Root that in view of the recent "Incident" he should not for the present make any change in Germany, and the President assured the former Secretary that Hill would be left in Berlin for at least a year. "You bid fair to stand almost alone amidst universal ruin," Root wrote to Hill, "for the new regime seems to involve quite general decapitation." Hill's mind was put still more at ease when he returned home on leave the next autumn and called at the White House to pay his respects. The President spoke of the excellent reports he had received about him and expressed the hope that he would remain at Berlin for a long time.[16]

Whatever the length of his mission, Hill was determined to give his country a dignified representation at the German capital while he was there. He would not live in a hotel or an apartment, as had all his predecessors before Charlemagne Tower, but would have a front door he could command. It was not fair to represent the German Emperor or people as desiring an American ambassador of great wealth to make a great display, he wrote to Root. "What touches them, and touches them deeply, is that the Government of the United States does not show them the same respect and consideration in providing for its diplomatic representatives that other countries show and that they show to the United States." The representations of the United States, he wrote to another government official, were often inferior to those of third- and fourth-class powers, and foreigners, faced with many evidences of American prosperity, drew the conclusion that Americans had little respect for other countries or even for their own officials.[17]

For a time it appeared that this might at last be understood in the United States. The "Hill Incident" had inspired a flood of editorials demanding that the government do something about the diplomatic service, and some of them had constructively suggested that the best way out of a deplorable situation would be for Congress to pass one of its pending bills to purchase embassy buildings in leading capitals, as other nations did, and then give ambassadors a salary adequate to their official needs.[18] A number of prominent citizens formed the American Embassy Association to lobby for the purchase of embassies, and from within Congress there came explosions of indignation that seemed to promise that this would happen. Yet, when Congressman Lowden of Illinois introduced a new bill authorizing the Secretary of State to acquire diplomatic and consular establishments, traditional indifference triumphed over momentary indignation and the measure was badly defeated. Fitting its tactics to political realities, the Embassy Association redoubled its efforts, arguing that better American representation abroad meant better foreign business, with the result that the Lowden Bill was passed in 1911. Its consequences, however, proved to be meager, for Congress still refused to accept a responsibility that every other great power and many of the smaller ones considered a simple matter of international courtesy, and because of niggardly appropriations most American diplomats were compelled to shift for themselves for many years to come. As to Berlin, the United States did not purchase an embassy there until 1931.[19]

During his first five months in Germany, Hill spent a part of almost every day walking through the residential streets of the capital, examining every available piece of property, looking for a residence roomy enough to accommodate not only his family but also the business offices of the embassy, which for years had occupied a cramped, dingy, and ill-furnished second-story flat above a bookstore on the Unter den Linden. Finding nothing within the means of an ambassador not possessing great wealth, he finally rented a house, a small brownstone structure with a dignified Italian Renaissance facade fronting on a plaza near the Reichstag buildings, which would at least make a respectable residence. He hoped that the State Department would allow him to apply $5,000 per annum toward the rent from the contingent fund of the embassy, but if it would not, he was prepared to pay the entire rent himself. As the real question in Berlin was not how the American ambassador lived but what provision his government made for him, he wrote to Root, he wanted to be able to say that, pending the purchase of a permanent American embassy, his government was providing its ambassador with suitable temporary quarters. The Department, which had recently increased the contingent fund from $4,000 to $10,000 partly for this purpose, not only gave its authorization but increased the contingent fund by another $5,000.[20]

But Hill's housing problems were still not over. Taking leave in the United States one year later, he returned to Berlin in December 1909 to find his house up for sale. It was sold in March, and he was notified to vacate by October. Forced again into a search, he found, in April, a house of the kind he had originally been looking for. Pleasantly located on a park-like lot in the Tiergarten, it had ample space for the embassy's offices on the ground floor and enough room for an ambassador with a small family on the two floors above. The Department permitted him to take a lease on it for three years on terms that cost the government no more than had his former residence alone. The house needed extensive repairs and improvements, perhaps explaining why it was available at a rent Hill could afford, but finally, in December 1910, the entire American embassy in Berlin was housed for the first time under one roof in surroundings creditable to the country it represented.[21]

The great task of American diplomacy on the continent of Europe, Hill had written to Carnegie during the Second Hague Conference, was to win Germany away from dependence upon militarism to the ways of arbitration. It now became his lot to share in this task personally. When he arrived in Berlin, negotiations, initiated by the United States a few months before, were under way between the two countries for a treaty of obligatory arbitration. The roots of these negotiations went back to the First Hague Conference, which had created the Permanent Court of Arbitration but had laid no obligation on the nations of the world to use it. President Roosevelt and Secretary Hay had been willing to accept such an obligation for the United States in certain categories of disputes, and in 1904 and 1905 Hay had negotiated treaties with eleven countries, including Germany, pledging to submit to the Hague Court differences of a legal nature or relating to the interpretation of treaties, provided they did not affect "the vital interests, the independence, or the honor" of the signatory states or concern the interests of third parties. The exemptions were sweeping enough to exempt any important question from the obligation to arbitrate, but as the treaties would have left this decision to the President alone, the Senate insisted upon amending them to require that in each case the *compromis* must be made with its advice and consent. Affronted by this presumption, Roosevelt withdrew the treaties from the Senate. Secretary Root, a jurist whose interest in arbitration was both more substantial and more realistic, persuaded Roosevelt that it was better to accept the Senate's constitutional prerogative than to wait for the impossible. Instructing the American delegates to the Second Hague Conference to propose a general treaty of obligatory arbitration as a means of strengthening the Permanent Court, Root stipulated that they were to reserve for the United States the Senate's right to approve the special agreements.[22] When the Hague attempt to fashion a general treaty failed, Root then sought, as Hay had done, to achieve the same results through bilateral treaties. With other countries making similar treaties among themselves, a network of obligations to arbitrate at least some international disputes would be created.

Most of the signatories of the Hay treaties agreed to add a clause specifying that the President would make special agreements with the advice and consent of the Senate, and a number of other countries agreed to negotiate similar treaties. Since a special agreement had to be negotiated for every arbitration, which gave each side an opportunity to escape from the compulsory feature of the treaties, the nations recognized that the new clause made no difference other than to satisfy the constitutional peculiarities of the United States. Even though not constitutionally obliged to do so, the executive of another country would unquestionably rely on some interested agency of his government for advice, and he could as easily prevent an arbitration as could the American constitutional treaty-making partners of the President and the Senate. The only state to object was Germany. The right to submit a special agreement to the Senate after it had been signed, Germany argued, would give the United States an opportunity for reconsidering and backing out that Germany would not have; Germany would be bound by the signing of the special agreement but the United States would not be bound. To meet this objection, Root suggested that an agreement should become binding only upon an exchange of notes. Each party would then have equal opportunity for further consideration and neither would be bound until the other was also ready to be bound.[23]

Unable to find fault with this proposal, Germany ignored it. Since the President was of the opinion that the chief value of the proposed agreement lay in the expression of good intentions, Germany said, it might be advisable to abandon the idea of a treaty and accomplish the same purpose by an exchange of notes stating that the two governments agreed in principle on the general subject of arbitration and were confident that any difficulties arising between them susceptible of its application would be settled that way. An exchange of notes, Root countered, would only cause the world to wonder why it was not possible for the United States to arrange a treaty with Germany as it was doing with other countries. Germany then agreed to conclude a treaty containing the clause relating to the Senate, provided the Hague court was empowered to arrange a special agreement if the two countries failed to come to an understanding.[24] The contradiction of purposes in the proposal, as Germany knew, ensured its rejection.

While these negotiations were taking place between Secretary Root and Speck von Sternberg in Washington, Root had directed Charlemagne Tower in Berlin to urge upon Foreign Secretary von Schoen his proposal that a *compromis* become binding only upon an exchange of notes. In one of his last despatches from the German capital, dated June 3, 1908, Tower reported that the Foreign Secretary had definitely assured him of the German government's acceptance of Root's plan in principle and of its decision to enter into an agreement in accordance with it. A German proposition, a few details of which still lacked the final decision of the legal authorities in the Foreign Office, would be ready within a short time.[25]

When Hill presented his credentials at the German Foreign Office on his arrival in Berlin nine days later, von Schoen immediately brought up the subject. There were still difficulties relating to the treaty that had been raised by German jurists, the Foreign Secretary explained. He was glad the American ambassador thoroughly understood the matter and hoped he would be able to meet these problems. "This I considered very auspicious as it indicates a disposition on the part of the German Government to meet our wishes," Hill wrote optimistically to Andrew Carnegie. "I do not doubt that with a little time we shall succeed."[26]

The legal adviser to the German government was Dr. M. Kriege, with whom Hill soon had several long talks. The German jurist, he discovered, was remarkably resourceful in throwing obstacles in the way of a treaty. Once a treaty of arbitration was concluded between the two states, Kriege first contended, the making of the *compromis* in a particular case was a matter for the two "governments," and consultation with the Senate would be invoking the participation of an entirely independent outside corporation.

When Hill explained that under the American constitution the Senate was an integral part of the "government" and a co-partner with the executive in foreign affairs, Kriege argued that a body of ninety men was impossible for purposes of negotiation. When Hill answered that the Senate would be consulted but would not negotiate, Kriege had still other objections. The Senate could arbitrarily reject propositions that jurists making an agreement thought right and reasonable, which would destroy the juristic conception as a basis of agreement between the two countries. Germany, Kriege also argued, would promptly pay any indemnity awarded by an arbitral court out of a large secret fund at the disposal of the Imperial authorities, whereas in the United States the money must be appropriated by Congress, which could delay or refuse payment. Since the United States had already made agreements with eleven powers of diversified political organizations and was negotiating similar treaties with many more, Hill observed, to argue the constitutional unfitness of the United States to enter into an obligatory arbitration treaty with the German Empire on equal terms was an extraordinary line to pursue.

The German jurist had still another objection, which was Germany's trump card in the game of evasion. The Senate, Kriege argued, was particularly disqualified for making decisions on special agreements because senators would never allow wrongs committed by the states they represented to be arbitrated. The United States would expect to arbitrate questions concerning the conduct of any part of the German Empire, but the German government would be told that the American constitution did not permit the central government to control the actions of the states. Kriege cited a specific case. In 1869 the state of Georgia had guaranteed the bonds of a local railroad, the Brunswick and Albany. The greater part of the issue of $3,300,000 was sold on the Frankfort stock exchange to German buyers. In 1872 the railroad went bankrupt, interest on the bonds ceased to be paid, and Georgia denied any responsibility for them, claiming that the guarantee law had been made under false pretenses. Later Georgia pleaded that the government of 1869 was a usurping government, and in 1877 the Georgia legislature declared the bonds voided. Since under the laws of the United States a state could be sued by a private person only with its own sanction, the German creditors were left without legal recourse. Germany could not deal directly with the state of Georgia, and the State Department declined to use its influence to persuade Georgia to meet its obligations.

Hill tried to dismiss this sticky objection by questioning the justice of the German claim. Surely the federal government could not be held responsible for the illegal pledging of public funds by a state legislature under circumstances which at best were doubtful and at worst intolerably corrupt, he argued. Moreover, the legal structure in America was well known to German lawyers who must have advised purchasers with regard to the legality of the bonds.

The problem was not whether there was any justice in the claim, replied Kriege, but that there was no way to ascertain if there was justice in it except before an international court of arbitration. While he might understand the matter, German subjects aggrieved at Georgia would not understand it. They would appeal to the Reichstag, and the government would be criticized for making a treaty of arbitration that excluded a case of immense interest to many long-suffering Germans. German bondholders were not being treated any differently than American bondholders, Hill retorted, and he did not believe the German people or the Reichstag would have any difficulty in understanding the situation.[27]

But by raising a minor issue of forty-year-old bonds, in the sale of which the irresponsibility of Frankfort bankers had probably matched that of Georgia, Kriege had ensured the failure of the negotiations. The Senate insisted on its right to approve special agreements of arbitration partly because of the fear of Southern senators that the President might consent to arbitrate just such questions of debts repudiated by the South's post-reconstruction governments. After several more months of futile discussion, Secretary Root informed Hill in January 1909 that because the difficulties in the way of reaching an agreement were so great, the State Department was abandoning the attempt for the time being.[28]

Outside of a few members of the Reichstag and a few professors,

Hill wrote to Carnegie, pouring out his disappointment, there was no enthusiasm in Germany for the great contemporary movement for international organization on judicial lines. It was no wonder that Germany felt isolated, for she was voluntarily cutting herself off from the great society of nations willing to work for the peaceful settlement of international differences. Perhaps Germany did not really intend to depend upon the sword instead of the courtroom, but certainly her great military strength and her indisposition to associate herself with the arbitration movement tended to justify the fear that she had little regard for international amenities.[29]

On May 1, 1909, Count Johann von Bernstorff, the new German ambassador to Washington, reopened negotiations on the treaty with the Secretary of State of the Taft administration, Philander C. Knox. "There are some pretty serious difficulties in the way," Hill wrote to Carnegie in a much more optimistic mood, "but I have at last persuaded the one man whom it is necessary to convince to get around the Senate obstacle. I dare not be too confident of results, but I believe it is only a question of *time*." It was his frank statement of American public opinion to Chancellor von Bülow, he explained, that had led to the reopening of negotiations. Americans would never be able to grasp why it was impossible to make a treaty with Germany, Hill had told the Chancellor, in view of the fact that a dozen other powers had not even suggested Dr. Kriege's "mental difficulties." "Do not despair of our G. friends," he encouraged Carnegie. "It is rather difficult to understand them and they move slowly, but they are not impossible."[30]

But the renewal of negotiations came to nothing. Kriege had already made it a precondition of any treaty that the case of the Georgia bonds be adjudicated, otherwise their owners would raise a row in the Reichstag. Von Bernstorff therefore merely reiterated Germany's objections to the participation of the Senate in arranging special agreements and Germany's insistence that the United States assume responsibility for the acts of individual states.[31]

Hill still hopefully continued to count on time. "I hear nothing of any further move in the general arbitration treaty between the U.S. and Germany," he wrote Carnegie in January, 1910, "but I am quietly doing what I can here. . . . We can afford to wait a little, and it may even prove a good thing. I see signs that Germany does not want to be left out of Mr. Root's system of treaties. All will come in time."[32]

A month later von Bernstorff was again instructed to resume discussions on the treaty. But as the Wilhelmstrasse officials still continued to insist upon a settlement of the Georgia railroad case, it was another fruitless gesture. Writing eight years later as a private citizen, Hill strongly hinted of collusion between the German Foreign Office and Frankfort bankers. The speculating bankers, he suspected, had paid little or nothing for the Georgia railroad bonds, and if the United States had accepted responsibility for them the next exhibit would have been a collection of Confederate notes from some museum.[33]

While the negotiations to make little more than obeisance to the principle of arbitration struggled to stay alive, Hill became involved in a far more ambitious scheme to win Germany to the ways of peace. The growing might of the German Empire had focused world apprehensions largely on the person of the Kaiser, the "War Lord" of Europe. Hill shared in these fears but at the same time found hope in the person of the Emperor. "Whenever I talk with him . . . I am impressed with his good intentions. I am sure he wants to preserve peace, but his position and his surroundings are peculiar," he wrote to Carnegie in June 1909. "Personally I am convinced that he means *peace*, but wishes to be *strong* that he may secure it," Hill wrote the ironmaster again a few weeks later. "I am confident that his heart is right, whatever we may think of the system of which he is the exponent." Carnegie, too, had faith in the Kaiser's peaceful intentions and he thought the Emperor might be won away from his reliance on military strength. The one man who could do this if anyone could, Carnegie believed, was Theodore Roosevelt. Upon laying down the Presidency in March 1909, Roosevelt had gone off to Africa to hunt big game for a year, after which he planned to make a whirlwind tour of the principal capitals of Europe on his way back to Oyster Bay. Writing to the Colonel at his hunting camp, Carnegie proposed that when he reached Berlin he persuade the Kaiser to take the lead in a world

movement for arbitration and disarmament, which would put to
an end the mounting tensions of Europe and the threat of war.
When His Majesty had given some intimation of assent, Roosevelt should then cross the Channel to plan with British statesmen
privy to the scheme the concrete proposals to bring about perpetual peace under the aegis of the "three branches of the Teutonic
race."[34]

Roosevelt promised to do what he could, but warned Carnegie
not to expect too sweeping results and that certain "cranks" must
have nothing to do with the plan. Carnegie assured the Colonel
that none of the participants in the scheme were the type of "peace
at any price" men Roosevelt so thoroughly detested. Elihu Root,
Nicholas Murray Butler, and President Taft were Carnegie's con-
fidants in the United States, and in England the leaders of the two
great political parties were brought in. It was arranged that Prime
Minister Asquith, Sir Edward Grey, Arthur Balfour, Lord Lands-
downe, Lord Morley, and Lord Haldane would meet with Roosevelt, Carnegie, and Ambassador Whitelaw Reid at Wrest Park,
the country residence of the ambassador, in the latter part of May
1910, when Roosevelt would come over from Germany.[35]

Hill's function in Berlin was to help make Roosevelt's mission
there a success; and as the famed traveler came out of Africa, in
February 1910, and cut a swath across Europe, telegrams and letters
poured in and out of the American embassy as the ambassador
struggled to harmonize the plans of the Colonel with the whims of
the Kaiser. Roosevelt originally planned to visit the German
capital in April. But the Kaiser said he would not be there until the
middle of May. Since Roosevelt was to deliver the Romanes Lecture at Oxford on May 18, the German Foreign Office moved
Wilhelm's return to Berlin up to May 10. Hill thereupon made
plans for Roosevelt and his family, who had joined him in Europe,
to be his guests at the embassy. The Kaiser then announced that he
would not return until May 12 and did not want the Colonel to
arrive before then. He wanted to greet Roosevelt personally at
the train, an honor hitherto accorded only to ruling monarchs,
and he wanted Roosevelt to be his guest for three days at the Imperial Palace, an invitation no one could remember having been

extended before to a person not of royal blood. Unless Mrs. Roosevelt were also invited, the Colonel answered, he would not stay at the Palace or anywhere else, and he still intended to reach Berlin on the evening of May 9 or the morning of the tenth.

Perhaps omitting his own part in the coincidence, Hill informed Roosevelt that his letter refusing the invitation to the *Schloss* had reached the embassy on the same day as a message from the Kaiser extending the invitation to Mrs. Roosevelt. He suggested that the Colonel still come to Berlin as he had planned on the ninth or tenth and stay at the embassy until he and Mrs. Roosevelt went with the Emperor to the Palace on the twelfth. This was agreeable to the Colonel but not to the Kaiser, who insisted upon meeting his guest personally at the station at the price of giving up two days of his vacation. He would reach the capital at nine o'clock on the morning of the tenth, and he asked Roosevelt not to arrive before then. Arranging special train accommodations from Stockholm for Roosevelt's party, Hill finally coordinated plans to everyone's satisfaction. The Kaiser would meet the Colonel at the station on the tenth and take him and Mrs. Roosevelt to the *Schloss* for the three-day visit, after which they would stay at the embassy until they departed for London on the fifteenth.[36]

In three months of hectic correspondence Carnegie's peace plan was never mentioned. But now that it was certain Roosevelt would have three days with the Kaiser at the *Schloss,* Hill wrote to the ironmaster: "There will be long and intimate intercourse, and I am certain much good will come of it."[37]

Then suddenly everything went wrong. Probably through the inadvertence of Carnegie himself, the newspapers reported that Roosevelt was going to speak to the Kaiser about peace and disarmament. The German Foreign Office became cool and the semi-official German press openly critical toward his visit. The press frowned and Berlin society rumbled over the intention of the Kaiser to entertain a mere untitled citizen at the *Schloss.* This unusual mark of distinction would not have been properly understood in America either, von Schoen recorded in his memoirs, and he was about to tell the Kaiser this, when news came of King Edward's death. The death of Edward VII of England on

May 6 was as convenient as it was sudden. The German court went into mourning, and Wilhelm could not greet Roosevelt at the train, attend dinners in his honor, or entertain him at the Palace.[38]

Roosevelt lunched with the Kaiser at Potsdam on the tenth and the next day went with him to Döberitz to witness military maneuvers. They had several private conversations, Hill wrote to Carnegie. He did not know what they said, but they were "very earnest and friendly." "They seemed very fond of each other," he observed hopefully, "and the friendship may yet mean much for the world's good."[39]

It was a pity, lamented Carnegie, that Roosevelt could not have been the Kaiser's guest for three days. But according to Roosevelt it would have made no difference. He had never believed that his speaking to the Kaiser about peace and disarmament would do any good, he recorded, and when officially inspired articles appeared in the German press to prevent him from speaking he felt relieved. "Not only Mr. Carnegie, but a multitude of well-meaning and ignorant people had wrought themselves into the belief that if I chose I could do something with the Emperor for peace; and I was glad to be able to point out to them this announcement from the German foreign office in advance of my visit, which saved me the necessity of trying to explain why I could accomplish nothing."[40]

"It all comes back to Germany," Carnegie and Root had said several times. Nevertheless, they had planned to hold the meeting at Wrest Park even if Roosevelt failed to get any encouragement in Berlin. "We shall try Britain and hope for the best," Carnegie had written to Hill. "Japan I take it would follow Britain and that would be a combination especially on the sea, which Germany would realize as one not to be ignored." For all his condemnation of armaments, Carnegie was evidently willing to see his own peace scheme rest on military power. But with the King dead, Britain's leading statesmen could not go off on what ostensibly was to be a gay social week-end, and the meeting at Wrest Park never took place.[41]

"We want the Germans in the Anglo-American agreement, but there is only one way to get them," Hill wrote to Carnegie in

March 1911. "I flatter myself that I have discovered what it is." It was through the power of a thesis he was currently presenting at Columbia University in a series of lectures under the auspices of the Carpentier Foundation. "It is intended to be, and I believe is," he told Carnegie, "the clearest and strongest argument yet written for an international court of arbitral justice." The Columbia University Press published the lectures under the title of *World Organization as Affected by the Nature of the Modern State*. They were also translated into French and German and published in Paris and Berlin.[42]

The development of a juristic conscience, Hill posited, had become practically worldwide and part of the heritage of every civilized nation. The growth of this jural consciousness, which ensured public order and was expressed in the positive law of substantially all modern states, certainly could not logically terminate in a refusal to recognize in international affairs the principles it had evoked and was applying nationally. It furnished, instead, the basis for a juristic world organization and for an international law, enforced, not by armies, but by common consent.

The groundwork for this judicial organization of world peace, Hill emphasized, was already more completely laid than would have been thought possible a mere two decades before. The Hague Conference of 1899 had, for the first time in history, given arbitration an organized and international form. The Second Hague Conference had markedly advanced the juristic idea by the establishment of an International Prize Court, an agreement not to collect debts by force unless arbitration were refused, and the acceptance in principle of a really permanent court of arbitral justice. Two hundred and eighty-eight treaties of obligatory arbitration for certain classes of cases had been registered in the Bureau of the Administrative Council of the Permanent Court at The Hague. While every agreement was in some way qualified, and according to the preference of each signatory could represent solid achievement or a mere dream, the treaties nevertheless represented progress toward the adoption of the juristic conception of the modern state as the basis of international relations.

The excessive armament of great powers, Hill admitted, was

exciting universal suspicion, creating alarm, and producing a situation both unreasonable and extremely dangerous. But to strive for disarmament as an ideal in itself was futile. Armies merely evidenced that nations were determined to maintain their rights by force so long as there was no other way of securing justice. The threat of war could never be expunged until a peaceful method of securing justice, in every instance, was found. The jural consciousness embodied in the modern state, he was confident, could provide that necessary effective guarantee of justice through a world organization based on law.[43]

"All will come in time," Hill had written to Carnegie the year before. "Patience, patience, quiet and steady loyalty to a great idea are what are needed."[44] But loyalty to the idea was never strong enough to translate it into reality—and time was running out.

8

Dismissed from the
Diplomatic Service

ON MARCH 6, 1911, HILL RECEIVED A TELEGRAM FROM ASSISTANT Secretary of State Huntington Wilson instructing him to return to Washington at his earliest convenience, "discreetly allowing the fact to become public that you have been called to the Department to confer regarding the potash case and other matters." The potash case was a diplomatic wrangle—"a case of greed against greed," President Taft had privately said to Hill—that had arisen over the alleged invalidation by the German government of American contracts for the purchase of that commodity.[1]

The production and sale of potash in Germany, which had a near monopoly of the salts, had for years been rigidly regulated by a syndicate of the mine owners. At midnight on June 30, 1909, however, the syndicate agreement had expired before mine representatives meeting in Berlin were able to reach a new understanding. In the small hours of the morning before the representatives could meet again the next day, two of the mines made large contracts, at prices about forty-five percent under those of the syndicate, with American buyers in Berlin who had been waiting for such an opportunity. For the next several months the mine owners continued to negotiate among themselves to form a new syndicate, and with the American buyers to cancel their contracts. According to Robert S. Bradley, Chairman of Board of the American Agricultural Chemical Company and chief spokesman of the American buyers, the Americans offered to give up two-thirds of the advantage they had obtained under their new agreements, but the mine owners arbitrarily demanded surrender of the contracts under threat of retaliation with the cooperation of the German government. On October 1 the owners formed a new syndicate, leaving out the two mines with the American contracts. These mines immediately made contracts with other American buyers at the same low prices, cornering about ninety percent of the American potash trade. The value of the contracts, including rights of option to extend them from one or two years to seven years, approximated thirty-five million dollars.[2]

The syndicate made good its threat. On May 10, 1910, the German Reichstag established a special board of government officials and mine owners to fix production quotas for all mines. Deliveries exceeding the quotas were to be heavily taxed. The Bundesrat, however, was empowered to reduce these duties so that final prices on deliveries to American buyers would be no higher than before July 1, 1909.

On instruction from Washington, Hill protested the passage of this legislation, and on May 12 von Schoen assured him that the American contracts would "in no respect be invalidated or impaired by the new law, which as finally modified puts it in the hands of the Bundesrat to fix prices so that the existing contracts will not be affected." Whatever this murky assurance meant, Hill had to advise the State Department that the German government was not invalidating the American contracts or doing anything it did not have a right to do. The contracts included an agreement to pay any government charges that might be imposed. This clause was not accidental but had been inspired by a statement made in the Reichstag, before the contracts were formally signed in New York, that a government duty for the purpose of securing equity in the potash industry might be enacted. The duty was imposed on the domestic producer, Hill pointed out, and if the foreign buyer had agreed beforehand to take the burden of it upon himself, that was a part of the contract and the action of the German government could not be construed as a violation of it. The American contractors, he hoped, would be satisfied with the provisions of the law, inserted as a result of his representations, that authorized the Bundesrat to pare the duties so that prices would be no higher than before the new contracts were made.[3]

The American buyers were far from satisfied. The State Department was deluged with complaints from chemical companies, congressmen, and state agricultural commissions,[4] and the dispute sharpened. Washington interpreted von Schoen's statement of May 12 as an official assurance that "existing prices" in the contracts would not be affected by the potash law. The German Foreign Office, referring to the clause relating to government charges, said there had been no invalidation of "existing contracts." This agreement, the State Department retorted, related to "a proper and moderate exercise," not to a duty greater than the price of the product itself. It protested that potash shipments were being subjected to the full tax, which meant prices far above the former syndicate level, and that because the mines with American contracts claimed they had no untaxed quotas for export, all deliveries were being taxed. Another dispute arose over whether the reduction of the duty applied to purchases on which buyers might exercise their rights of option. The Foreign Office contended that the reduction could be applied only to quantities of potash that the buyers were actually obliged to accept. The State Department, on the other hand, insisted that the rights of option were integral parts of the contracts.

Under instructions from the Department, Hill argued its position. The Bundesrat, however, would agree to reduce duties only to the point of maintaining the level of syndicate prices, and it made even this contingent on conditions the State Department was unwilling to accept.[5]

A private conference of the interested parties, Hill several times suggested to Washington, would be the most satisfactory way to settle the controversy. The German Foreign Office appeared receptive to the proposal, but the State Department was not. Acting at the request of Robert Bradley that it send a special agent to Berlin, it sent over Mack H. Davis of the Bureau of Trade Relations, in September 1910, to press official negotiations with greater force.[6]

Hill agreed that Davis might bring pressure on the German government through discreet suggestions that the United States might invoke certain provisions of its anti-trust and tariff laws. But taking an offensively threatening attitude, Davis overplayed his hand. After only two interviews with Dr. Sydow, Minister of Commerce for Prussia, he came to the end of his string, unable to see any higher official. Drawing up a report for Washington recommending retaliatory measures, Davis consented, however, to withhold it until Hill communicated with the Department again. Enclosing a synopsis of Davis's recommendations in his despatch, Hill cautioned against precipitous action. As the problem would probably be resolved by some working arrangement between the parties involved, he advised, it would be highly inexpedient for the United States by the actual invocation of anti-trust or tariff laws prematurely to set in motion machinery it could not afterwards stop without embarrassment. And again he asked to be allowed to arrange a private conference by speaking personally to the Chancellor of the Empire.[7]

Its tough approach having failed, the Department consented. Acting as an unofficial mediator, Hill reached an agreement with Dr. Sydow whereby the independent mines would transfer their contracts to the syndicate, which in turn would pool the quotas of all the mines so that in making American deliveries no taxes on excesses of quotas would be due. On the question of prices, the American buyers offered to divide the difference between their contract prices and the prices that had prevailed earlier, but the syndicate, entrenched in the potash law, refused to compromise, bringing the negotiations to an end.[8]

"I never worked harder in my life," Hill commented to a former official of the embassy. "It is possible that we got a bad start. I think several of the Americans took that view." One American who did was Robert Bradley. After instigating the presence of Mack Davis in Berlin, he felt that Davis only aggravated the situation and the negotiations might have turned out differently had Hill been left alone.[9]

Davis, however, was more than ever for strong action. Further overtures for a friendly settlement, he advised the State Department, would only be interpreted as evidence of weakness. The

influence of the syndicate on the German government could be overcome only by a positive declaration that extreme retaliatory measures were imminent, and Ambassador Hill should be instructed to
inform the Chancellor that the maximum American tariff would be
imposed on German imports. Modulating this combativeness only
slightly, the Department instructed Hill in December to present an
aide memoire to the German government strongly hinting at such
action unless Germany became more cooperative.[10]

Germany responded in a memorandum handed by Bernstorff
to Acting Secretary Wilson on January 31, 1911. The document
made plain that Germany had not appreciated the representations
of Davis in Berlin, that it did not consider the American contractors to have suffered any actual loss, and that it regarded the potash law as a purely domestic matter completely unrelated to tariff
regulations. If the tax fell on the American buyers it was because
they had voluntarily agreed to pay it in their private contracts.
Nevertheless, the memorandum continued, Germany was willing
to help find an equitable solution of conflicting interests. Once it
were determined by arbitration that the American buyers were
liable under the terms of the contracts for the payment of the tax
(Germany later said a formal admission of liability would be
acceptable), Germany would reopen negotiations on the basis of
the terms reached privately by Ambassador Hill and Minister
Sydow. When the two governments came to an agreement fair to
both sides on the remaining question of prices, they would use their
influence with the interested parties to have it accepted.

Wilson replied on March 9. He was disappointed over Germany's prerequisite to a final settlement (which would have seriously prejudiced the American case). But inasmuch as Germany
had reiterated its willingness to use its influence with the potash
interests, would it not join with the United States, he asked, in
bringing the interested parties to another conference for a direct
private adjustment of their differences?[11]

Such was the state of the potash negotiations when Hill was
summoned to Washington on March 6 with orders to publicize
that it was to discuss them. He had already booked passage to
sail for New York on March 10 to deliver the Carpentier Founda-

tion Lectures, his plans had been approved by the Department, and they were publicly known. To state now that he was returning home for another reason seemed unnecessary, but he followed instructions and gave an announcement to the German press. He later learned that a similar statement was published in the United States on March 9, the same day that Wilson's note to Germany seemed to remove any reason for discussing the potash question with him.[12]

Arriving in New York on March 20, Hill inquired if it would cause any inconvenience if he did not come to Washington until he had finished his lectures on April 1. On the advice of Mack Davis that they should have his intimate knowledge of current official sentiment in Germany before then, Wilson asked him to come to Washington sometime before the end of the week.[13] The great urgency was never explained.

On March 24 Hill met in Washington with Wilson and Messrs. Davis and John Osborne of the Bureau of Trade Relations. The Department had abandoned its previous strenuous policy, he discovered, and they all agreed to proceed along the lines of his unofficial discussions with Dr. Sydow the previous autumn. This was the manner in which the controversy was eventually settled and which had always been his view of the proper course to take. The newspapers the next day, however, attributed the decision exclusively to "Washington officials" and inferred that he was a hard-liner who had been called home to be overruled.[14]

On March 28 Hill received a note from Secretary Knox saying that the President had decided to appoint his successor at Berlin. The decision was not in any way connected with the manner in which he had discharged his mission, Knox assured him. The President simply wished to make certain new appointments. Hill could make public his resignation any time before the middle of May, whereupon the Department would ask agreement and announce the name of the new ambassador.[15]

Returning to Washington after completing his lectures, Hill saw Knox on April 11. When the Secretary again assured him there had been no criticism of his mission, he asked bluntly why the President wanted him to resign. "These high positions are political assets and they are very much needed at this time," Knox answered with equal directness. The next day Hill sent the President his resignation, to take effect July 1, and to Knox he sent permission to make it known immediately. On April 14 the *Washington Evening Star* published his letter to the President and Taft's reply, which he had not yet received, and attributed his resignation to the potash dispute. The following day other newspapers carried the story, most of them also conjecturing that the potash controversy was the most likely reason for his leaving the diplomatic service. The New York *Herald,* however, asserted positively, on the authority of "officials," that Hill's hard-line handling of the dispute, which was characterized in the Washington discussion he was called home to attend as "a pretty mess," was indeed the reason why Taft and Knox had demanded his retirement.[16]

Everything favored the theory, Hill saw. He had been called home to discuss potash; the Department had changed its policy; and as he had recently fitted up a new residence in Berlin, his resignation was obviously not voluntary. It was all too neat not to have been arranged, he thought, a suspicion that prompted him to record in detail all the events surrounding his dismissal. Upon reading Taft's letter, he noted, he was struck by the President's apparent unawareness that his resignation had been demanded. It was "with great reluctance" that he accepted it, Taft had written, adding that he was glad Hill would remain at his post until July. Hill's first reaction was that he was dealing with two persons, one of whom had peremptorily dismissed him from the diplomatic service while the other expressed regret over his determination to leave. But on reading the papers further he saw what was afoot: to hide the real reason for his dismissal he was being tarred with the failure of a high-handed policy he had in fact always advised against.[17]

His suspicions were clinched when he discovered at the Bureau of Trade Relations on April 15 that the instructions given to Davis upon being sent to Berlin and Davis's bellicose report to the Department had been removed from the records of the case. Storming to the State Department and not finding Knox in, he threatened Assistant Secretary Wilson with publishing the whole official correspondence of the case if the potash theory of his resignation were not denied. Going next to the White House, he refused to be content with Taft's oral statement that potash had nothing to do with the termination of his mission and wrung from the President a promise to say so in writing.[18]

The next day, April 16, the newspapers carried the following brief release from the State Department: "The Department of State is entirely satisfied with Dr. Hill's handling of the potash controversy, and the ambassador is not at all blamed for the long delay in settling the case, which continues to receive the earnest attention of the Department. The origin of the press reports to the contrary is not understood." The Department's failure to deny unequivocally that the potash story had been inspired from official sources, and the absence of any statement at all from the White House, convinced Hill the more that it had been deliberately planted. The press labeled the Department's statement perfunctory and continued to keep the potash theory alive. On April 21 Congressmen William Brantley of Georgia and Asbury Lever of South Carolina, representing states that imported large quantities of potash, introduced a resolution in the House calling on the President to disclose whether differences of opinion over the potash controversy had caused him to request Hill's resignation. But as the congressmen withdrew the resolution a week or so later when Taft privately assured them that there was no connection, the potash story continued to thrive. Hill could have quickly killed it himself by publishing Knox's demand for his resignation, but not wanting to embarrass the President, he held his peace and returned to Berlin.[19]

On May 21 Taft sent the letter he had promised Hill five weeks before. "I promised to write you before you went away and to announce the name of your successor," Taft began. "Complications growing out of the extra session have prevented my making the somewhat extended changes in the diplomatic corps which I have in mind and I have, therefore, delayed my annnouncement of your successor's name which was an essential link in the chain of adjustment." Neither potash nor any other question had anything to do with the resignation, the President said. The first time Hill had offered his resignation he had felt that justice required he not accept it. "When you a second time presented your resignation," Taft went on, "I felt impelled to accept it because of plans that I had made for promotion in the service and for changes and readjustments in the corps, which a vacancy at Berlin would permit and facilitate."[20]

The letter struck Hill the same as Taft's first letter had struck him initially. The President seemed not to know that he had been ordered to resign. It did not seem possible that Taft could have written this letter if he had known of Knox's note of March 28 or of the Secretary's explanation of why a vacancy at Berlin was wanted. The letter seemed to bear out, moreover, an authorized statement from the White House published in the New York *Sun* on April 25 denying reports that Taft had requested his resignation in order to make a place for a political follower to whom he was under obligation. The President, the item in fact noted, had twenty-three prominent men under consideration for the post.[21]

"I believe you are right in thinking that the President was not the *real cause* of the note I got demanding my resignation," Hill wrote to Andrew Carnegie on June 3. "It is evident the President is placed in embarrassment about it, and it looks as if he had been tricked by someone. I have been absolutely loyal to the President, in whom I believe as a good and just man, and no eye but mine has ever seen the summary demand for my resignation, which all his correspondence with me indicates he does not even know about." "I am convinced by information that has recently come to my knowledge," he wrote to Carnegie a week later, "that there was an *intrigue*, and a disagreeable one." On July 4 Hill again wrote to the ironmaster, "I cannot get over the idea that there was something mysteriously dark in the action of Mr. Knox. His letters and the President's do not hang together."[22]

Soon, however, as reports that the President wanted his place for political reasons continued to circulate, Hill's suspicions of Taft's complicity began to revive. On July 18 he wrote to Carnegie: "Without any expression from me, the public has come, I think, to understand that my place was wanted for political purposes. . . . I have felt that, unless my reputation were to suffer severely by silence, I could not, as Mr. Taft's friend, repeat what Mr. K said to me when he gave as the sole reason for my displacement that the place was a 'political asset.' Still, if it were *not* so, the President could easily when he makes his readjustment of the service, retain me in it, but I do not believe he will.'"[23]

Spending the summer in Switzerland, Hill returned to the United States in November. One of his first acts was to request Carnegie to ask Taft directly why he was ordered to resign. "The Senators were complaining that there were three ambassadors from the State of New York in the three best places in the diplomatic service, and they felt this was not fair," the President told the ironmaster. "I promised them I would change that. I could not dismiss Bacon, whom I sent to Paris, because I appointed him in fulfilment of a promise to Roosevelt. I tried to change Reid, [at London], but I could not find anyone to take his place. In fulfilment of my promise to the Senators I had to displace H, and I did it reluctantly. But I let him stay long enough to vindicate fully his appointment." Although Carnegie thought that Taft had given him the truth of the matter, Hill was skeptical. He had never heard or seen this reason alluded to before. But it was no longer possible to doubt that Taft was responsible for his dismissal from the diplomatic service.[24]

Rumors that Hill was the victim of a political payoff were given more definite form the following summer by the findings of a Senate committee investigating the Republican campaign fund of 1908. The inquiry disclosed that Taft's close personal friend Larz Anderson had thrown $25,000—one of the largest individual contributions—into the party chest. From this disclosure the story was developed that when Taft's manager began preparations for the 1912 campaign, they looked to Anderson, and to put him in the proper generous mood decided to give him a foreign embassy. None was vacant, but the least productive from the standpoint of campaign contributions was the one at Berlin. Because of the publicity given to Hill's ouster, however, the scheme had to be changed. Anderson, who had been prominently mentioned for Berlin, was sent to Brussels instead, with the understanding that he would eventually be transferred to the German capital. Meantime, Ambassador Leishman was moved up from Rome to become Hill's successor.[25]

Of more Machiavellian proportions was the explanation, never made public, that Hill himself arrived at as the pieces of evidence began to fit together in his mind. On March 28 the President through Secretary Knox had asked for his resignation in order to make some new appointments by the middle of May. On April 4 Taft called an extra session of Congress to pass a bill for tariff reciprocity with Canada, a measure which many Republicans, especially in the Senate, opposed. Taft's purpose, as Hill saw it, was to offset public disapproval of his vacillating attitude toward the tariff. "It was expected to be his political justification before the people, and its success, it was believed, would make him the inevitable canditate in the next presidential election. He was determined by all means to pass the bill through the Senate, to drive its opponents out of the party, and to make himself the standard-bearer of a new political alignment." On April 12 Taft had the Berlin embassy to offer; and by April 24, according to the "authorized statement" appearing in the New York *Sun*, he had twenty-three prominent men under consideration to fill it. Yet by the mid-May deadline Knox had given Hill to make his resignation public, the President had not made an appointment. The delay, Taft explained in his letter to Hill of May 21, was caused by "complications growing out of the extra session." How these "complications" were related to changes in the diplomatic corps soon became evident. On July 22 the tariff reciprocity bill was rammed through the Republican-controlled Senate by a minority of Republicans assisted by practically all the Democrats. Two weeks later Taft made the long-delayed diplomatic appointments, and by transfers in the service two vacancies were created. One was filled by Larz Anderson, and the other by a former Democratic congressman from New York without previous diplomatic experience.

The administration announced in explanation that it intended to make the diplomatic service a nonpartisan body based entirely on merit and qualification. This was a late and interesting conversion to a sound principle, Hill observed, but what was to be said of the method by which it was reached? "Why was it important to have a diplomatic vacancy just at the beginning of an extra session of Congress? Why was it necessary to deny that a vacancy had been purposely created at that time? Why should there have been any evasion of the manner in which it had been obtained? Why, if there were good reasons for creating it, was it not promptly filled when it was obtained? Why were diplomatic appointments in a service based on merit mixed up with complications connected with the passing of a bill? And, finally, why, when the bill was passed by a Democratic majority against a Republican majority in the Senate, was a Democratic politician without experience in the diplomatic corps appointed from a state which, the President says, already had too many high positions in that service?"[26]

As neither the President, the State Department, nor Hill ever explained why he had resigned, the press, not content with merely potash or politics, surrounded his departure from Berlin with as many rumors as they had his arrival: he was to succeed Knox as Secretary of State; he had quarreled with his British colleague; he objected to Knox's policy of making ambassadors the errand boys of business interest. Inevitably, imaginative newsmen also reached back to 1908 for explanations: Hill could not afford the post; the Kaiser's clumsy utterances before his arrival had always made his position untenable; the hostility of the Imperial Court toward his simplicity and absence of great fortune had finally had its effect; he had become persona non grata to the Emperor. The Kaiser, explained the New York *World* with still more enterprise, resented Hill's disinclination to regard him as the instrument of heaven.[27]

The German press, equally at loss for a reliable explanation, similarly indulged in many surmises, but on one point all the Berlin papers agreed: they had a high estimate of Hill as a man, a scholar, and a diplomat. They were astonished at his retirement and made it plain that they would like to have him stay.[28]

The Kaiser's reaction was the same. Hill had won the Emperor's liking and confidence, and His Majesty invariably singled him out at social and state functions to talk to him longer than to anyone else, Joseph C. Grew, then the embassy's second secretary, had written to his mother over a year before. Learning of Hill's resignation, Wilhelm telegraphed Chancellor von Bülow from his yacht at Corfu: "We are very sorry Hill is going to leave us. What is the matter? We are anxious about it." Some weeks later the Emperor entertained William M. Sloane, professor of history at Columbia

University and president of the American Historical Association, aboard his yacht at the Baltic port of Travemünde. "Tell me about Hill," the Kaiser pressed the visiting scholar. "Why is he leaving? . . . I do not understand it at all. . . . I respect and admire him. What pleasant talks we have had in the quiet of a window at Court visits and balls! I like the man and appreciate him most highly. What does it mean?"[29]

Without being effusive, the Kaiser a week before had expressed his feelings to Hill personally. Inviting the Ambassador to Kiel for the week of the regatta, his great naval festival held annually at the end of June, Wilhelm had seated Hill beside him at the yacht club banquet and offered to decorate him with the Grand Cross of the Red Eagle, one of Europe's most coveted orders. Although Hill could not resist thinking what it might mean to his children and grandchildren to possess the broad sash of the order, bestowed by the hand of a great sovereign, he tactfully explained that as an officer of the United States he was prohibited from accepting the honor.[30] Because the Kaiser had made the gesture, however, Hill could depart from Germany, where he was originally not wanted, with something much more precious than a piece of ribbon.

9

Publicism and Politics

BEFORE HIS APPOINTMENT TO BERLIN, HILL HAD WORKED OUT THE PLAN OF volume three of his diplomatic history of Europe, collected most of the material, and written about a hundred pages; then because of the heavier schedule of work and social obligations at the German capital, he had been forced to lay the project aside. He planned to return to it as soon as he had the time, he wrote to a publisher in 1910, for he intended to make his history the chief monument to his life's work.[1] Summering in Switzerland and wintering in Paris or Washington for several years after his retirement from the diplomatic service, Hill completed volume three and saw it published in 1914.

Surveying Europe from the Peace of Westphalia to the eve of the French Revolution, *The Diplomacy of the Age of Absolutism* covered an eventful age crowded with men who for initiative, finesse, and chicanery in the game of diplomacy have probably never been surpassed. In complex struggles for dynastic aggrandizement, alliances and ententes were momentarily formed, only to be dissolved and formed anew. European diplomacy was an extraordinarily tangled skein, and to synthesize the mountains of material on it was a formidable task that reviewers thought Hill accomplished admirably. Writing in the *American Historical Review,* Sydney B. Fay considered the book probably the best in English for the period it took under review.[2]

It was to be the last volume. Returning to the United States from Switzerland in November 1914, following the outbreak of war in Europe, Hill put volume four, on which he had already begun work, aside. "I have since devoted my time, as I felt it a patriotic duty to do, to the discussion in periodicals and books, as well as by the living voice, of the questions international or national, growing out of the Great War," he wrote to James Brown Scott eight years later. Reluctant in 1922 to pick up his history again at the age of seventy-two, and doubtful that he could personally complete it, he hoped that the Carnegie Endowment for International Peace, of which he was a trustee, might subsidize a younger man to carry it on.[3] Though the Endowment was receptive to the proposal, apparently no satisfactory arrangements could be made, and the history was never finished.

In shelving past diplomacy, Hill was perhaps as impatient with scholastic retirement as driven by patriotism. In any event, it was not the war alone that was responsible. Progressivism abroad in the land and Woodrow Wilson in the White House were affronts to Hill's political conservatism that had already begun to draw him away from the Muse of history. "The year 1913 was marked by the rising of a tide of radicalism in political thought in the country such as had not been known since the establishment of the Federal Constitution," he wrote some years later. "The electoral campaign of the previous year had been notable for its appeal by more than one political party for the votes of the discontented. Such expedients as the free employment of the popular initiative and referendum, the recall of judges or of judicial decisions, and the limitation of the powers of the Supreme Court of the United States had been proposed and advocated. A 'New Freedom' had been announced as about to supersede the constitutional system as it had been developed in this country. As for that document itself, it was declared that it was 'an outgrown eighteenth century conception,' and that the Constitution as it stood was 'fit to be relegated to the scrap-heap.'"[4]

A tide of disintegrating influences was menacing the Republic, and in the December 1913 issue of George Harvey's conservative *North American Review* Hill came to its defense. Laying bare "The Crisis in Constitutionalism," he placed honesty and patriotism wholly on the side of the political status quo and hung the stigma of personal ambition and interest on almost all urgers of change. "It is . . . a matter of sincere congratulation that he has returned to his own country at a time when the wisdom derived from thought and experience is sadly needed," commented Colonel Harvey editorially, and conservative newspapers throughout the country agreed. "The day will come," wrote Senate minority leader Jacob H. Gallinger to Hill in congratulation, "when the views that you have so forcibly expressed will find a lodgment in the minds of the American people, and we will get rid of the nonsense that is now being preached by a great many public men." Senator Frank B. Brandegee read the article into the *Congressional Record* and franked over eight thousand copies to his home state of Connecticut. Ten thousand more copies, also under Brandegee's frank, were sent throughout New York at the request of its Republican committee.[5] America's conservatives had found a new spokesman.

For the nearly twenty years left to his life Hill defended "constitutional" government with an outpouring of articles and addresses that attested to remarkable vigor and industry. The substance of what he had to say, however, appeared early in two small books: *The People's Government* (1915) and *Americanism: What It Is* (1916).[6]

The distinguishing characteristic of American government, Hill contended, was the recognition of certain inherent and inalienable rights, including the security of life and liberty and the prerogative of acquiring, possessing, and enjoying property, upon which government could not infringe. The American people in their constitutions had sought to exclude absolutism in every form from government and establish a system of just laws and principles in place of mere arbitrary will. In so doing they had renounced the absolute power of majorities over individual rights and liberties and had safeguarded them against overthrow by mere majority legislation by entrusting the judiciary with final authority in declaring the law. This constitutional system of government, Hill warned, was now being threatened by radical attacks on property inspired largely by foreign influences and promoted by power-hungry demagogues.

The initiative, referendum, and recall were to progressive reformers answers to boss rule, venal legislatures, and exploitative corporations entrenched behind sympathetic courts. To Hill they were loose and irresponsible measures inconceivable by honest men. The initiative and referendum would replace deliberate, well-considered public action by responsible representatives with hasty and confused fumbling by inexpert and inexperienced masses. To diminish the power of the courts through recall would be even more disastrous, for the judicial authority to interpret the law, uninfluenced by waves of popular excitement, was the palladium of American liberties.[7]

Hill viewed all proposals for constitutional amendment with an equally hostile eye. "Individuals and classes who desire to dominate," he charged, "and demagogues who wish to rise to power by appealing to the sordid interests of a numerical majority, regardless of minority rights, may be expected to use every means to break down the constitutional obstructions to their designs; and for that purpose make it an easy matter to destroy, one by one, through constitutional amendments, the existing guarantees."[8]

It was perhaps too early to demonstrate the full results of two recent amendments, Hill wrote in 1913, but it remained to be seen if the people could elect worthier senators than the legislatures or if the power to impose a graduated income tax would not become the instrument of class and sectional legislation. Several years later he was less restrained: the income tax amendment had placed absolute and unlimited power in the hands of a few hundred men in Washington (elsewhere called responsible representatives) to take from the whole population any portion of their earnings or proceeds of their business they chose and use it for any purpose they saw fit: "The American people had, without protest, and even without qualification, consented to a form of control over their lives, their liberties, and their means of happiness more absolute than any monarch of modern times has ever presumed to assert or demand."[9]

What was demanded by those who found themselves obstructed by the American constitutional system of government, Hill explained, was not equal law but laws of equalization. "Equality of law merely gives the prize to industry, thrift, enterprise and economy.... It recognizes, promotes and rewards superiority. It condemns and indirectly punishes incapacity." Enemies of the Constitution, however, wanted laws that would "distribute to each from the common stock according to his needs."[10] "Is it conceivable," he asked, the problem of the distribution of the nation's wealth still as uncomplicated to him in 1915 as it had been thirty years before, "that the industrious and the idle, the thrifty and the wasteful, the provident and the improvident should possess and enjoy the same desiderata of life?"[11]

Hill's essays appealed to the conservative mind in America, and his books were popular. *Americanism: What It Is* was adopted by reading circles in several states and went into a fourth printing in little more than a year.[12] But blind even to the slightest need for reform, Hill never understood the progressive current that had swept through the nation and both major political parties. He railed against it but never descended from the level of abstractions and generalities to come to grips with its specific complaints; and aside from a few extremists, his polemics were directed against men of straw. Sensing no striving to preserve traditional American ideals, he saw only foreign-inspired, socialistic agitation fomented by dishonest or misled men. Americanism, which recognized the inherent and inalienable rights of the individual that no majority could abridge, was thus threatened and he became its champion. Still, one looks in vain for any individual right about which he showed concern except the right of property.

Thoughtful readers, wrote Philip Littell in the liberal *New Republic*, might call it unaccountable that a man of Hill's broad experience should publish, in the sixty-seventh year of his life, "a book in which almost all the proposers of constitutional change have interested motives, and in which reason and will are separated so neatly." But they should not be surprised, Littell went on, for it was not by accident that Dr. Hill had come into the world. Nature had decided to have him.

> "I will make," she said, "the perfect standpatter. He shall be exposed to the fires of experience, and not a hair of his head shall be singed. He shall be predestined to worship inherency and inalienability, and nothing that happens to him, nothing he reads or sees or hears, shall sully the glassy purity of his devotion. In him shall burn, unbent by any draught from any open mental door, the faith that wealth belongs 'to those who by their enterprise, skill and industry have produced it, or who by their abstinence from consuming it have kept it in existence.' If men appear who say that the individual's right to his wealth may justly be abridged, this perfect standpatter shall accuse them all, agitators on the make and quiet economists alike, of interested motives. . . . But this perfect standpatter," Nature added, "shall also be a disinterested standpatter. He shall not belong to the class of hawkeyed marauders who have much to lose by change. His departure from this type shall be wide. He shall be a student, a man of books, a writer. . . . To David Jayne Hill, LL.D., I point with pride. Here is the standpatter, perfect, disinterested, blind to light, yet having nothing to gain from a darkness he loves without hope of reward. He is what he is because I chose to make him that way."[13]

Even as a young man, although liberal in religious and educational matters, Hill had been strongly conservative in his political views. And he had often tended to be dogmatic and doctrinaire, an inclination which age, success, and acquaintance with the mighty had done nothing to lessen. "Accuracy at the expense of elegance," wrote Chase Osborn, former governor of Michigan and regent of the state university, who had gone to Berlin in 1909 to size up Hill for the university's presidency, "requires me to record that I reported to the board of regents that Mr. Hill had taken on too much weight of all kinds."[14]

With the eclipse of progressivism, Hill's fears of an omnipotent state, socialism, and alien ideas found a new focus: it was no longer a misguided majority that imperiled constitutional government but organized minorities. Along with many Americans in the immediate postwar years, Hill saw bolshevists and socialists under every bed. "If the guarantees of the Constitution can be gradually destroyed," he warned in 1919, "the revolution will be readily accomplished whenever an active and persistent minority chooses to impose it." But there were other minorities as well that would bend government to their own interests. "We are threatened with government by private groups and blocs, composed of vociferous and irresponsible minorities, which undertake to force or to prevent legislation, conformable to their private interests or their arbitrary will," he told the faculty and students of Bucknell University in 1924. "These blocs do not reason, they command. They do not debate, they threaten. We have the Farm Bloc, the Labor Bloc, the Peace Bloc, the Bureaucratic Bloc, aiming to control legislation, to dictate the economic policies of the country, and even to influence so delicate a matter as its foreign policy."[15] Hill characteristically did not discern even the existence of a Business Bloc.

Sounding a call to action in "The Crisis in Constitutionalism" in the *North American Review* of December 1913, Hill had recalled the citizens' clubs formed during the Civil War to help preserve the Union and suggested a similar movement to preserve constitutional government at a new hour of crisis. The next month several men living in Washington met at his home under a sense of urgency. A National Popular Government League had recently been organized to espouse the initiative, referendum, and recall, and to advocate constitutional amendment by majority vote. It was an attack on the constitutional system, Hill's guests agreed, which must be opposed by the formation of an association at once. On April 27, 1914, the group, enlarged to twenty, met again at Hill's house to found The National Association for Constitutional Government. Dr. Henry Campbell Black, author of several books on constitutional law, and Charles Ray Dean, Hill's former secretary at the State Department, now practicing law, were charged with preparing a constitution. Meeting again on May 6, the concerned gentlemen adopted the constitution and elected Hill the president of their society.[16]

The purpose of the Association, its constitution stated, was "to propagate a wider and more accurate knowledge of the Constitution of the United States, and of the distinctive features of constitutional government as conceived by the founders of the Republic; to inculcate an intelligent and genuine respect for the organic law of the land; to bring the minds of the people to a realization of the vital necessity of preserving it unimpaired, and particularly in respect to its broad limitations upon the legislative power and its guarantees of the fundamental rights of life, liberty, and property; to oppose attempted changes in it which tend to destroy or impair the efficacy of those guarantees, or which are not founded upon the mature consideration and deliberate choice of the people as a whole . . . ."[17]

For over fifteen years the Association issued leaflets and pamphlets that conservatively defined the American constitutional system and inveighed against anarchism, bolshevism, socialism, syndicalism, alien radicals, the National Popular Government League, the American Federation of Labor, the I.W.W., and other alleged menaces to America's well-being. It distributed over one hundred thousand copies of a *Pocket Edition of the Constitution,* complete with an explanatory introduction to its "real meaning," many of which were bought at the cost of printing by business firms and patriotic societies. In April 1917, the Association began publishing *The Constitutional Review: A Quarterly Magazine Advocating the Maintenance of Constitutional Government and Recording its Progress at Home and Abroad.* Under the editorship of Dr. Black until his death in 1927, then under the direction of Dr. Herbert F. Wright, professor of political science at George Washington University, the *Review,* self-described as "the implacable and outspoken enemy of bolshevism, socialism, and other forms of extreme radicalism," was intended to supply quotable material to newspapers as well as circulate to members and libraries.[18]

Membership in the Association, however, was never large nor its influence extensive. To launch the organization, its founders sent invitations to one hundred fifty prominent citizens to become members of an Advisory Committee of One Hundred. Of the thirty who responded, only six accepted. Because of slowness in attracting members it was not until May 1916, when membership had reached four hundred, that the formation of the Association was publicly announced at a formal banquet featuring Senator Henry Cabot Lodge as the principal speaker. "What we need in our movement," wrote Charles Ray Dean to Hill in August of that year, "is some live, constructive idea which will appeal to the young and vigorous element in our national life." Two years later membership had risen to only 548. "We have been thus far too academic and have not exerted the popular influence which the Association ought to exert. This larger work we desire now to undertake," Hill wrote to Nicholas Murray Butler in September 1918. But efforts to give the Association a broader base failed. "We have tried to organize local committees or societies in the large cities—without success," Dr. Black wrote to a friend in August 1919. Men of property and affairs, Charles Ray Dean wrote to Hill a week later, were apathetic about vicious and revolutionary propaganda being spread throughout the country and were too inert. "Our own Association," he complained, "is itself too inert, I think, and is to academic to reach great numbers of people." In 1926, twelve years after its founding, membership in the Association stood at 1160. The next year it fell to 1053, and in 1930 to 831.[19]

With dues set at two dollars annually for regular members, five dollars for its few sustaining members, and one payment of one hundred dollars for its even fewer life members, the amount of educational work the Association could carry on was severely limited. Had he been less principled, Hill could have had substantial backing from the beginning. Shortly after the initial organizational meeting in his home he was called on by one Levi Cook, counsel of the National Liquor Association, who pleaded interest on partiotic grounds in his recent article in the *North American Review*. The people he represented, Cook explained, were opposed to a federal law prohibiting the manufacture and sale of intoxicating liquors, and if Hill would organize the constitutional clubs proposed in the article he would finance the cause, which of course could be done confidentially. The idea of his coming to see Hill, it came out, had been suggested by Senator Root. If Root wished to aid the cause he had rich friends who could start the organization, Hill retorted, but he did not intend to ally his proposal with private interests.[20]

Looking to more respectable sources, Hill tried unsuccessfully in 1916 to interest the Rockefeller family. The next year he managed to get a small annual subvention from the Carnegie Corporation, which kept the Association alive but hardly more. In 1920 Hill's first vice-president, Archibald Hopkins, suggested a merger with the Constitutional League, a recently organized society with parallel aims, which appeared to be well financed and had gotten very much in the limelight. But nothing came of the proposal, and when the Carnegie Corporation withdrew its subvention in 1924 the future of the Association looked black. Trying to get the subvention renewed in 1926, Hill explained to Dr. Henry S. Pritchett, an officer of the Corporation, that through the funding of dues paid by life members the Association had eleven thousand dollars in capital. But for the coming year its receipts would be approximately $4,150 and its expenditures $7,392. "With this budget we can not go on without consuming our permanent fund—and then dissolution!"[21]

Earlier that year Hill had proposed merging with the National Security League, which after the war had turned its attention from military preparedness to combating bolshevism. The League's president, S. Stanwood Menken, was warm to the suggestion, but when it turned out that his organization was scarcely more solvent than the Association, the scheme died. The next year Hill considered merging with the Constitutional Anniversary Association, an organization of dubious substance under the presidency of Harry F. Atwood, a Chicagoan who styled himself on his letterheads as lecturer and consultant on patriotism. This too failed, for Hill and Atwood had little to offer each other beyond their own super-patriotism. "Out of a thousand letters setting forth the aims and purposes of our Association," Hill had complained to Dr. Pritchett a few months before, "I have not received twenty-five manifesting any intelligent apprehension of what it is all about accompanied with any substantial encouragement. . . . I do not feel that I can give up while I live this Association for Constitutional Government. I am going to try to find someone or several unitedly to help us tide it over."[22]

But failing to find a patron, Hill was at last forced, in December 1929, to inform the Association's members that without new funds it would be impossible to continue beyond the end of the year without running into debt. Suggesting that dues be increased to five dollars and that every member enlist at least one new member before January, the executive committee asked for immediate replies so that it might know what resources could be depended upon for the coming year. Seventy-seven of the Association's 850 members replied, subscribing totally $1,275. The amount needed for 1930 was $6,500. After more futile correspondence with Harry Atwood about a merger, Hill dissolved the Association on April 30, 1930. George Washington University agreed to take over publication of the *Constitutional Review,* but that too died when the University could find no one to edit it.[23] The Association had already outlived its time: the New Freedom and the Red Scare had long been relegated to history, and for a decade political conservatives in the United States had had little cause to fear or complain. The New Deal, which was to upset them again, still lay in an unpredicted future.

An uncompromising Republican of the Old Guard tradition, as well as a scholar and diplomat who fitted the image of the highest type of public servant, Hill was bound to be promoted for political office. Early in 1912 Francis Mitchell suggested in the *Post Express* that the Republicans of New York nominate the former ambassador, who continued to retain his legal residence in Rochester, for governor. Because the delegates to the state convention, which was to meet on September 25, were for the first time chosen through primary elections, there was some press speculation, in which Hill's name figured, about the possibility of their naming a dark horse candidate. On the day the convention opened the New York *Evening Telegram* carried the front-page, full-spread headline, "'UNBOSSED' REPUBLICANS MAY NOMINATE DR.

DAVID J. HILL." But Hill's name was not even placed in nomination.[24] In Switzerland, all the while, Hill apparently had not been approached by anyone, and had himself said nothing.

Two years later, however, Hill was not in the dark when Mitchell, James G. Cutler, and Lewis P. Ross suggested sending him to the United States Senate. Reading their commendations in copies of the *Post Express* sent to him in mid-summer 1914, he reiterated views he had expressed to them earlier in the year before leaving for Europe. If he were the spontaneous choice of the Republicans of New York for the office he would deem it a privilege to run, but he would never personally enter a primary race as now required for the nomination. The primary was totally different from an election contest once a man had been nominated by his party. To campaign on the platform of one's party in order to carry its principles into effect was as worthy as any public act could be; but to enter a merely personal struggle for place in opposition to others perhaps equally qualified involved a lowering of one's self-respect and disloyalty to party unity. The members of the party should be left free to make their choice without any urgency or expenditure of time and money by the candidates. Any other course destroyed all the benefits the nominating primary was intended to bestow and made the voter the victim of self-advertisement. If he did not know whom he should nominate when left alone, then the nominating primary was an illusion and a snare, and it would be better to revert to a nominating convention where the eligibility of men could be determined by those who knew them. Without putting up a fight in the primaries he could not, perhaps, expect to be nominated, Hill added, therefore he was not taking the matter very seriously.[25] Still, he did not ask his friends to drop their plans.

Despite the handicap imposed, Rochester Republicans had already organized a Hill Nomination Committee to circulate a petition to place his name on the primary ballot. It was a strange candidacy, and one bound to arouse apprehensions. The chairman of the Republican State Committee, William Barnes, Jr., who offered Hill the temporary chairmanship of the state convention meeting in Saratoga in August, was afraid that it would sap the strength of his own senatorial candidate, James W. Wadsworth, former speaker of the New York Assembly. Nicholas Murray Butler, always with a finger in state and national Republican politics, also feared that the petition was being circulated, without Hill's consent, simply to hurt Wadsworth's chances in Rochester. Since he would be compelled by law to run in the primaries if the petition were filed, Butler cabled Hill in Switzerland, he would act for him to prevent filing if Hill really did not want to be nominated. "The party must freely select its candidate," Hill cabled back. The next day he followed up this refusal to withdraw from the race with a letter explaining his refusal to campaign, which he suggested Butler give to all the news associations. He sent copies to Mitchell and Cutler to publish should Butler not do so.[26] Although pleading that this measure was to avoid being placed in a false light, Hill appeared to be trying to issue at least one campaign document.

The Hill petition was filed with a required three thousand signatures in time to meet the September deadline, and in the ensuing primary Hill received over thirty-seven thousand votes, carrying Rochester and Monroe County almost unanimously. For a restricted, eleventh-hour candidacy it was a respectable showing. The two other contenders, Wadsworth and William M. Calder of Brooklyn, had been campaigning for five or six months with generous financial backing. The Hill Nomination Committee had been in existence only three weeks, its campaign fund had been less than three thousand dollars, and since its candidate had refused to stump, its campaign had been confined solely to the distribution of literature. Culter, who chaired the committee, was nevertheless disappointed, but consoled himself with the thought that a good foundation had been laid for running Hill again when the next senatorial vacancy opened in two years. Hill warned Cutler and Mitchell, however, not to expect his attitude toward the primaries to change. If he were the spontaneous nominee of the party he would gladly and earnestly work for election, but he would never press his own candidacy for nomination.[27]

He stood ready to serve if his services were wanted, Hill had said, and in a less obvious way he had already that year served his party. Through arrangements made by Charles H. Sherrill, lawyer, diplomat, and G.O.P. influential, he had met Theodore Roosevelt on June 13, 1914, at Dover, England, while the Colonel was traveling to Spain to attend the wedding of his son Kermit and he was en route to Switzerland, to make the first direct effort to bring the former President and his Progressive followers back into the Republican fold. Riding on the train to London and breakfasting together, he and Roosevelt discussed the possibility of a fusion of Progressives with regular Republicans in the New York elections. The Colonel thought his party might support a regular Republican of "the right type" for governor if he would stand for Progressive aims without necessarily adopting Progressive formulas. He was personally willing to support a regular Republican, if his party did not insist upon putting up a candidate of its own, Roosevelt added, provided he did not favor the leadership of William Barnes. Since Barnes had a strong grip on the party's state machine, Roosevelt's enmity toward him, which Barnes cordially reciprocated, presented a serious obstacle. Without conciliation there was no hope for either party, Hill argued. Could not personalities be left out and an attempt made to unite on common principles? The antagonism of Barnes to himself, and that of some members of his party to Barnes, the Colonel replied, was so bitter that he did not see how open conflict could be avoided. He could not conciliate alone, and he would not be disloyal to his associates.

Nonetheless, Roosevelt had indicated his willingness to support a fusion ticket, and Hill could report to Sherrill, who was waiting in Paris, that the Colonel was not averse to advances and conciliation was not impossible. Were "Mr̃. M" to urge a union of the parties in New York for the election of a governor and a senator acceptable to both groups, Hill thought Roosevelt would approve.[28]

Mr. M was Frank A. Munsey, the millionaire publisher who had thrown his editorial pages and checkbook into the Progressive campaign of 1912. A businessman devoted to contemporary business ideals, he was an admirer of Roosevelt rather than of reform, and soon repenting his hasty promise to support the new party had as early as February 1913 proposed in his magazine that it repair to the Republican standard. William J. Dalliba, the American Express Company agent in Paris and another confidant in Sherrill's scheme, now cabled Munsey that a "breach healing plan" had been approved by the Colonel,[29] information that brought Munsey to Paris to meet with Sherrill on July 11.

Before sailing, Munsey discussed Sherrill's plan with George W. Perkins. A partner of J. P. Morgan and director of the United States Steel Corporation and the International Harvester Company, Perkins too had been more taken with Roosevelt than with Progressive ideals, and although second only to Roosevelt in command, he had never been comfortable in the party and was as eager as Munsey to bring its existence to an end. Favoring Sherrill's plan, Munsey and Perkins were nevertheless cautious. "Although apparently they both thought well of it," Sherrill informed Hill, "they seem both of the opinion that our Republican friends are so confident that they set little store by anybody's endorsement of our candidates. The impression left upon me was that they 'would be willing,' but felt that our should be the first move. Is there anyone to whom you could suggest this confidentially in New York?"[30]

This Hill had already taken the opportunity to do in replying to Barnes's bid to come to the Saratoga convention. Many Progressive leaders, if not too much antagonized, he had written the state chairman, would be glad to find a way to retreat from their excessive attitudes, and it would be a good idea to welcome them back. Otherwise Republicans would not find a majority at the elections. It would therefore be expedient to invite their cooperation in designating candidates and framing a platform that both parties could support. But Barnes, as Munsey and Perkins had surmised, was not inclined to make any concessions. "I agree with you entirely on your main proposition," the chairman replied. "But I do not think you take into consideration the number of former Democrats who are bitterly aroused against the present administration and who say they will never vote a Democratic ticket again." Barnes also threw cold water on the possibility of any personal truce with Roosevelt. "My great fear," he added, "is the establishment of an autocracy in America. We have so democratized our Democracy that people otherwise sane are looking toward an autocracy as a relief—and Roosevelt stands in the shadow ready to grasp it. To prevent that I believe to be the primal consideration."[31]

Barnes or no Barnes, Roosevelt was still ready to start moving back into the Republican party. Upon returning from Spain he suggested that New York Progressives combine with the progressive Republican element in the state, and despite the opposition of a majority of the state's Progressive leaders, tried to arrange a fusion candidate for governor. The attempt, though failing, signaled the end of the Progressive party. A hitherto suppressed fusionist faction was by implication given the Colonel's blessing, with the result that fusion tickets appeared in several states and in a number of New York assembly districts. Regular Progressive candidates everywhere, moreover, were dealt a fatal blow. Their Republican opponents derided Roosevelt's maneuver in New York as the act of a party on its deathbed, and the results of the November elections gave proof to their claims.[32]

In a less personal manner, Hill became involved in still another political episode in 1914: the contest over the repeal of the Panama Canal Act of 1912, which had exempted American coastwise shipping from the payment of tolls. The British Foreign Office had protested the Act, claiming that the exemption violated the Hay-Pauncefote Treaty of 1901, which had provided that all nations observing certain rules for the neutralization of the canal would be treated on terms of entire equality. Although in the election of 1912 both major parties had approved the Act, President Wilson became persuaded that national honor required its repeal and made this recommendation to Congress in March 1914.[33]

Taking issue with the President, Hill sent George H. Lorimer, the arch-conservative editor of the *Saturday Evening Post*, an article on "The Meaning of the Hay-Pauncefote Treaty," which Lorimer published in mid-May. By the provisions of the treaty the United States had not surrendered its right to prescribe the terms on which its own domestic shipping might use the canal, Hill argued. The nature and logic of the treaty demonstrated that the stipulated equality of treatment applied only to the nations that agreed to observe the rules of neutralization, and an analysis of the rules showed that they had "from their very nature no application to the United States, which, therefore, can not fairly be regarded as included in the expression 'all nations which shall agree to support these rules.'" To reinforce this construction that the treaty's negotiators never intended that other nations should have entire equality with the United States, Hill quoted extensively from communications drafted at the time by Secretary Hay, Ambassador Pauncefote, and Foreign Secretary Lansdowne.[34]

The opponents of repeal seized upon the article eagerly. Newspapers throughout the country quoted from it, and James A. O'Gorman of New York, who led the fight against repeal in the Senate, and Congressman William S. Greene of Massachusetts each inserted it in the *Congressional Record*. But their fight was already lost. The House had passed the repeal bill six weeks before, and when its supporters were finally able to bring it to a vote in the Senate on June 11, 1914, they won an easy victory.[35] Considerations of principle, patronage, and support for Wilson's overall foreign policy readily outmatched some party defection, the opposition of Irish-Americans, and the quasi-legalistic arguments of a well-publicized former ambassador.

"Having chosen those who are to represent us in the shaping of international policies," Hill had admonished the Rochester Chamber of Commerce in December 1913, "it is only weakening our cause to divide into hostile camps and issue volumes of criticism upon foreign relations. Our duty is to stand by the President because he is our President and we have put him there for that purpose and we ignominiously weaken him by criticising his policies. It follows as a corollary that it is foolish for any man not omniscient to criticise a foreign policy because the heads of government are so much better informed than private individuals that it is an act of prudence not to indulge in this criticism."[36] Whatever the value of this advice, it was more than Hill himself could live up to. Wilson seemingly plotted against him by doing everything wrong in foreign affairs just as he was doing everything wrong in domestic affairs. Possibly a lesser factor was that through a series of articles Hill published in *Harper's Magazine* on the functions and needs of the diplomatic service[37] he discovered that "instructive" comment on foreign policy was a good way to supplement his income. In any event, in his new role of publicist he was soon criticizing other aspects of Wilson's foreign policy, and by 1916 there was no phase of it he was not condemning. Writing frequently for the *North American Review*, whose publisher, George Harvey, hated Wilson with all the intensity of a defected partisan, he produced a particularly scathing two-part article for September and October 1916, timed for maximum effect in the presidential election.

Wilson's determination to overthrow the Mexican dictator Victoriano Huerta in order to encourage a form of government that had never existed in Mexico, Hill found totally indefensible. Huerta's government was vindicated by the fact that the lives and property of Americans were protected wherever its authority extended while being menaced and outraged elsewhere by the bands or irresponsible revolutionaries whom Wilson was assisting. While boasting of having "kept out of war" when no nation wanted war with the United States, Wilson had provoked a dangerous situation with a friendly country and committed every act characteristic of war. Though earlier in the year Hill had criticized Wilson for pursuing toward Mexico "a policy of passive delay . . . in the midst of extraordinary provocations,"[38] the President's more vigorous stance now led him to condemn it as a humiliating catalogue of errors of judgment and caprices of policy without parallel in American history.

Secretary of State William Jennings Bryan's conciliation treaties were equal objects of Hill's scorn. The Secretary, in his noble infatuation to become the hero of peace, had pledged the United States not to resist any insult, injury, or humiliation, however grave, but to make only verbal protest until an entire year had elapsed. By renouncing the right to take preventive measures at the proper time, the treaties would permit great powers to inflict irreparable injury upon the United States and small powers to escape punishment by subsequent apology or change of government. The treaties therefore eliminated from the thoughts and plans of other governments, which had hitherto been restrained by consideration of what action the United States might take, all concern regarding the opinion and aims of the administration at Washington.

Leaving the signatories of the treaties free to do whatever they pleased, Bryan's scheme had precisely the effect that might have been foreseen. "It was an act of self-effacement on the part of a great nation in the midst of world conflict; in which there was no need that it should participate, but which a valiant and self-reliant nation of the magnitude and former prestige of the United States might have influenced in important ways, had it not previously and voluntarily exposed itself to the complete neglect of other nations." America might have made itself the effective guardian of neutral rights, which were being violated in every manner conceivable. "But," complained Hill, "knowing beforehand that the United States, whatever happened, would positively take no action, the merely formal protests of our Government have been treated with inattention, and sometimes with open and continued defiance."

Duty and self-interest had required the American government to speak out at once even at the risk of war, Hill insisted, when Germany violated the neutrality of Belgium in defiance of the Hague Convention respecting the rights and duties of neutrals, to which the United States and all the belligerents were parties. But the administration had remained silent. "*Our* law, the law of the whole civilized world, trampled upon, and no whisper even of remonstrance!" A prompt and earnest protest would not have involved the United States in war, however. "It would have given us at once the moral leadership of the world, and made the United States the friend and rallying centre of all the neutral countries. It would have done more: it would have given us the balance of power during the war in international affairs; and, even in the fearful turmoil of conflict, the belligerents would have sought our approval in choosing their methods of procedure."

Having endowed American pronouncements with such extraordinary power, Hill interpreted Wilson's "strict accountability" note of February 10, 1915, as signifying merely an intention of precise bookkeeping and a later demand for payment of money indemnities. Again the administration had failed the American people. The situation had demanded plain, frank, and resolute speaking: the German Ambassador should have been told that if an American life was taken by a submarine on the high seas, diplomatic relations would be severed at once. It was his firm belief, Hill asserted, that if such warning had been given, followed by a telegram to the German Emperor appealing to the Kaiser's good sense and friendly disposition toward the United States, "not a single ship known or believed to carry American passengers would ever have been sunk without warning." But because of Wilson's policies ships were sunk, and the President then failed his country again. His response to the sinking of the *Lusitania* with a speech about being "too proud to fight" was fatal to the prestige and influence of the nation. It was a pusillanimous invitation to further humiliation, "an assurance of license to every extremity." The Wilson administration did threaten to sever diplomatic relations with Germany following the *Sussex* attack, Hill admitted, but it deserved no credit for finally putting an end to its temporizing. The note of April 18, 1916, was sent because the administration had been "swept forward by an irresistible tide of public sentiment that could not be curbed."[39]

"Your friend who remarked that these articles read like a criminal indictment is precisely right," wrote William R. Willcox, chairman of the Republican National Committee. Having made arrangements with Hill some weeks before, the committee was ready to distribute several hundred thousand copies of the indictment in pamphlet form immediately after the second installment appeared in the *Review*.[40]

Demanding a tougher policy toward Germany, Hill also urged building up America's weak military posture, and as a member of the Navy League, a National Committeeman of the National Security League, Chairman of the Advisory board of the National Defense Society, and Chairman of the Whitman Committee appointed by the governor of New York to encourage adequate defense, he took a leading part in the preparedness controversy that raged from the outbreak of the war through 1916. In articles, books, and motion pictures a host of panicky preparedness advocates were predicting attacks on American territory, the renewal of national piracy on the seas, and the forcible wresting of colonies from civilized peoples. Hill considered such hysterical arguments detrimental to the cause of national defense. It was the right of innocent passage and commerce on the free ocean and the invisible bulwarks of liberty and self-government that called for defense. As a great power that could not decently throw the whole burden on little nations, it was America's duty to stand for law and humanity and be a positive and effective influence in the world. Hill also saw the possibility of disputes arising over the safety of American life and property in ill-governed countries, over the right of other nations to establish bases and defenses in territories near those of the United States, over naval movements in waters where the United States wanted no warlike operations, or over some other right of Americans or people within America's sphere of influence that the United States would not be able to settle amicably without strength formidable enough to make its words and standards of conduct universally respected.[41]

Adequate defense, Hill maintained, required not only increased armaments but also a system of compulsory military training, the existence of which would cause any power to reflect long before it disregarded the rights of American citizens. Opponents of compulsory military service, usually fired with progressive enthusiasm for governmental regulation in other areas, raised the contention that there were distinct limits to the state's power over the individual. But any relationship of this argument to his own expostulations on the limits of state authority Hill would have denied, for he saw military service as a personal duty one owed to the nation and distinctly provided for in the eighth section of the first article of the Federal Constitution.[42]

For these progressive peace advocates, who by preventing adequate military preparedness had brought the nation "first into humiliation, and finally into a confession of our helplessness," Hill had bitterly scornful words. "What could be expected of people who were declaiming against the rights of individuals, and denying that any person possessés any rights except those a majority chooses to grant?" he asked the Washington Chapter of the Sons of the American Revolution. "What then if a few hundred men, women, and children were sunk in the sea? Let them stay at home, and leave the sea to the free activity of the German submarine!" "They think that our weakness is in no respect an exposure, but even a security," he told a New York meeting of the American Defense Society. "They have a sublime and abiding confidence in the goodness, purity, and righteousness of all the over-armed nations of the earth on land and sea. It is impossible, they think, that any one of these should ever wish to do us any wrong; and, if they did, it would be better not to resist it. We have only to be very civil and very complaisant and nothing will ever happen to us. But regarding the people of the United States these persons have a different feeling. It would be positively dangerous, they say, if *we* were strong. We should be so arrogant, so fiery, so selfish, so unjust, and so ambitious, that we should be engaged in constant wars. And so they sing the traitorous ditty, 'I did not Raise My Boy to Be a Soldier,' and try to seduce our young men to the treasonable act of solemnly pledging themselves never to take part in any war, even though it be in defense of our soil against an invading enemy. I do not know what to say of such people, except God have mercy on their craven souls. . . . The nation has no need of them, for they are not of it. They are only parasites upon it."[43]

America must gird itself not only for military defense, Hill warned, but also for industrial defense. Victorious or defeated, Germany would emerge from the war with its mightily organized industrial-commercial-financial mechanism practically unimpaired. Before the war Germany had been rapidly conquering the world's markets. After the war, excluded from allied European markets, it would look to neutral countries and would converge its enormous producing and distributing power largely upon the United States, the neutral country with the greatest capacity for absorbing its goods. America would be subjected to an unprecedented campaign of underselling for possession of its markets—to wholesale dumping. To maintain its own industrial and commercial interests, and the standard of living of its working classes, the United States would be forced to restore a protective tariff. But it was as unprepared for taking such economic measures as it was for taking military measures. The existing tariff legislation had no scientific relation whatever to the facts of international industry and commerce. It was a piece of congressional guesswork from which all substantial evidence had been systematically excluded. While other governments were employing their intelligence and exerting their influence to encourage the highest efficiency of industry, the government of the United States was applying a dogma that had repeatedly been refuted.[44]

Voicing this perception of "An Impending Danger to the Republic" at the Merchants' Club of Boston in October 1915, and publishing it in the December issue of the *North American Review,* Hill soon defined the economic threat hanging over the United States as more ominous still. The war was at bottom a battle for trade and control of trade routes, he explained to the Home Market Club of Boston and the Economic Club of Portland, Maine, in February 1916, and later wrote in *Americanism: What It Is.* Whether its outcome was German domination of the greatest continental and maritime empire that had ever existed or undisputed British supremacy on every sea, the United States must be strong enough to insist upon equality with all other nations in the commerce of the world or that equality would be denied to it. The signing of peace treaties would end only the military phase of the war. There would then open a battle for recuperation—a race for preponderance in the world's markets. With centralized, state-controlled organization and supervision of industry and commerce already highly developed in Germany, and rapidly evolving in the other countries at war, commerce and industry would be "militarized" as never before in history. The Entente nations would be Germany's strenuous and efficient rivals in every mart of the world, and there would thus be an unprecedented attempt by several nations to dump their products on American shores and vie with America for all foreign trade.[45]

Taking issue with the generalizations and superficial trade statistics of Hill's article in the *North American Review,* the New York *Journal of Commerce* analyzed the nature of Germany's prewar exports and dumping policies to show that the former ambassador's apprehensions were greatly exaggerated,[46] but most journals accepted his arguments at face value.[47] That Europe's postwar recovery would be made at the expense of the United States was a popular conception, and one not confined solely to high protectionists dismayed by the apostasy of the Underwood tariff.

Secretary of Commerce William C. Redfield had already suggested the enactment of "anti-dumping" laws, which would declare under-selling illegal on the ground of unfair competition. This alternative to a protective tariff Hill assailed as ridiculous. "While there is a sovereign right to impose customs duties, and this no responsible government will dispute, . . . it is a different matter positively to prohibit trade with a foreign country," he argued. "It is an act of economic war, which would not only destroy our most important source for the raising of revenue, but involve us in controversies and complications with countries with which we desire to deal, and expose us to reprisals that would seriously damage our export trade with our best customers."[48]

This was partisan and protectionist reasoning that would not wash. To prevent foreign goods from being sold cheaply in the United States by denying them entry if below a certain price, Hill was contending, would destroy the nation's most important source of revenue and expose it to economic reprisals, but to exclude those same goods by a protective tariff would somehow produce revenue and international amity. But protectionists were not inclined to be critical of Hill's pronouncements. Thomas O. Marvin, editor of the *Protectionist* and secretary of the Home Market Club of Boston, was deluged with requests for copies of the address Hill delivered to the Club, one enthusiast arranging for the reprint and circulation of a hundred thousand copies. When Hill delivered essentially the same message of high tariff or economic disaster to clubs of the Hughes Business Men's League in Rochester, New York, and Waterbury, Connecticut, in October and November, Marvin gave it wide distribution in the *Protectionist* and as a campaign pamphlet.[49]

Marvin, who considered Hill "probably the best informed man in the country" on the tariff question, thought he should be the nation's next President. Hill was not setting his sights that high, but did hope to be named a New York delegate-at-large to the Republican national convention at Chicago in June. As one of the "Big Four" he would be in the spotlight in New York politics and perhaps the state party organization's choice for the Senate. At an unofficial convention held in Carnegie Hall in February to select the delegates-at-large, who would then be "recommended" to the voters in the primary, Hill was the choice of Governor Whitman, George Aldridge, and a number of other country leaders, but was opposed by William Barnes. Although Barnes had been ousted from the state chairmanship by the Whitman faction, he still commanded a powerful bloc within the party, and he was not willing to send to Chicago a friend of Theodore Roosevelt, who, almost inevitably, was being mentioned for the nomination. Barnes at first backed William Berri of Brooklyn. But when the recommendations committee, which chose the other three delegates without contest, deadlocked over Hill and Berri, Barnes threw his support to Elon R. Brown of Watertown, Republican majority leader in the state senate, who won out by a switch of one vote.[50]

There was nothing personal in Barnes's objection to Hill, and when the Albany leader saw a chance to use the Ambassador to grind another axe, he tried to do it. By July it appeared that William M. Calder, who had helped Whitman overthrow Barnes, would get the Republican senatorial nomination without opposition in the primaries. This prospect brought Elon Brown to Cohasset, Massachusetts, where Hill was spending the summer, to ask if he would run against Calder. He would have the support of practically all the people who had been for Wadsworth two years before, Brown assured him, making his election certain. Because he belonged to no faction and wished to use his influence for party unity, Hill responded, he could not accept a candidacy without a spontaneous call for it and general agreement that it was in the interests of the party. Since the Ambassador did not actually refuse to be a candidate, but only to run personally in the primaries, Brown suggested that he inform Colonel Roosevelt, Chairman Willcox, Frank Mitchell, and James Cutler of the proposal and rely on their advice. In any case, Brown wanted Hill to let George Aldridge know of his visit and that the men who had overriden his advocacy of Hill for a delegate-at-large were now well-disposed.[51]

Aldridge, to whom Calder was no more acceptable than to Barnes, was ready to bury the hatchet with the Albany politician, and he thought Hill should take the matter up with Roosevelt and Willcox as Brown had suggested. Yet he had to advise that since Hill refused to campaign and Calder had been busily promoting himself for the past two years, the situation did not warrant his becoming a candidate. Since Barnes wanted to stop Calder through the primary system rather than bemoan it, he felt the same way. After intimating to Hill that if he really wanted to run he had better say so quickly for time was growing short, Barnes found a candidate of prestige and respectability, and one with no objection to running in primaries, in the person of Robert Bacon, former financier and diplomat. As former diplomatic colleagues, Hill and Elihu Root personally endorsed Bacon when he announced his last-minute challenge to the regular party organization late in August.[52] From the beginning, however, Barnes had never had much chance of upsetting Calder, and Hill was just as well out of this personal vendetta.

Active and to some degree ambitious in the electoral campaigns of 1916, Hill took no part whatever in the contests of 1918. In ill health, he spent the summer at the White Mountain resort of Bethlehem, New Hampshire, where he went "to forget everything but breathing." He had little interest anyway in state politics per se. And he had become increasingly disgusted with Republican acceptance in New York of the nominating primary. When financier John A. Stewart asked him to join with other prominent Republicans in calling an unofficial state convention to endorse not more than two primary candidates from several in the field for governor, Hill gave vent to his feelings. "Why not a real convention . . . ?" he asked. For popular effect, Republican politicians had allowed the party to be disintegrated and almost destroyed by legislation that necessarily divided it, he scolded. "We shall have to learn by experience the result of destroying responsible representative party government. The truth is, we Republicans have surrendered our principles, in order to win Democratic votes. We do not really believe in this system, which divides our house against itself and leaves us on election day composed of a victorious and a defeated faction. Until we abandon it and reconstitute the party on lines of unity, loyalty, responsibility, and the selection of candidates by the party as such, I shall entertain little hope of enthusiasm in State politics." Since an unofficial convention would only end in divisions more open and bitter than already existed, he could not, he said, join in the call for one.[53]

The call nevertheless was successful, and the unofficial convention met at Saratoga Springs in mid-July. The Republican Committee of Monroe County elected Hill a delegate, but he wired Aldridge his regrets. A week later, Aldridge telegraphed to offer him the district's congressional nomination. Since there would be no contest in the primaries, and the Republican nomination was equivalent to election, Hill had a seat in Congress for the taking. Yet he again wired his regrets.[54] If a senatorial nomination had been handed to him this way, he would have seized it, but in a lesser office he was not interested.

10

The Fight against the League

PRESIDENT WILSON'S CONDUCT OF AMERICAN FOREIGN POLICY WAS NO more satisfactory to David Jayne Hill after the United States entered the European war in April 1917 than it had been before. His earlier affection for Germany overcome by ingrained ultranationalism and emotions roused by war, he objected particularly to the President's ideas on making a just and permanent peace. Rejecting Wilson's contention that America's quarrel was with the German government and not with the German people, he called for peace terms that were unmistakably punitive. "The people of Germany are more loyal to the Emperor than the Democratic Party is to Wilson today," he told the trustees of the American Defense Society a few weeks after the United States had declared war. "The President has said that we have no hostility toward the German people, but do not the German people support the Imperial Government to a man? Didn't a wave of general rejoicing go through Germany when the Lusitania went down? How many Germans in Germany can you find who are not imperialistic? I have never found one."[1]

In articles in the *New York Times Magazine, Current History,* and *Har-*

per's Magazine in 1917 and 1918, Hill portrayed the German people as no less hypnotized than their Kaiser by a false conception of government and an obsession for world power and territorial spoils.[2] In 1918 he published most of these and a few other essays in a book entitled *Impressions of the Kaiser.* An analysis of the predominant influence of the Kaiser in shaping the government and the foreign policy of Imperial Germany, the volume nowhere recorded the impressions Hill had sent to Carnegie from the German Court. Rather than portraying Wilhelm as sincerely wanting peace, it convincingly and crushingly indicted him for deliberately instigating war.[3]

When the war came to an end, Hill turned his literary guns on the conference at Paris, criticizing the President's every act. Especially opposed to the creation of the League of Nations, he began attacking that organization monthly in the *North American Review* from the moment of its conception. Many of these articles, together with a number of addresses, he published in two books: *Present Problems in Foreign Policy,* which came out in May 1919, the month the Senate undertook consideration of the Versailles Treaty, and *American World Policies,* which appeared in June 1920, timed for the presidential election campaign.

Hill condemned the peacemakers at Paris for failing to resume the movement toward world organization based on law as conceived by the Hague Conferences. The League of Nations was not an institution of justice—there were no provisions whatsoever in its Covenant for the formulation or revision of international law—but an instrument of power. It was an imperial syndicate for ruling the world, controlled by a few great powers determined to project their territorial possessions. A supergovernment nowhere pledged to recognize the inherent rights of nations, it intended to abolish neutrality, coerce sovereign nonmember states, and govern absolutely the peoples who were placed under its mandate by conquest. The United States could not participate in such an imperium over the whole earth without violating its Constitution and surrendering its national independence and freedom.

In addition to this main theme, Hill raised every other objection to the League that a hostile mind could conceive. The United

States would be required to surrender all control over foreign affairs to a council in which it would have but a single voice, the exclusive direction of which would endow the President with excessive power. It would be drawn automatically into foreign wars with which it had no concern, including every Balkan frontier quarrel arising from the errors of the misguided cartographers at Paris. It would have to forfeit its healthy isolation from the hostilities, intrigues, and ambitions of the Old World and permit the intrusion of an international body into a sphere hitherto regarded as exclusively American. Possessing neither imperial interests nor traditions, it would nevertheless be compelled to guarantee the territorial possessions of the great powers of Europe, which were all either actual empires or aspirants to imperial dominion, no matter how iniquitously these territories were obtained, how they were ruled, or what violence was done to the principle of self-determination. The Covenant of the League would also make the United States the executor and guarantor of secret compacts dividing the spoils of war, as demonstrated by the Shantung article and General Smuts's system of mandated territories. In this connection Hill saw a sinister conspiracy in the selection of the term "regional understandings" in Article XXI of the revised draft of the Covenant, which provided that nothing in that compact would "affect the validity of international engagements, such as treaties of arbitration or regional understandings like the Monroe Doctrine, for securing the maintenance of peace." Ostensibly designed to recognize the Monroe Doctrine, its real purpose, Hill suspected, was to protect the secret imperial agreements dividing the German and Turkish empires. The League, Hill also presumed, would arbitrarily settle the great questions of world trade as well as those of territory and war.[4]

Hill's objections to the League were attended by equally strong strictures of President Wilson, whom he portrayed as a devious, egoistic, anti-democratic, would-be dictator. The League was the result of an abstract plan of world reconstruction the President had sought to impose upon the nations at Paris, and although as the price of its adoption it had been transformed into something very different from his original purpose, Wilson was insisting that the American people accept it because acceptance was necessary to his prestige. The President's call for a "great and solemn referendum" on the League was the stratagem of an autocrat. To attempt by plebiscite to set aside the constitutional powers of the Senate and force it to approve the treaty without change was comparable to the appeals of Louis Bonaparte to the "will of the people" and was intended to serve the same purpose. If the referendum sustained Wilson, he would be a hero even while subverting the Constitution; if it went against him, he would escape the blame that the Allies and history would place upon him for preventing ratification of the treaty and at the same time receive the plaudits of the people for yielding to their will. The next plebiscite, Hill warned ominously, might easily be on the question of whether the President should make laws without the sanction of Congress.[5]

Criticism of the League was to be expected from someone who for years had advocated a strictly judicial form of world organization. But Hill did not write and speak merely as a proponent of the World Court idea. A political conservative affronted by the progressivism Wilson had come to symbolize, he disliked the President with an obsession that debarred any fair appraisal of his efforts at Paris. A frank and decided Republican partisan, he could not accept the League Covenant as Wilson brought it home, yet could find reason to approve it if given a Republican stamp. Most fundamental of all, he was an ultra-nationalist who, while professing internationalism with complete sincerity, could not really brook any restraints on the will of the United States. The result was that his advocacy of an international rule of law was often bewildering in its twists and turns.

Since his Carpentier Lectures of 1911, Hill had written several essays on the problem of world organization,[6] capping them in 1917 with *The Rebuilding of Europe,* a collection of eight papers, six of which he had originally delivered as lectures at Johns Hopkins University on the Schouler Foundation.[7] Taking issue in that volume with the League to Enforce Peace, which had been organized two years before, he argued that a general international organization was neither desirable nor possible. Any plan establishing not only an international legislature and judiciary, but also an executive controlling an effective police, would institute a superstate annihilating all the national characteristics of its federated political units. To propose it would invoke universal resistance. It would be impossible, he also insisted, discarding the whole theme of his Carpentier Lectures of a universal development of juristic conscience, to unite absolute and constitutional states into one league. Absolute states would not accept restrictions placed upon them by general principles of law, while constitutional states would doubt the good faith of powers adhering to a conception of sovereignty whereby they were bound only by their own will. The inequality of states in size and power presented still another obstacle, for it would be very difficult to apportion representation in a general organization in a manner satisfactory to all.[8]

"It is to the great Powers that mankind must look for both peace and justice, for they alone can impose them," Hill had declared to the American Society of International Law in 1916. "If they could act together the problem might be quickly solved. . . . The final triumph of international law, if it is finally to prove victorious, will, no doubt, be brought about by the great Powers."[9] Developing this idea in *The Rebuilding of Europe*, Hill contended that the most to be expected in the form of an international organization, at least in the beginning, would be a strong but limited group of powers around which all responsible and socially inclined nations might ultimately unite. "It would not necessarily be a federation, which would imply the creation of a new state, nor even an alliance," he theorized. "It might be in substance merely the formal recognition of the existence of a real, as distinguished from a purely fictitious, society of states based upon common intentions and a declaration of definite principles of right which the members were willing to accept, to observe, and to defend." Such a society of states, however, would be a mere fiction of the mind unless it possessed some kind of legislative, judicial, and executive power, and it would have to be sufficiently powerful to defend its members from attack and protect smaller states wishing to join it. "But it is quite possible," he maintained, "that a society of states should in some degree possess such powers without in reality constituting a new state. The establishment of new relations is not equivalent to the creation of a new entity, and it is merely the establishment of new relations that is here contemplated.

There would be no new sovereignty developed, but merely the concurrent action of preexistent sovereignties. For constitutional states there is virtually no surrender of sovereign authority in submitting to international law, because, being themselves constituted for justice as the end of their existence, international law contradicts nothing essential to them."

International law could easily be perfected at international conferences, Hill went on, if the universal character and requirement of unanimity that had hamstrung the Hague Conferences were given up and nations admitted their obligation to obey international legislation that had received preponderant assent. The solution to this problem lay in the expression, "decisions in the nature of general laws," for constitutional states had no reason not to accept such laws as binding if agreed to by a large majority. With a body of international law developed, the necessary machinery of international government would be extremely simple, for responsible governments, when the law was clear, would willingly submit disputes of a justiciable character to an international tribunal. The problem of forming a competent court would also be solved. Because the vagueness of existing law consigned disputes to the private judgment of jurists who might be influenced by their national prejudices, every state demanded a representative on an international bench who could sit in its own case. Such a court was impracticable in every way. But if the law were clear and complete, national prejudice would be excluded. A decision would become merely a question of ascertaining the facts and applying the law to the circumstances of the case. The requirements of a good international judge would be simply common honesty and clear intelligence.

Since constitutional states were habituated to accepting the decisions of properly constituted courts, and absolutist governments were by definition excluded from the society of states he conceived, Hill dismissed problems of enforcing international law as mostly imaginary. A state that refused to respect the decision of an international tribunal would be considered an international outlaw and might properly be treated as such. But the use of military force to enforce international obligations would not be practicable. No wise nation, he argued, would "enter into any general compact to 'enforce peace,' which in view of actual facts might bind it to the most odious obligations against its own judgment and conscience. Such an agreement would, moreover, bind itself and its cosignatories by a solemn compact to preserve the *status quo,* for a time at least, in every unjust situation.'' It was inconceivable, he thought, that prudent statesmen would ever agree to go to war under circumstances wholly unknown to them and not directly affecting their own interests.[10]

The Rebuilding of Europe, said the editors of the crusading periodical *The World Court,* ''seems to us to be the most important contribution to sound thinking about the underlying problems of international reconstruction and reorganization which has been published in this country.'' Other reviews also found it profound and lucid.[11] But, critically examined, it was not an impressive discussion of international organization. Hill's assertion, on the one hand, that a general international organization would constitute a superstate annihilating all national characteristics, and his metaphysical explanation, on the other hand, as to why a more limited organization of great states possessing the same powers would not even imply the creation of a new political entity, were neither convincing nor even comprehensible. By suggesting that smaller states might enter into the compact of the strong powers, he ignored the obstacle of representation he had thrown in the way of a general union of nations. He solved the problem of formulating international law with the expression, ''decisions in the nature of general laws,'' then solved the problem of establishing a court by presuming for international law a degree of precision and refinement that no civil system of legislation had been able to achieve. The problem of enforcing international law he solved by excluding absolutist states that refused to recognize it—the major threats to world peace—from his considerations. In ruling out the use of force by states presumed to have an exemplary devotion to law, he unwittingly questioned the practicability of the whole juridical approach to world organization; for if international law could be made so clear and complete that constitutional governments would unhesitatingly submit their disputes to its application, how could a general compact to enforce that law bind a nation to odious obligations, to preserve an unjust

status quo, or to go to war under wholly unknown circumstances?
Moreover, if states could be expected to act only in their own interests, the analogy to civil society on which his whole scheme of a
law-abiding international society was based fell apart, for it was
the violation of the law rather than the specific act that had to be
reprobated. Although the theme of *The Rebuilding of Europe* was that
the theory of absolute sovereignty belonged to the past, Hill shied
away from effectively challenging it.

Whatever the weaknesses of Hill's scheme, its central proposition
was clear: peace and justice in the world under a rule of law depended solely upon the great powers. This idea, however, he seemed to
want to repudiate in *Present Problems in Foreign Policy*. He would maintain the thesis, he stated in its preface, "that without the rule of law
there is no hope of permanent peace; and that International Law,
being the affair of all nations, requires for its enforcement that all
nations, and not a single group organized in their own interests,
shall freely have a part in the formulation and protection of it."
Even if the League of Nations were to make law and not power the
chief object of its existence, he insisted, it could not long remain
merely as a "League," or group of powers within the general society
of states. The equality before the law of all sovereign states required
the union, not the division, of that society.[12]

Having thus disavowed an organization of great powers, Hill
proceeded to advocate exactly that. The policy of the United States,
he advised, should be to sustain the unwritten charter of union that
constituted the "Entente of Free Nations." Uncovenanted armies
had gathered from every quarter of the globe to assert the determination of the free nations that the rule of arbitrary force shoud be
ended. A new brotherhood of man had come into being, and its
simplicity should not be marred by attempting to force upon the
victorious co-belligerents any untried theory of legal union that
might be honestly rejected or accepted with doubt and reluctance.
The minimum functions that he would assign to the Entente, however, included maintaining a supremacy of force to guard the Peace
of Versailles, the examination and mediation of international disputes, consultation on measures to be taken if any nations went to
war, suppression of persistently turbulent or aggressive states, and

the rewriting of international law, powers that were not less than those assigned to the League of Nations. But they would involve no limitation of national freedom or alienation of sovereignty, Hill explained, for the practice of the Entente would be guided solely by a declaration of principles, with a solemn pledge to respect and defend them, leaving the decision of the action to be taken in every case to the participating nations. Whether or not a super-government existed depended upon the degree of discretion and freedom of action retained by the nations. An Entente of Free Nations would leave the nations entirely free; the League of Nations bound its members to predetermined action. The League did not invite, it commanded.[13]

Irrespective of the validity of this distinction—which he elsewhere negated—Hill was the victim of an age-old dual concept of morality: that which was permissible in the service of the faith was morally reprehensible among infidels. He had no criticism, he wrote, of "an effort to preserve the peace of the world by the consultation and cooperation of the Great Powers, or an organized agreement on their part to pursue, condemn, and punish an outlaw. . . . Such an agreement is imperatively demanded; but it should be dedicated without equivocation or reserve to the service of the law . . . ." In criticism of the League, however, he repeatedly insisted that any limited international organization violated the concept of international law. The conference at Paris, he charged, had not been engaged in "the formation of a universal Society of States, such as that contemplated by International Law, but the creation of a predominant group within this more general association." Advocating the Entente, he declared that a union for the maintenance of law now happily existed. "It consists of the nations that have had the force and the courage to enter the war, in order to bring the law-breakers to justice, and of no others. I say of no others, because a nation is of value in providing a real sanction to the authority of law only when it is ready to defend the law. A neutral nation at best only renders a passive respect to the authority of the Law of Nations. In the cause of equity it is not an asset, it is only a liability." The danger of war would be minimized, he agreed with Lord Parker, if it were made clear that in the future there could be no neutrality. But

speaking of the League, he insisted that since it would be "an exclusive corporation, to which only those it is willing to receive can
be admitted, it is evident that by itself it will not be a body competent to make laws." Even if it consisted of a majority of states it
would still not be competent. "It may through its preponderance of
power be able to command, and even to enforce its will, but law does
not rightly issue from mere power, or rest on power." And the policy of the League, he observed a few pages further on, appeared to
be that neutrality would be abolished. "By what right," he demanded to know, "can this League declare that there are no neutrals?"
That was imperialism.[14]

Hill drew almost passionate contrasts between European imperialism and American principles; their incompatibility was necessary
to most of his arguments against the League. This led him into more
contradictions. To demonstrate that the League of Nations was in
itself a sovereign and imperial power, he held that the territories and
islands conquered from Germany would be placed "completely
under the sovereignty of the League," to be governed by its council
through its appointed agents. But in warning that it was the individual imperial interests of the great powers and not principles that
were to be protected by the League, he said of these same mandates:
"Theoretically, the League of Nations is to issue 'Acts and Charters'
for the administration of those countries; but practically they will be
portioned out to the 'Big Five' in accordance with 'understandings'
already agreed upon." England, he said, "gets the German colonies
under a mandate of the League just as effectively as if they were
taken by direct annexation." Seizing upon General Smuts's compar-
ison of the mandate system with the government of the British
Empire, he spent several pages denouncing the "un-American,"
absolutist rule exercised by England over her empire. In *The Rebuilding of Europe* he had spent twice as many pages demonstrating
that the British Empire was no longer really an empire but actually
a confederation of autonomous, self-governing republics. Again
and again he laid down positively the principles of American policy, explained the true nature of the Monroe Doctrine, and spoke of
"Americanizing" the treaty of peace. Yet he stated in the epilogue
of *Americal World Policies:* "By every test that can be applied to the

foreign relations of the United States at the present time, it is evident that there is in this country no definite and settled policy whatever upon which any foreign nation can depend, except perhaps the
Monroe Doctrine, whatever that may imply."[15] He had been pro-
pounding, this seemed to say, not American principles but his own
principles.

But the most fundamental contradiction was inherent in Hill's
advocacy of an Entente of Free Nations. As members of the League,
the great powers were intent on sequestering the spoils of war and
establishing a preponderance of power in order to keep their subject nations in hand and control the commerce of the world. Their
professions of idealistic purposes were no more to be trusted than
those of the Holy Alliance a hundred years before. Yet as uncovenanted members of an Entente of Free Nations, restrained only by
a pledge, they became the indispensable defenders of justice. "If
the Entente Allies, who have fought together in this war to vindicate
the rights of nations, are not to be trusted, and there is in them no
soul of honor, then the outlook for mankind is, indeed, a hopeless
one."[16]

Like other opponents of the League, Hill fastened his glare stern-
ly on Article X, which stated: "The Members of the League undertake to respect and preserve as against external aggression the territorial integrity and existing political independence of all Members
of the League. In case of any such aggression or in case of any threat
or danger of such aggression the Council shall advise upon the
means by which this obligation shall be fulfilled." At first he did not
attach to it any sinister significance: it was "a mere agreement between sovereign states for their mutual defense." Shortly, however,
he perceived, with an ingenious twist of reasoning, that it was really
an imperial insurance policy, which the United States was being
asked to underwrite: "Article X does not, it is true, require aid to a
sovereign State in suppressing an unsuccessful revolution; but if
any portion of it should attain its independence and the mother
country continued at war with it, 'external aggression' would be
alleged; and the aid of all the High Contracting Parties, economic
and even military, could then be invoked against the new claimant
of independence." Then came the discovery that Article X would

bind the United States to preserve every circumscription of territory written into the peace treaty by the arbitrary decree of three or four powers regardless of the wishes of the populations involved; provisions, he thought it needless to affirm, "in contradiction to every policy and every principle hitherto known as American." Completing his examination of Article X, Hill found it to be the most important cog of an automatic machinery that would deprive the United States of all control over its foreign policy, strip Congress of its constitutional powers, and turn every war into a world war.[17]

But Article X was a chameleon that changed color with Hill's arguments. Calling President Wilson's contention that the League Council could only advise, not command, member states absurd, he interpreted the words "advise upon" to mean not advice to the nations but that the members of the Council would take counsel together. Yet, arguing elsewhere that the League would be a useless instrument to execute the Treaty of Versailles, he construed "advise upon" to mean advising the nations and waiting to see if any were disposed to act. If the League were efficient enough to involve the United States in every foreign war by automatic action, yet incapable of keeping the peace treaty because its members could ignore the Council's advice, Hill confused the issue still further by maintaining that the advice of the Council, and by extension the whole prescribed peace-keeping machinery of the League, was irrelevant to the obligation that would be undertaken. The obligation to preserve against external aggression the territorial integrity and political independence of every member of the League by whatever means necessary would not be created by a decision of the Council but was fixed in the first sentence of Article X itself, he argued in a newspaper debate in the Boston *Herald* in September 1920. The guarantee made by each signatory was absolute and could not be set aside by a decision of the Council, or by refusal of Congress to act, without abrogating the treaty. If the means advised upon by the Council were inadequate, and war was necessary to fulfill the obligation, Congress would be bound by contract to support war. And regardless of the disposition of Congress, if the Covenant became the "supreme law of the land" as part of the treaty, the Executive would be bound to execute it.[18]

Hill had again argued himself into contradictions. Article X was now onerous, not because it would take the decision to make war out of the hands of Congress and place it in the hands of a council in which the representative of the United States would be appointed by the President, nor because it would commit the United States to prescribed actions that would lead to war, but because it would pledge the United States to proceed independently, if need be to the ratio ultima of war against the advice of the League Council, to fulfill an independent obligation. But according to this interpretation, Article X was no different from an agreement by an Entente that "certain principles are to be sacredly respected and defended, leaving the decision of the manner of action to the participants, in view of the circumstances that may arise."[19] The obligation assumed by the United States in each case would be just as absolute and war might be just as necessary to fulfill it.

Looking for trouble in every line of the peace treaty, hypercritical of Wilson and the "potterers at Paris," too ingenious in his arguments, and often appearing not very well informed, Hill fell into inconsistencies and contradictions *ad nauseam*. Less obvious perhaps in his serial publications, it was readily apparent when they were collected into volumes. "Harveyized propaganda prepared for immediate consumption does not appear at its best in stiff covers," remarked historian Frederick J. Teggart. "Dr. Hill's sentences, treating of problems for which some of us feel that we ought almost to seek a solution on our knees," commented Lord Eustace Percy, a member of the British delegation to the peace conference, "seem often to wash about between his chapter headings like water in a half-empty bucket."[20]

Despite his excesses, Hill did present a serious criticism of the work of the peace conference from the legalistic point of view. Still, there was an enormous discrepancy between his brushing aside as inconsequential and uncertain the provisions for arbitration in Articles XII and XIII of the League Covenant and the directive of Article XIV for the establishment of a Permanent Court of International Justice and his contentment with the far smaller gains of the Hague Conferences. At the same time that he cried "back to The Hague," he demanded of the League the millennium or nothing at all. Moreover, if the people at Paris had believed that history was against exclusive reliance on the world court idea, he had conceded as much himself only a few years before. While a world court could settle justiciable disputes, he had written in at least two articles, such cases were not the chief causes of international conflict. These were to be found in national policies, which no court could ever settle. And as for American policies, certainly no one was more determined than he to keep them from *any* form of international scrutiny. The United States had attached to each of the Hague Conventions a statement exempting the Monroe Doctrine from international jurisdiction, and Hill would qualify American participation even in his proposed Entente in precisely the same way.[21]

Hill's antipathy toward the League appeared beyond the power of any amount of remodeling to abate. Yet he was ready to accept it when Elihu Root proposed three reservations, which would reject Article X, insure the right of withdrawal, and exclude from League control questions the United States deemed to be purely American. Later he was willing to go along with the lengthier list of Lodge reservations. Neither proposal would come close to removing all the constitutional and other objections he had raised, but he rationalized that with these reservations the Covenant of the League would approximate the character of a written Entente.[22]

Hill probably contributed more words to the League debate than any other publicist, and private anti-Leaguers and the Republican party organization gave them wide dissemination.

In April 1919, Hill delivered two lectures, "The Corporate Character of the League of Nations" and "The Treaty-Making Power under the Constitution of the United States," at George Washington University. William Collier, former Assistant Attorney-General and minister to Spain and now president of the university, sent copies to every senator and congressman and at the request of the secretary of the Republican National Committee provided copies for the national committeemen and the chairmen of state committees. Collier also furnished two thousand copies to the League for the Preservation of American Independence, of which Hill was a director, printing them as university bulletins but sending them without covers lest he be accused of making the institution an agency for propaganda.[23]

The League for the Preservation of American Independence also distributed ten thousand copies each of three articles, "The President's Challenge to the Senate," "In the Valley of Decision," and "Americanizing the Treaty," which were published in the *North American Review* in June, July, and August 1919. When "Americanizing the Treaty" appeared in the *Review*, someone thinking it especially effective sent a copy to every member of the Senate. Later, when Hill explained "The Senate's Service to the Nation" in the January 1920, *Review*, Senator Henry W. Keyes of New Hampshire asked the editors to send him a half-dozen copies.[24]

"I think your articles constitute not only the most notable, but the most informing and comprehensive review of the foreign policy of this Administration. In writing them you have rendered a great service to your country," Charles Evans Hughes wrote to Hill in June 1920. A few days later Colonel Harvey asked if Hill could let the *Review* have an article each month of the campaign, giving scope to his views at will. He would see that they had wide dissemination through the channels of the Republican National Committee, Harvey promised.[25]

Early the next month Truxton Beale, a millionaire admirer of Herbert Spencer and David Jayne Hill, instructed the publishers of *American World Policies*, which was just off the press, to send the Republican National Committee five hundred copies. He also directed them to send the committee ten thousand copies each of two chapters—retitled "The League Un-American" and "Covenant or Constitution"—made up as pamphlets. Beale and Hill personally also sent large numbers of these pamphlets to various Republican state committees.[26].

In mid-July the New York State Republican Executive Committee, after a stormy session, named Hill temporary chairman of the state convention opening at Saratoga Springs on the twenty-seventh. Suggested by George Aldridge, his selection was pushed through by the Old Guard over the opposition of younger elements in the party, who wanted someone of less standpat persuasion. "In picking David Jayne Hill we have chosen a big man of the calibre of Elihu Root," the chairman of the executive committee explained. "He is capable of writing a message that will become a campaign document."[27]

With this end in view the state committee chairman instructed Hill to concentrate on national issues in his keynote address. Unlikely to have done differently anyhow, Hill delivered a partisan broadside against the League. Though toned to the occasion, its arguments were already old and it was not in any case the kind of address to excite a convention to cheers. By the time he had finished, according to the pro-League *New York Times,* few people except delegates remained in the hall and two-thirds of the seats on the platform were empty. But as campaign literature it was the stuff the Republican high command wanted and the National Committee distributed it in huge quantitites. "I have had a large experience in League speeches," Henry Cabot Lodge wrote to Hill, "and I do not think I have ever seen our case stated so conclusively with equal conciseness. I have put it aside and shall unblushingly rob it of some of the references, which were so extraordinarily well chosen." Since he was about to convey something from the speech into his own, Lodge wrote to Juliet a few days later, the least he could do was thank Hill for it and for his great service to constitutional government and the protection of the country against the League. "His writings have been of the very highest value to us. . . ."[28]

The National Committee printed several more of Hill's *North American Review* articles, a small leaflet, *Selling Out America,* which committee chairman Will Hays had asked him to write as simply as possible for wide distribution among people who did not read very carefully explaining just why Mr. Wilson's League was bad, and, on the same shallow level and most in demand of all, *The Peace Family and the League of Nations.* Hill had originally published *The Peace Family* in the *Boston Evening Transcipt,* and Truxton Beale had brought it to the committee suggesting that it put it on the Keith vaudeville circuit. Apparently this would have been done had there been time enough to justify the expense. Cast in the form of a dialogue between Mr. and Mrs. Peace and a professor of history whom they consulted about the League, it was aimed at America's new voters on the distaff side. Mr. Peace was naively enthusiastic about the League Covenant just as Wilson had brought it back from Paris, but Mrs. Peace was skeptical; and it was she who saw from their conversation with the professor that the League was really a military alliance to protect the spoils of war by new wars and what the world needed was to get back to the idea of the Hague Conventions. "John and I are going to vote against this Article X," she finally announced. "It is a death-trap."[29]

"We have put nothing out on which there have been more calls than the several things worked out by you," wrote Ralph V. Sollett, head of the National Committee's distribution department. "Especially has this been true of the Peace family." The committee sent out three hundred thousand copies. As intended, it appealed especially to women. The women's division of the Republican state committee of Massachusetts had its own reprints made directly from the *Transcript* article. "It is simply splendid," gushed Mrs. Warren G. Harding, "perfectly capital!"[30]

Following the election Hill received many letters of congratulation. Among the most unstinting in praise were those from Cambridge intellectuals and United States senators. "More than anyone else," wrote novelist Basil King of the Republican victory, "you have helped to secure it, when it comes to the higher, more intellectual, and more statesmanlike lines of effort." Biographer William Roscoe Thayer also thought Hill among the foremost of those who brought victory about: "Your articles in the *North American Review*, for the past year, have been the most powerful I have seen to expose the dangers of Wilson's schemes." Senator Charles S. Thomas of Colorado thought "The Betrayal of the Monroe Doctrine," the lead article in the November issue of the *Review*, was Hill's masterpiece: "It is absolutely unanswerable." "Indeed," wrote Senator Wadsworth of New York, "a good deal was done in your writings and speeches to clarify the public thought." President-elect Harding was also laudatory: "It was a great victory, and your part in it was an important one, as your words upon the League of Nations were wise and weighty."[31] Many of Hill's correspondents wondered what post he would receive in the new administration.

Hill wanted to be Secretary of State. Privy to this ambition a full year before, William Collier had suggested that he use his availability for the Senate to insure that Senator Wadsworth, who was up for reelection, and William Barnes would use all their influence to get him the appointment. Because Wadsworth had the state organization so solidly behind him that his opponents could find no one willing to challenge him in the primaries, which Hill had already twice refused personally to enter, the idea was quite impracticable. When a delegation of political dissidents from New York came to Washington to urge the former ambassador to run, he declined with the comment that no self-respecting man could enter such a contest. Hill and Collier had also discussed Hill's availability for the presidency. Since sentiment did not seem to be crystallizing in favor of any particular Republican candidate there was a chance, they figured, that if he were sent to the Chicago convention as one of New York's "Big Four" and made chairman of a committee or given the opportunity to speak, he might so impress the delegates that they would swing to him as they had to Garfield in 1880. Collier proposed this strategy to George Aldridge and Lafayette B. Gleason, secretary of the New York State Republican Committee, adding that Hill's presence at Chicago would probably at least help make him Secretary of State. Although Aldridge said he would see what he could do, the plan died there.[32]

A month before the election, Harding had invited Hill to his home at Marion, Ohio, and afterwards invited him back with the host of political figures who came to pay their respects, give advice, or seek positions in the new administration. In press speculation over whom the Ohioan would appoint Secretary of State, Hill was generally given an edge over Elihu Root, Philander C. Knox, and Charles Evans Hughes, despite increasingly frequent mention of the last. "Within the past week," wrote Frederick W. Wile in the *Washington Herald* on January 8, 1921, "there has been a decided slump in the stock of Charles Evans Hughes. David Jayne Hill now looms." "Quite seriously," Wile wrote to Hill the same day, "I have heard more David Jayne Hill talk in Washington this week than for some time past."[33]

Although for the next month newspapers rumors ceased to show any discernible trend toward one name, it was reported that Republican senators, especially the Irreconcilables, favored Hill. He agreed with their ideas on foreign policy, and while he was a fine, respectable figure with sufficient experience to make his appointment justifiable, he had no political following to make him cocky. He would be, as columnist Mark Sullivan quoted the senators apocryphally, "a man who will take orders." Nicholas Murray Butler, to whom Harding first offered the secretaryship, later recorded in his memoirs that Hill had the urgent and organized support of an influential group of senators, and he was seriously considered before the post was offered to Hughes.[34]

Speculation ended when Harding announced on February 11 that Hughes was to confer with him at his vacation retreat at St. Augustine, Florida. Newsmen now thought that Hill might be named Under Secretary; and John Barrett reported to Hill from St. Augustine that Harding was enthusiastic about this possibility when members of his party suggested that the Ambassador might accept the lesser post. But soon rumors centered on Hill's appointment to a foreign post, probably Berlin, perhaps Tokyo. Preferring Europe and particularly France, Hill made this known to Hughes through William Willcox and secured promises from New York's Senators Wadsworth and Calder to speak to the President about it.[35]

On May 3 Hill was lunching at the Metropolitan Club in Washington when Hughes approached his table and drew him aside to inform him that he had cabled his name to Tokyo for the assent of the Japanese government. Hill's surprise in turn astonished the Secretary. Harding had directed him to cable for the agrément, Hughes explained, and he had supposed that the President had already spoken to him. Hill seems to have had little enthusiasm for the Japanese mission, but he felt compelled in any case to decline it. His son David had recently fallen seriously ill while sojourning in France, and Hill had booked passage to sail there on the twenty-first. Present relations between the United States and Japan made the mission to Tokyo the most important one the President had to offer, Hughes urged, and both he and the President wanted a man of experience and one in whom the Japanese government could have confidence. Finally the Secretary persuaded Hill to consider the matter further and consult his wife.

The next day Hill informed Hughes that he and Juliet had decided that it was imperative that they follow their plans. He could not immediately accept the Japanese post, and would not be available before September. This he regretted, he explained, for an opportunity seemed to him to exist for replacing the Anglo-Japanese Alliance with a tri-power entente, making it possible through reciprocal security, but without involving any military or political alliance, to maintain permanent peace in the Pacific. But since the President no doubt wished to send his appointments to the Senate very soon, he could not suggest delay. Hughes, still unwilling to accept a negative answer, asked Hill to see him again before sailing, after he had had another talk with the President. A week later, however, the *New York Times* reported that Hill had turned down the appointment.[36]

11

The Washington Conference
and the World Court

ARRIVING IN EUROPE LATE IN MAY 1921, DAVID AND JULIET spent several weeks in Paris arranging for the care of David, Jr. Not knowing how long it would be before they could bring him home, and wanting to be not more than a short journey away, Hill spent the summer on the Continent, looking and listening and recording his observations of the tense and unstable postwar situation in Europe. Every week or two he sent lengthy reports to Secretary Hughes, who had asked to be kept posted on what he learned abroad.

In the political and academic circles of Paris, Hill found a deep fear of future German hostility and a determination to strengthen France and weaken Germany as the only hope of French security. He spent three days touring the devastated regions of France and several more days at Coblenz, Germany, with the army of occupation. There he was again impressed by the French conviction that a future war with Germany was inevitable unless France made good use of its present superiority of power to keep Germany helpless. He spent a week in Berlin, where he talked with many prominent Germans, including Chancellor Wirth and Walther Rathenau, the Minister of Reconstruction. Struck by the apparent determination of the Wirth government to meet Germany's reparation obligations, he prepared a special report to Hughes on how it planned to do it. It was an effort that must not fail, he warned. Both the monarchist right and the communist-socialist left expected it to fail and stood ready to seize power, but because neither group was capable of forming a government, the result would be anarchy that would have to be crushed by force. He was also struck by the virulence of German resentment over France's determination to chain Germany's military and economic power, and how French policy thus nourished the hostility that France feared. From Berlin Hill went to Geneva, the "observatory of Europe," where he remained until autumn, writing lengthy missives to Secretary Hughes that contained considerably more advice than hard information.

The United States could best help the war-torn and mutually suspicious nations of Europe through a steadying and restraining moral influence rather than by any economic schemes, Hill counseled Hughes. Europe must save herself or she could not be saved, and she must learn a lesson from her present distress. The United States would do well also, Hill advised, to avoid complicity in the new Permanent Court of International Justice. Since it was the private tribunal of the League of Nations it offered no hope for the judicial organization of peace. The United States should insist on an association of nations based on the idea of voluntary submission to judicial decisions in justiciable matters. Until this was realized every nation would try to be as strong as ·it could for its own defense and all hope of disarmament and peace was illusory.

The principal topic of international interest in Europe at the moment was the disarmament conference to be held in Washington at the end of the year, and on this too Hill had much advice to give. European disarmament was for the present out of the question unless the United States was ready to guarantee the security of Europe, especially France, he told the Secretary. But if European disarmament were discussed and not accomplished, Europe would regard the whole conference, whatever its other results, a failure. The conference should confine itself solely to assuring peace in the Pacific Ocean through the creation of an "Entente of the Pacific."

This "Peace of the Pacific," he suggested, should be based on the principles that all responsible sovereign states bordering on the Pacific reciprocally recognize each others political equality and territorial sovereignty, that an act of aggression against the sovereign rights of any of them be regarded as of interest to all, and that each should have the right at any time to bring any case of aggression to the attention of a council in which all were equally represented.

Should the conference score a great success for the United States by assuring peace in the Pacific, Hill prognosticated, the way would be prepared for the United States to take the initiative in forming a more general international association than the League of Nations. The United States was presently regarded in Europe as delinquent and self-centered because of its abandonment of the League. But with renewed confidence in the ability of America to lead, and recognizing the impotence of the League, Europe would be ready to follow the United States in a still broader movement for peace.[1]

Thus through the magic of agreements that pledged nothing would Hill establish peace in the Pacific, deal a death blow to the League, and place world leadership where it rightly belonged.

Early in November Hill returned to the United States to cover the Washington Conference for a news syndicate formed by the New York *Tribune*. In several preliminary articles despatched earlier from Europe he maintained, as he had to Hughes privately, that the most urgent problem facing the gathering was not mainly one of armaments but the peace of the Pacific Ocean, which could be achieved by replacing the imperialistic Anglo-Japanese Alliance with an "honorable entente." But an entente alone was not enough, he soon admonished. It was a lesson of history that international friendships did not rest on mere sentiment; there must be disarmament as well. The League of Nations could never limit armaments through its methods of force, and they could not presently be limited on land in Europe, but at the Washington Conference a few maritime powers attending to their own interests could limit naval armaments. "The nations bordering on the Pacific Ocean," he argued, are so far advanced in civilization, their interest in peaceful industry and trade is so much greater than any advantage they could derive from war, that here at last the experiment of limit-ing armaments might well be made."[2]

When the conference opened on November 12, Hill hailed Secre-tary Hughes's unprecedented proposal for the actual scrapping of capital ships as "a splendid gesture." By itself it would leave the international situation essentially unchanged, but he was sure the Secretary did not intend to let the conference adjourn without settling related Far Eastern questions. But after a few days with no new developments, Hill's tone became scolding. The United States was assigning to an imperial alliance, if the Anglo-Japanese Treaty were to endure, twice the naval strength it would itself be allowed to possess. It was renouncing its leadership and turning it over to maritime powers that might at any time shut off American trade with the whole continent of Asia. The American people should de-mand that the imperial policy existing in the Pacific be changed under threat of a United States counter policy. "There should be no political compact regarding the Pacific in which the United States . . . cannot have an equal place; and upon this policy our government should straight-way insist." The conference was now in its fourth week, Hill wrote on December 8, and neither Britain nor Japan appeared inclined to come to an understanding with the United States. "Let it not be thought that American idealism is inexhaustible," he warned. "There are things that America can do, if the necessity is thrust upon her, alone and in her own strength."[3]

Two days later came the announcement of the conclusion be-tween the United States, Great Britain, Japan, and France of a Four Power Treaty. The fruition of labors to modify the Anglo-Japanese Alliance begun by Secretary Hughes long before the con-ference assembled,[4] it obliged the powers to respect each other's rights in their insular possessions and dominions in the region of the Pacific Ocean, to consult with one another in joint conference when controversies over Pacific questions arising between any of them were not settled by diplomacy, and to communicate with each other on measures to be taken in case of an aggressive threat by an outside power. Upon ratification of the treaty the Anglo-Japanese Alliance would terminate.

Hill very much approved. The pact was in harmony with his

principles for an Entente of the Pacific and embodied his ideal of treaties for peace. It involved no obligation to make war but aimed through common counsel to avert it. "If war is necessary to defend the rights of the contractants," he explained, "each is left at perfect liberty, under its own constitutional limitations, to engage or not engage in armed conflict. The provisions of the new agreement are wholly for peace and in no sense for war."[5]

Some newsmen and politicians were not so sure. Were not the contracting parties under at least a moral obligation to use armed force if it became necessary to fulfil the purpose of the treaty? And if so, was not the treaty an alliance? Hill had no patience with such doubters, who gave a wrong idea of the new agreement. There was no obligation in it, expressed or implied, he assured his readers, that went beyond a promise to try to arrive at an understanding in case the rights of any party were threatened. Whatever moral obligation to go to war there might be would rest not upon the treaty but upon the particular situation and would be just as imperative if no treaty existed. The signatories were pledged only to respect each other's rights in the Pacific, not to any definite action in defense of them.[6]

Hill also had little patience with another attitude assumed by statesmen and newsmen in the course of the conference. When Secretary Hughes proposed to limit French strength in capital ships to 175,000 tons and submarines to 31,500 tons, the French delegation objected and demanded the right to twice that tonnage. Charged with threatening to disrupt the conference, France became the object of an almost universal chorus of obloquy. Supporting the French position, Hill argued that every nation had the right to judge for itself its requirements for defense, and that every justification for Britain's claim to 500,000 tons of capital ships and 90,000 tons of submarines—the extent of its coasts and the far-flung position of its colonies and sea lanes—applied equally well to France. It was nonsensical to maintain that France required only half as powerful a navy as Japan, which had only a limited area to guard with no powerful enemy near, and this in a region to be protected from attack by the pledges of the other naval powers.[7]

The argument was perfectly sound—and Hill could as easily have compared French naval needs with those of the United States, which Jules Jusserand, the French ambassador, did in a letter to him. But it applied the very standard of determining relative naval strength that Secretary Hughes had concluded would lead straight to failure, for the nations would never come to agreement on national defense *needs*. The only hope of ending naval competition was to induce the powers to stop their building programs where they were, and Hughes had felt that no power could seriously object to a quota that preserved its relative strength as it then existed. Yet as Jusserand wrote to Hill, during the war when France was necessarily devoting all her resources to land armaments, and after the war when she was voluntarily scrapping five battleships in various stages of completion, the other powers were rapidly increasing their naval strength. Hill agreed with Jusserand's implication. France would not have fallen under disapprobation if she had not already practiced what the other powers were not holding up as the virtue of nonconstruction, he wrote in a subsequent article. "From pre-eminence in what they now denounce as a vice of national ambition and warlike menace the great powers claim and receive their reward in a large allotment of ships, while the virtue of previous abstention is construed as a reason for permanent declassment, and the claim of theoretical equality is reproved as if it were an example of obstinacy and insolence."[8]

Since Hill almost alone in the American press defended France, the French and friends of France were deeply appreciative. "Your article is so admirable and so timely," wrote Ambassador Jusserand the day after Hill's first column on the subject, "that I have cabled a summary of it to my Government; it will cheer them at a moment when nothing very cheering has come to them from this country for a while." Maurice Leon, a Wall Street attorney, wrote that if the United States came through the conference with any honor left it would be due more to Hill than to anyone else. "More than ever," he added, "I lament the fact that you are not our Secretary of State but rejoice that we have the benefit of your leadership in a private capacity." Walter Berry, president of the American Chamber of Commerce in France, was at loss to understand why the Harding administration had not availed itself of the services of one of the most level-headed, clear-sighted statesmen he knew.[9]

Late in the spring of 1922 Hill and Juliet again went to Europe, staying until the end of October. A few months after returning to Washington Juliet was struck by a delivery truck as she stepped from the curb in front of her home at 1745 Rhode Island Avenue. She died the next day, January 16, 1923. Until his own death nine years later, Hill continued to live in his Washington home, his inevitable loneliness lessened by the devotion of his daughter. Now married to Dr. John A. Tillema, a professor at George Washington University, Catherine lived in an apartment nearby and came in to read to her father evenings when he was home. In 1930 Hill spent the summer in Europe with his son Walter. Other summers were spent more quietly with Catherine and her family at Camden, Maine.[10]

Membership in numerous academic, patriotic, defense, peace, law, international friendship, and other societies occupied some of Hill's time. For several years he was retained by an American syndicate claiming certain property rights in former territories of the Austro-Hungarian Empire to intercede with the State Department in its behalf. He also represented a coal company for whom he contacted diplomatic representatives of foreign governments in Washington about exports and bunkering ships.[11] The most significant activity of his septuagenarian years, however, was standing against any American involvement with the League of Nations by joining the newly established Permanent Court of International Justice.

Acting under Article XIV of the Covenant, the League Council immediately after its organization had appointed an Advisory Committee of Jurists, of which Elihu Root was a member, to provide plans for a permenent court. The resulting Court Statute, after being revised to make a provision for compulsory jurisdiction in certain classes of disputes optional with each adhering state, was approved by the Assembly in December 1920. It was then brought into force by the individual ratification of an attached Protocol of Signature by a majority of League members. Specifically to permit the United States to join the Court without joining the League, the Assembly had provided that the Protocol was also open to the signature of "States mentioned in the Annex to the Covenant," a list of the original signatories of the Versailles Treaty, all of whom had become members of the League except the United States, Ecuador, and Hedjaz.[12]

By 1923 forty-six of the League's fifty-two members had signed the Protocol. At the urging of Secretary Hughes, President Harding asked the Senate in February that year to consent to American participation in the Court with four reservations prepared by Hughes. They provided that the United States assumed no legal relation to or obligations of the League, that it should participate equally in the election of the Court's judges, that it should pay fair share of the Court's expenses, and that the Statute of the Court should not be amended without its consent.[13]

On February 26 Senator William King of Utah submitted a resolution for adherence to the Court under these terms. Instead of the usual procedure of having it referred to the Committee on Foreign Relations for report, he asked to have it read and put on the table until the next day. He delayed calling for its consideration, however, until March 3, the day before the close of the congressional session. His motion was defeated forty-nine to twenty-four, with some senators voting nay, however, only because the question could not possibly be disposed of in the few remaining and crowded hours of the short session.[14] The Court proposal was thus deferred until Congress met in December.

In the August, October, and November numbers of the *Saturday Evening Post,* Hill took issue with the President's recommendation. His fundamental complaint was that the World Court was the "league's private court." It had been brought into existence by the League, its judges were chosen and paid by the League, and it would have to defend and support the Covenant of the League, which was its fundamental law, above all other international law. Yet it was the new construction of world relations in the Covenant, which American acceptance of the Court would solidify and perpetuate, he warned, that was the chief danger to the interests of the United States.

The most important recommendations of the Committee of Jurists, Hill further complained, had not been followed. Its proposal that in strictly legal cases an aggrieved member could take its complaint to the Court and cite the aggressor to appear there without delay had been set aside, so the Court offered no sure redress against the illegal conduct of a state that preferred to decide a dispute for itself by superior force. The League had also rejected the Committee's proposal for a new Hague conference to clarify and extend international law, Hill charged. An international court required principles of law that had been clearly defined and previously accepted, but the League obviously intended the Court to develop international law by its own decrees or be guided by the quasi-legislation of the Council and Assembly, which, being exclusive political bodies of a military alliance, were not competent to make international law.

To enforce upon a nation a law that it had not accepted—especially one decreed by an arbitrary body composed almost exclusively of foreigners representing various forms of jurisprudence—would inevitably require armed force, but nations that would not willingly obey a law would not enforce it unless their own interests were involved, Hill continued with a familiar argument, mindless of the voluntary nature of the Court that he had just decried. The only hope for peace in the world lay in the growth of a juristic sense and a disposition to be governed by law; and while awaiting this consummation a wise nation would do well to look to its own defense.

The Court was the official legal adviser of the League, Hill also noted, hitting the point that was to become most important in the Court debate. As a member of the Court the United States would be legally and honorably bound by a mere advisory opinion to assist the League in acts that might be both unjust and disadvantageous. Many American states were members of the League, and the League's right to intervene in the western hemisphere with regard to them would have to be sustained by the Court, he specifically warned. The United States could find itself forced to abandon the Monroe Doctrine.

The indispensable first step to American membership in the Court, Hill pronounced, was that it be detached from the League and made a true world court in which all recognized sovereign states would share in the selection of judges and be judged under a common law. Compulsory jurisdiction might perhaps be suspended until rules of law were more clearly defined by new Hague conferences, but with the understanding that all strictly justiciable questions were to be adjudicated. "The world would thus have as much peace as it is prepared for and as the great powers would permit."[15]

Irreconcilable senators on the strategic Foreign Relations Committee—who would be quick to reject the compulsory jurisdiction of any court—thought Hill's criticisms splendid. William E. Borah of Idaho, Medill McCormick of Illinois, John K. Shields of Tennessee, and Chairman Henry Cabot Lodge of Massachusetts extended their congratulations for having presented the most important and searching analysis of the League's Court they had ever seen. Lodge and Borah thought it unanswerable. He had procured extra copies, Lodge wrote, and had them ready for use. "By 'use' I mean robbery!" he explained.[16]

In his annual message to Congress on December 6, President Coolidge, who had come into office upon Harding's death in August, reminded the Senate that it had the Court proposal before it. Although the League issue was closed, it had long been American policy to seek the establishment of a permanent world court of justice, he observed, and the Senate should discuss the question without partisanship or prejudice. "As I wish to see a court established, and as the proposal presents the only practical plan on which many nations have ever agreed, though it may not meet every desire, I therefore commend it to the favorable consideration of the Senate, with the proposed reservations clearly indicating our refusal to adhere to the League of Nations."[17]

What the President meant, Hill explained in the *Boston Transcript* the next day, was that out of courtesy to his predecessor and to the nations adhering to the Court he was commending the proposal for the Senate's favorable consideration, but after the Senate had discussed it with entire candor it should propose that the League's Court be expanded into a real world court. Sending a copy to Lodge, Hill explained the merits of this course of action: "If the League should say 'No' to a proposal coming from the United States to create a real World Court, it would give the League the *coup de grace* in American opinion and clear the air completely. If it did not refuse, the procedure would record an American victory."[18]

James T. Williams, Jr., the *Transcript's* bitter-end editor, was so pleased with Hill's fanciful interpretation of what Coolidge had said that he asked the Ambassador to continue the discussion in several more editorials. "What I wish to do is to wring the neck of Europe's rag doll, (to quote Senator Moses) but to do it in a genteel and polite way." Senator Lodge was equally approving. His committee would "not support a League Court in any form, but we ought to give it full consideration, just as you suggest," he wrote. It was absolutely necessary, Lodge thought, that the committee offer a true world court as a substitute for the League's court. If the League rejected it, that was their affair. He was glad Hill was going to write more articles for the *Transcript*, Lodge wrote a week later. "You have already made the best analysis of the Court that I have seen," he added, referring to the *Saturday Evening Post* articles, "and I find that many Senators are reading it. I must have it put in document form so that it can be sent out." Inserting the articles in the *Congressional Record*, Lodge had Senator Moses of New Hampshire order them printed as a senate document so they could be distributed under congressional frank.[19]

"I ought to say frankly that I favor a real world court," Hill replied to Williams. "I believe that strategically as a matter of good policy the Senate can best evade the League's Court by proposing a real World Court, and put the League to shame if it does not accept it." The *Transcript* editorials, therefore, justified America's right to offer a new court, which the rest of the world could take or leave. The League, Hill argued, was usurping the right to maintain an exclusive international judicature, and if the United States had not been listed in the Annex to the Covenant as one of the League's "original members" the Court would not be open to it. "Clearly, the United States can have no position of dignity in this court. . . . No foreign agency is empowered, or can be permitted, to determine which recognized sovereign states shall be associated in a World Court, and above all to fix the terms on which the United States shall be admitted as a member of such a court." It was impossible anyway, Hill contended, to accept the proposition that a world court could be organized and the United States not have anything to say regarding its creation. The Senate must have the privilege of passing on and amending each step taken in the formation of the Court, which was really the right to propose a real world court in line with traditional American policy.[20]

The point that the United States could come into the Court only under the Annex was "most ingenious," congratulated Senator Lodge. He had not seen it suggested anywhere and had not thought of it himself. It was a "very effective and important" argument. When the editorials were completed, the Senator wrote several times, he was going to put them in the *Congressional Record* and order pamphlets for distribution. On February 18, 1924, however, Lodge wrote that he was holding them back. "We have been so submerged in oil," he explained, referring to the sensational Teapot Dome investigations, that he was afraid they would not be noticed as he wanted them to be. "They will count a great deal more when we get around to that court, if we ever do."[21]

Lodge's committee had now been sitting on the Court question for more than two months. On December 10 Senator King had resubmitted his proposal to join the Court with the Hughes reservations and Senator Irvine Lenroot of Wisconsin had proposed joining under a plan that would separate the Court from the League by a new scheme of electing its judges. Both resolutions had been referred to the Foreign Relations Committee, whose failure to "get around" to them had prompted Lodge on this occasion to write to Hill; he wanted advice on how to answer insistent letters from a prominent advocate of the Court.[22]

Pressed by strong pro-Court sentiment in the country, Lodge finally appointed a subcommittee chaired by George Wharton Pepper of Pennsylvania, which began public hearings on April 30, 1924. Pepper asked Hill if he would come and speak against the Court. The condition of his health would probably prevent his appearance, Hill replied. "I do not greatly believe in the direct action of theorists and persons representing particular interests upon the organs of government," he added. Because responsible representative government should not yield to the pressure of private groups, he had "never felt called upon to offer any advice to the established authorities of government." If the committee was seeking information and not merely balancing preferences, he would be glad to furnish any information he could, but he was "indisposed to join the ranks of those who desire to bring pressure upon the constituted authorities by the weight of their wills." This surprising declaration over, Hill offered the Senator several pages of advice on the kind of court the American people really wanted. "It would be a great achievement," he also commented, "if the present Administration could have the courage to lay down a really American program in which it would participate and let the world pursue its own course until it is accepted."[23]

Anti-Leaguers on the Foreign Relations Committee succeeded in postponing consideration of any program at all. On May 5 Claude Swanson of Virginia, a pro-Court Democrat on the committee, submitted another resolution to join the Court with the Hughes reservations. Lodge countered a few days later by proposing a third Hague conference to "transform the present league court into a world court of justice as a part of the Hague peace organization." Williams of the *Boston Transcript* wired Hill for an editorial on Lodge's plan, which Hill declined to write. "The plan is good," he told Williams, "but it cannot be put through and is not expected to be." With the latter part of this statement editorial opinion in the nation overwhelmingly concurred, finding that Lodge's only purpose was to muddle the court proposal and defeat it. On May 22 Senator King, commenting that Lodge's purpose was to torpedo any rational scheme, proposed changing the Hughes reservations to amendments of the Court Statute. Lodge then withdrew his plan in favor of one submitted by Pepper, which would sever the Court from the League with less trouble than his own scheme by rewriting the Court Statute and Protocol. On May 24 the Foreign Relations Committee rejected Swanson's resolution ten to eight and voted out Pepper's ten to six. The sole effect of its action, Swanson commented, was to defeat any hope of approval of the Hughes plan that session.[24]

In their 1924 campaign platforms both major parties endorsed the Court. Following the November elections the Republican party was thus at least morally committed to American membership. With only one or two exceptions, however, the Senate opponents of the Court were Republicans, and Coolidge was anxious to find a course that would satisfy them. Having read Hill's articles in the *Saturday Evening Post,* he sent George Harvey, now America's ambassador to England, on November 21 to talk with the author of them. Later in the day Coolidge invited Hill to dine that evening at the White House to continue the discussion personally. The President, Hill recorded upon returning home, seemed much impressed with his advice to propose a real world court, independent of the League, in which the United States could participate and would have a part in establishing.[25]

But Coolidge took other counsel. In his annual message to Congress two weeks later he again urged adherence to the Court on Hughes's terms, this time with a fifth reservation providing that the United States would not be bound by advisory opinions on questions it had not voluntarily submitted to the Court. Senators on the Foreign Relations Committee had raised the fear that the Court might hand down an opinion relating to American immigration laws or some other matter considered none of the League's business, and before the committee had voted down Swanson's resolution the previous May, Swanson had added the reservation that the President now endorsed.[26]

The Foreign Relations Committee, chaired by William E. Borah after Lodge's death in November, still took no action. When the Pepper resolution it had already reported out came up on the Senate calendar late in the evening on February 27, 1925, Senator King objected to its consideration and proposed that his earlier resolution in line with the President's recommendation be substituted. To this Borah objected. And before most senators even realized that the Court question had been broached, it had been passed by.[27]

But by this time scores of business, professional, labor, veterans, fraternal, women's, and religious organizations, and four-fifths of the nation's press were clamoring for membership in the Court. On March 3 the House of Representatives voted for adherence 303 to 28. The next day in his inaugural address Coolidge spoke out bluntly against the use of sophistries and subterfuges to argue away the duty of the United States. On March 13 the Senate, held over in special session to pass necessary revenue measures, voted to take up on December 17, soon after the next session began, a new resolution offered by Swanson for adherence to the Court with the fifth reservation relating to advisory opinions.[28]

When Congress met in December, President Coolidge emphasized the Court question in his annual message. Answering the major objections raised against the Court, Coolidge said he did not see how safeguards could better have been provided for maintaining its independence from the League than through the procedures by which its judges were nominated, elected, and paid, nor did he see how the Court's advisory function impaired its independence. He warned against demanding a court "which we have set up alone or which reflects only our ideals . . . or under which we assume absolutely no obligations."[29]

In two issues of the *Saturday Evening Post* in January 1926, Hill gave the Senate and the American people different advice. Sending copies of the articles to Coolidge and Borah, he suggested to the latter that they be called to the attention of every senator before the resolution was brought to a vote. Senator Gerald P. Nye of North Dakota immediately inserted them in the *Congressional Record*.[30]

The imperfections of the Court—its lack of compulsory jurisdiction and an adequate law—might be overcome through future development, Hill now conceded. The Statute of the Court had never been an object of criticism in the United States, and there probably could be no other court, he further admitted. What was objectionable was that the Court had been created by the League and the United States could come into it only under the Annex to the Covenant. Why the Assembly had opened the Protocol of Signature to states listed in the Annex, thus permitting the United States to enter this "closed and impenetrable organization," was a question that begged an answer, and Hill now supplied it with an ingenious syllogism: A "protocol" was by definition an implementary document to a treaty. The Protocol of Signature was a supplementary document necessary to the execution of the Treaty of Versailles. Therefore as signatories to the Treaty of Versailles, the United States, Ecuador, and Hedjaz could not be ignored. That under the terms of Article XIV of the Covenant the Assembly could have adopted the Court Statute by its own action; that when it decided instead to use a separate instrument it attached no significance to its title; and that the object of opening the Protocol to the signature of states listed in the Annex, as expressly explained to the Assembly, was to permit the United States to adhere to the Statute, were considerations Hill disregarded. Insisting that the Court must be detached from the League and that the United States must join it on terms of entire equality, but having no real criticism of the Court itself, Hill proposed a new protocol for the signature of all eligible states, which differed from the Protocol of Signature with the American reservations mainly in that it made no reference to whether the states had signed the Treaty of Versailles.[31]

In letters to Senators Borah, Pepper, Moses, and George H. Williams of Missouri, Hill said much the same thing. To sign the Protocol as it stood and enter the League's Court on unequal terms solely by right of being mentioned in the Annex would be a national humiliation. But it would also be humiliating, and ridiculous and discourteous besides, to join the League's Court while declaring by reservations total independence of the League, though this would be necessary if the United States were not to be bound morally and legally to the League. The United States must therefore settle for nothing less than a new protocol that would transform the League's Court into a real World Court. If the League were not willing, it would demonstrate its intention to keep the Court under its domination and be a superstate.[32]

The senators agreed that Hill advocated the best course but differed as to its practicability. Moses, who had sent to Hill for suggestions the draft of a speech he planned to make in the Senate, would, like Hill, still settle for nothing less than cutting the Court completely away from the League. Hill sent him a copy of the new protocol he had drafted, but the New Hampshire senator chose instead to reintroduce the passed-over Pepper plan. On the last day of the Senate debate on the Court, however, Senator Williams, who had called on Hill personally to discuss the Court, introduced his protocol in a speech that followed almost verbatim Hill's letters to him.[33]

Senator Borah thought that it was impossible to do anything "constructive" since both parties had endorsed the Court program and were unwilling to consider any other. "But your letter will be helpful in any opportunity to work out anything worth while," he wrote. "If we can get the matter to a point where we can check the present program, we can do something."[34]

Senator Pepper felt that since the attempt to arouse popular interest in disassociating the Court from the League had failed, the issue was reduced to joining or not joining, and he believed it was best to join "if we can do so with safety to our own independence of action." He thought the most practicable terms of adherence were embodied in the draft of a resolution he sent to Hill. The draft, he confided, was from the pen of John Bassett Moore, who had authorized him to use it but did not want his name publicly associated with it.[35]

John Bassett Moore, who had preceded Hill as Assistant Secretary of State in 1898, was an eminent American authority on international law who had been elected to the bench of the Court upon its organization. He disapproved of the Court's advisory function because he believed that the giving of opinions with no binding force would impair the advance of the judicial principle and the development of international law. This would certainly be so, he feared, if the advisory function lacked the usual safeguards of judicial action. The Court had laid down in its rules that advisory opinions would be given in open and full court and that the same procedures would be followed as in rendering judgments. It had also refused by a vote of seven to four in 1923 to give an advisory opinion on a dispute between Russia and Finland over Eastern Carelia when Russia, which was not a member of the League, had withheld its assent. But these were practices that could be reversed, and Moore would make them permanently binding on the Court by including them in the American terms of adherence. His proposed terms were that the Court was not obliged to render opinions on request; that it would never give any secret or confidential opinion or advice; that it would not give an opinion on any question to which the United States was a party without the consent of the United States (a different rule could then hardly be applied to any other non-member of the League); and that the United States disclaimed all responsibility for opinions it had not joined in requesting.[36]

On December 21, four days after the Senate opened debate on the

Swanson resolution, Pepper recommended, without making a specific proposal, that the resolution be modified in accordance with Moore's suggestions.[37] Five weeks later, on January 27, 1926, after witnessing appeals to isolationism and racial prejudice, attempts to bury the proposal for another year, the defeat of a filibuster by cloture, the personal appearance in Washington of Judge Moore, and the insertion by Borah in the *Congressional Record* of an anonymous memorandum, the recommendations of which were identical with those the jurist had given to Pepper and which everyone attributed to Moore, the Senate voted seventy-six to seventeen to give its consent to United States adherence to the Court under the terms of the Swanson resolution, but with the fifth reservation significantly altered.[38]

As originally proposed by Swanson, the fifth reservation had provided that the United States would "be in no manner bound" by advisory opinions it had not joined in requesting. Legally, advisory opinions were not binding on either the League or the states concerned anyhow, but as none had been ignored, and some members of the Court and the League were coming to regard them as equivalent to judgments,[39] this provision was not considered a sufficient safeguard by either the Court's opponents in the Senate or most of its friends. In his apparently very influential memorandum, Judge Moore advised that the United States should assure to itself the same right of self-protection possessed by great power members of the League who could block requests for opinions on questions vitally affecting their interests. Although this line of reasoning dominated the Senate debate, the Senate became determined to assure to the United States a veto power on opinions to which it objected regardless of whether or not it was possessed by other states. Senators Swanson and Thomas J. Walsh of Montana, another strong supporter of the Court, assisted, it was reported in the *New York Times,* by Judge Moore, accordingly stiffened the fifth reservation to provide "that the court shall not render any advisory opinion except publicly after due notice to all states adhering to the court and to all interested states and after public hearing or opportunity for hearing given to any state concerned; nor shall it, without the consent of the United States, entertain any request for an advisory opinion touching any dispute or question in which the United States has or claims an interest."[40]

In the *Saturday Evening Post* of April 3, 1926, Hill compared the Senate to the distraught mother in a current popular limerick who permitted her darling daughter to go out for a swim but forbade her to go near the water. The Senate did not have the courage to refuse knocking at the door of the League for admission to its Court, yet still had not approved of it, said Hill. Although American ideals had been frustrated and abandoned in both the League and its Court, the influence of organized propaganda by friends of the League looking to enter it by a back door had decided the debate before it began. The Senate therefore took little interest in it. But when it was brought out that the Court was the League's Court and not the world court its protagonists had represented, proponents of the Swanson resolution, embarrassed by the country's reaction and anxious to close the debate, decided to sign the League's Protocol before a substitute protocol (obviously meaning the one written by Hill and introduced by Senator Williams on the last day of debate) could get underway. Yet the resolution showed where the Senate stood. It distrusted the League, would have as little to do with the Court as possible, and would see to it that that little was controlled by itself. "The wisdom of the Senate is not to be decried," Hill pronounced. "It has committed the country to nothing of importance."[41]

One might boggle at an account of how the Senate, after three years of delay, hastily approved a resolution it disliked before an awakened public could prevent it. But not opponents of the Court. "You have written many splendid articles upon this subject but it seemed to me that this was one of the very best," wrote Senator Borah. "It was magnificent." But he did not agree that the Senate had committed the country to nothing of importance. The United States would not exercise the veto power under the fifth reservation one time in a hundred when it should, and there would be many instances when it would have no right to exercise it, he complained. The Court would be prostituted into being an attorney on political matters, and in time the United States would be drawn thoroughly into Europe's political affairs.[42]

But Borah was wrong, for decision by the United States Senate did not settle the matter. In amending the Swanson resolution the Senate had stipulated that its conditions were to be accepted by each of the powers signatory to the Protocol through an exchange of notes. But since the Protocol was a multilateral agreement, the League Council reasoned that modification of it called for consultation among the interested states and multilateral assent. Consultation seemed especially necessary since reservation five might hamper the work of the League, which had already in several instances been greatly facilitated by advisory opinions. The Council therefore invited the United States to meet with the signatory states in Geneva on September 1 to clarify the meaning of the fifth reservation and frame a supplementary agreement.

The administration in Washington, trimming between pro-Court and anti-League pressures, treated the Council's invitation as uncalled-for League intervention. He would not send a representative to Geneva, the President declared, and Secretary of State Frank B. Kellogg answered that the reservations were "plain and unequivocal," he had no authority to modify or interpret them, and they must be accepted in the manner prescribed by the Senate.

Representatives of forty nations nevertheless met at Geneva to work out an agreement. They accepted the first four reservations without difficulty.[43] With reference to the first part of the fifth reservation they agreed to consider incorporating in the agreement the principles that the Court had already fixed in its rules. With reference to its second part they agreed that the decision of the Eastern Carelia case should satisfy the United States that in a dispute to which it was a party the Court would not give an advisory opinion without its consent. On a question to which the United States was not a party but claimed an interest, they agreed to assure to the United States a position of equality with members of the League. Contrary to the assumption of the Senate and Judge Moore, it had not been determined whether unanimity was required to request an opinion, and the conference therefore agreed that an objection by the United States should have the same force as a vote against a request by a member of the Council or Assembly. Because this right would effect the functioning of the League rather than the Court, the conference suggested that the manner of exercising it be arranged between the United States and the Council.

These recommendations were not well received in Washington. President Coolidge publicly refused to send them to the Senate, stating that he did not believe it would take action on them. Unless the Senate's requirements were met by the other nations, he saw no prospect, he said, of America's joining the Court. Pro-Court Senators Swanson and Walsh joined with Irreconcilables Borah and Moses in approving his stand.[44]

The following spring Hill published his last book, *The Problem of a World Court: The Story of an Unrealized American Idea.* Adding an explication of the "Great Assize'" at Geneva to his *Saturday Evening Post* articles of the previous year—which the New York *Herald Tribune* called "famous"—he defended the continued refusal of the United States to join the Court on any but its own terms. The deliberations of the League Council in September furnished indisputable proof, he found, that the alleged World Court was not a true world court. It had been constituted for the express purpose of furnishing advisory opinions to the Council and Assembly in order to clothe the actions of a political and military alliance with the prestige and authority of a nominally judicial tribunal. But the United States had no intentions of subjecting its national policies to the intrusion of a foreign body of men acting in a quasi-political capacity or permitting imperialist Europe to use this private court politically to invade America. The fifth reservation of the Senate's resolution did not demand a vote on particular advisory opinions but a veto on the use of the Court as an agency of international control. "It is not equality," he explained, "it is independence that is involved in this reservation." The idea of a World Court was an American idea, growing out of its distinctive institutions, which the League was trying to pervert, Hill caviled. By treating the Court as its auxiliary and instrument the League was trying to usurp the authority of "the real, the morally indestructible Society of States," which had been legitimately represented at the Second Hague Conference and from which the United States could not be deprived of its rightful place. The world must therefore turn from

Geneva and go back to The Hague if there were to be a true world court and a true world law.[45]

The Problem of a World Court was the most comprehensive statement against the Court to appear. But it was conspicuously a piece of special pleading, which the London *Saturday Review* described as "the excursion of the one hundred per cent. American into foreign affairs."[46] Hill genuinely wanted a world court and a world law, but they must be entirely in accord with the wishes of his own country as he interpreted them, there must be no sacrifice of American sovereignty, and there must be no contact with the League.

For several more years Hill continued to write prolifically on questions of foreign policy, publishing his articles in the *Saturday Evening Post, Current History,* and the *American Journal of International Law.* As in his earlier writings, he often seemed unable or unwilling to see beyond one argument at a time, a failing he was generally quick to attribute to anyone who disagreed with him. Thus he scoffed at the idea of outlawing war as an example of loose thinking and questioned the constitutional right of the United States to accept French Foreign Minister Briand's "proposal of perpetual peace," yet he hailed the consequent Pact of Paris as "a great advance in the cause of international peace" and "a solid foundation for inaugurating a new era in the life of mankind." Writing of the restrictions on military action that governments had already voluntarily accepted, he said of the provision of the Bryan treaties for delayed action, which he had so caustically attacked in 1916: "It was a wise provision—the best perhaps now actually operative, since it gives opportunity to utilize all others." An even more apparent feature of these last essays was that irrespective of his topic, Hill's message was always the same: the "organization of peace" could be achieved only by the substitution of cooperation and voluntary mutual agreement on the codification of international law and the employment of legal and judicial procedures, with no impairment of national sovereignty, for the methods of coercion and enforcement of obligations represented by the League of Nations and its private and subservient court.[47]

In doggedly adhering to the old American ideal of peace through international law, Hill manifested a noble impulse. But it closed his mind to many realities. His representation of the League as an exclusive alliance had always been at best a strained assumption, but with the admission of Germany in 1926 and the extension of the League's hands to the few states still outside, it became a gross distortion of fact. He claimed that the League had created a "closed and exclusive" court, yet the Court was open to every state in the world on terms of equality, and in its first case Germany had come before it with a German judge sitting *ad hoc*. He charged that the League was using the advisory function of the Court as a screen for dubious political action, yet every opinion requested of the Court had related to a point of law and the Court had scrupulously discharged its advisory function by strictly judicial methods.[48] He bewailed the Court's inability to cite a state to appear before it, yet the optional provision for obligatory jurisdiction was more in keeping with his fundamental concept of voluntary international organization.

Hill never ceased asserting that the League, in order to give the Court a free hand under the League Covenant, had rejected the recommendation of the Advisory Committee of Jurists for a new Hague conference to codify international law. The League Assembly had not, in fact, taken immediate action on the recommendation, considering it best to wait until wartime emotions had subsided. In 1924, however, it requested the Council to convene a committee of experts, to which an American was appointed, to arrange for the progressive codification of international law by international conferences. Following a directive of the Assembly based on the recommendation of the Advisory Committee, the committee of experts invited the cooperation of the institutes and societies of international law throughout the world, as well as the collaboration of all governments.[49] The executive council of the American Society of International Law accepted this invitation at the society's annual meeting in 1925, and the society's *Journal* that year discussed these developments in every issue. Hill was a vice-president of the society and member of the executive council, he was present at the 1925 annual meeting, and he was an editor of the *Journal*. Yet the only reference he ever made to these painstaking preparations was to comment: "The Council of the League of

Nations . . . has become aware that it must adjust its policies to the demands of self-governing nations; with the result that, despite the rejection of the chief recommendation of the Commission of Jurists, it has announced its determination to supervise the codification of international law; quite plainly taking care that the process does not proceed so far as to affect any matter which is vital to the interests of the League, such as its own right to make war to enforce peace, or to impose it upon unwilling States."[50]

While Hill continued to insist that the essential prerequisite of a real world court was the codification of international law by further conferences at The Hague, the Court was functioning to the satisfaction of its almost fifty members and finding no lack of law to apply in an enormous accumulation of international conventions and customs, generally recognized principles of law and equity, judicial decisions of international and national tribunals, and applicable national legislation. Moreover, international law was being steadily codified at Geneva, and with far more success than had been possible at The Hague. For the first time in history a permanent agency, representing more nations than had ever gathered at The Hague, existed to assemble international meetings and enable them to work effectively; and numerous conferences and commissions meeting at the Swiss city were producing conventions on a broad spectrum of important subjects.[51] Despite Hill's theoretical barrages, the League of Nations was the closest approximation to a real "Society of States" the world had ever seen, and if the international court it had made possible was not a "true world court" it was only because Americans like himself kept the United States out of it.

Hill did not cease publishing two or three articles a year relating to international organization until the end of 1930, when he was eighty years of age. Although still vigorous intellectually and physically, he had little more than a year to live. On the afternoon of Washington's Birthday 1932, he went driving with his son Walter, who had come to the Capital from his home in Scranton, Pennsylvania, to attend the Washington bicentennial celebration. He planned to go walking with Walter the next day, but was taken ill. He died eight days later, on March 2, 1932.[52]

David Jayne Hill's abilities were large. A gifted college president, he infused two small and failing schools with new vitality, opening their development into modern and strong institutions of higher learning. An able diplomat, he handled foreign policy questions intelligently and represented his country with dignity and tact. Those who dealt with him liked and respected him. As a champion of peace through law, he labored for one of man's noblest ideals. A scholar of distinction, he devoted years to the study of religion and philosophy and later won acclaim as a historian.

Hill was a remarkably industrious and efficient individual. He was also an ambitious one. He aspired for recognition as a scholar, sought high place in the diplomatic service, and would have welcomed high office in government—provided attaining it did not violate his canons of responsible political behavior. He did not relish the game of politics, but he was never reluctant to debate certain large political issues. He felt it was a patriotic duty—and he enjoyed it. Prone to question the motives of those with other views, he was not a charitable opponent. The censoriousness that marked many of his public utterances, however, had no place in his personal relationships. He easily won friends by qualities of integrity, charm, humor, and kindliness, his company was valued, and his home was noted for its hospitality.

In the last two decades of his life Hill became a leading spokesman for the conservative opposition to progressivism, the League of Nations, and the World Court, all of which he believed threatened Americanism. Hill had serious faults as well as great abilities, and never were they more apparent than in this last of his several careers. He was a dogmatic and partisan publicist, his reasoning was often more ingenious than sound, and his blind spots were massive. But vision is seldom clarified by the belief that values and principles of vital importance are at stake, and few if any of those who stood on the other side of issues were free of the same human failings. Verbal warriors, moreover, are particularly vulnerable victims of historical scrutiny, especially when their causes are less popular with a later generation.

Hill was spared seeing another reforming Democrat in the White House and his concepts of Americanism threatened by the New

Deal. He did live long enough to witness the outbreak of naked aggression in Asia. If the League of Nations was exposed as irresolute, the alternative approach to peace represented by treaties depending solely on universal recognition of the benefits of playing the game according to the rules—the approach to which he so unreservedly subscribed—was exposed as a delusion.

Notes

The following abbreviations have been used in the notes:

HP	David Jayne Hill Papers, University of Rochester Library.
HC	David Jayne Hill Collection, Bucknell University Library.
WP	Andrew D. White Papers, Cornell University Library.
CP	Andrew Carnegie Papers, Library of Congress.
RDS	Records of the Department of State, Record Group 59, National Archives.
SDNF 1906–10	State Department Numerical File 1906–10, Record Group 59, National Archives.
SDDF 1910–29	State Department Decimal File 1910–29, Record Group 59, National Archives.

CHAPTER 1

1. William C. Morey, "David Jayne Hill," University of Rochester *Interpres* 50 (1909): 9.

2. David Jayne Hill, "As It Seemed to Me: Confidences Regarding the Inner and Outer Phases of a Varied Life" (also titled "Confidences of a Grandfather"),

typescript memoir to 1896, HC, pp. 4–96; David Jayne Hill, "The Ancestry of David Jayne Hill," typescript, HC; David Jayne Hill, "A Typical Preacher of the Nineteenth Century," *Centenary, First Baptist Church, Plainfield, New Jersey, 1818–1918, November 24th, 25th 1918* (privately printed, n.d.), pp. 15–25.

3. Lewisburg *Union County Whig,* Aug. 28, 1851, *Lewisburg Chronicle,* Mar. 25, 1859, quoted in J. Orin Oliphant, ed., *The Beginnings of Bucknell University: A Sampling of the Documents* (Lewisburg, Pa.: Bucknell University Press, 1954), pp. 55, 72; University at Lewisburg, *Catalogue* (1852–53), pp. 7, 28; *ibid.* (1870–71), pp. 5, 11–13, 24; University Female Institue at Lewisburg, *Catalogue* (1871), pp. 10–13.

4. Hill, "Confidences," pp. 105, 114, 124–43, 149.

5. *College Herald,* Oct. 1875, p. 31; Oct. 1877, pp. 108, 111; June 1878, pp. 5–6; University at Lewisburg, *Catalogue* (1877–78), pp. 5, 17, 25, 38; "Sketch of the Life of David Jayne Hill, LL.D," Bucknell University, *l'Agenda* (1888), p. 82.

6. Hill, "Confidences," pp. 144–46; *College Herald,* Oct. 1878, p. 23; Mar. 1879, pp. 54–55.

7. Hill, "Confidences," pp. 147–48. See HP for numerous reviews and HC for chapters on Poe.

8. *Memorials of Bucknell University, 1849–1896* (Lewisburg, Pa.: Published by the University, 1896), p. 28; University at Lewisburg, *Catalogues* (1851–52 to 1877–78), *passim;* University at Lewisburg, Minutes of the Trustees, Aug. 20, 1851, June 29, 1875.

9. Minutes of the Trustees, Apr. 10, 1866; Hill, "Confidences," p. 155; William C. Bartol, "Looking Backward," *Bucknellian* 21 (Mar. 1, 1928): 7; (Apr. 13, 1928): 7.

10. Minutes of the Trustees, May 5, 1863, Apr. 4, 1865, Jan. 7, 1873, June 27, 1876, June 26, 1877, June 25, 1878; University at Lewisburg, *Abstract of Treasurer's Report,* June 1, 1879, pp. 13–14; O.W. Spratt, *The University at Lewisburg, Report of the Twenty-Fourth Annual Commencement, Lewisburg, Pa., June 19–24, 1874* (Philadelphia, 1874), pp. 20–21, 34–35.

11. Minutes of the Trustees, July 27, 28, 1869, June 27, 28, 1870, June 25, 1872, June 24, 1873, June 29, 1875, June 25, 1878; Philadelphia *National Baptist,* Sept. 7, 1876, July 10, 1879, Apr. 28, 1881.

12. Minutes of the Trustees, June 26, July 24, Sept. 3, 1877, June 25, Dec. 27, 1878; J. Orin Oliphant, *The Rise of Bucknell University* (New York: Appleton-Century-Crofts, 1965), pp. 130–36; Lewis E. Theiss, *Centennial History of Bucknell University, 1846–1946* (Lewisburg, Pa.: Bucknell University, 1946), pp. 173–75.

13. Minutes of the Trustees, Dec. 27, 1878, Mar. 11, 1879; Hill, "Confidences," pp. 152–55.

14. *College Herald,* Mar. 1879, pp. 53–55; Jan. 1880, pp. 100–101; *Lewisburg Chronicle,* Mar. 20, 1879; Hill, "Confidences," p. 155; University at Lewisburg, *Catalogue* (1879–80), pp. 18–21.

15. Minutes of the Trustees, Dec. 30, 1879, June 22, Dec. 29, 1880; Philadelphia *National Baptist,* July 14, 1881; Hill, "Confidences," p. 156.

16. Philadelphia *Inquirer,* May 21, 30, 1879; [David J. Hill], MS of Address to the Baptist Social Union, HC; "Inaugural Address of President David J. Hill," Philadelphia *National Baptist,* July 10, 1879.

17. Minutes of the Trustees, Mar. 31, May 5, July 28, 1863, June 24, 1879, June 22, 1880, Apr. 21, 1881; Hill, "Confidences," pp. 494–96.

18. Minutes of the Trustees, June 28, Oct. 12, 1881, Mar. 7, June 27, 1882; Philadelphia *National Baptist*, Oct. 27, Nov. 10, 1881; James S. Swartz to Hill, Mar. 27, 1923, HP; Oliphant, *Rise of Bucknell,* p. 146.

19. Minutes of the Trustees, June 26, 1883, Jan. 10, 1884, June 23, 1885, June 22, 1886, June 28, 1887, June 26, 1888, June 23, 1891; "In Memoriam, William Bucknell," *University Mirror,* Apr. 1890, p. 211.

20. University at Lewisburg (after 1886, Bucknell University), *Catalogues* (1879–80 to *1887–88*), *passim;* editorial, "The Growth of Our University," *University Mirror,* June 1888, pp. 111–12; Theiss, *History of Bucknell,* pp. 201–2; J. Orin Oliphant, *The Library of Bucknell University* (Lewisburg, Pa.: Bucknell University Press, 1962), pp. 49–55, 67–83.

21. D.J.H., "The Elective System," *College Herald,* Feb. 1875, pp. 57–58; "Inaugural Address of President David J. Hill," Philadelphia *National Baptist,* July 10, 1879; Buckness University, *Catalogue* (1887–1888), pp. 17–20.

22. University at Lewisburg, *Catalogue* (1878–79), pp. 10–15; *ibid.* (1879–80), p. 17; *ibid.* (1880–81), pp. 19, 21; *ibid.* (1882–83), pp. 22, 25; Bucknell University, *Catalogue* (1887–88), pp. 17–20; George P. Schmidt, *The Old Time College President* (New York: Columbia University Press, 1930), chap. 4; Gladys Bryson, "The Comparable Interests of the Old Moral Philosophy and the Modern Social Sciences," *Social Forces* 11 (Oct., 1932): 19–27; "Dr. David Jayne Hill," Elmira (New York) *Journal* 1 (June 1894): 1.

23. Hill, "Confidences," pp. 192–201.

24. "Inaugural Address of President David J. Hill," Philadelphia *National Baptist,* July 10, 1879; University at Lewisburg, *Catalogue* (1882–83), p. 69; *ibid.* (1884–85), p. 68; Minutes of the Trustees, June 27, 1882, June 26, 1883, June 24, 1884; Philadelphia *National Baptist,* Sept. 27, 1883; Oliphant, *Rise of Bucknell,* p. 155.

25. Theiss, *History of Bucknell,* pp. 199–200, 207; Oliphant, *Rise of Bucknell,* pp. 173–77; Hill, "Confidences," p. 538.

26. John B. Cooke to Walter Hill, Apr. 6, 1932, HC; *College Herald,* Oct., 1879, p. 84; William C. Bartol, "Looking Backward," *Bucknellian* 31 (Apr. 26, 1928): 7; Theiss, *History of Bucknell,* p. 210.

27. Ernest Earnest, *Academic Procession: An Informal History of the American College, 1636–1953* (Indianapolis: Bobbs-Merrill, 1953), pp. 89–90; E. Dodge to Hill, June 22, 1883, HP. *The College Herald, University Mirror,* and newspaper clippings in HP contain numerous notations of Hill's speeches.

28. Hill to M.B. Anderson, Mar. 24, 1888, Anderson Papers, University of Rochester Library; Charles H. Hopkins, *The Rise of the Soical Gospel in American Protestantism, 1865–1915* (New Haven: Yale University Press, 1940), pp. 67–97; Hill, "Confidences," p. 500; "Sketch of David Jayne Hill," p. 82; David J. Hill, "Socialism: False and True," *Proceeding of the Fourth Baptist Congress, . . . New York, Nov. 1885* (New York: Century Co., 1886), pp. 23–28.

29. David J. Hill, *The Principles and Fallacies of Socialism,* no. 533 of *Lovell's Library* (New York: John W. Lovell Co., 1885), pp. 68–71 and *passim:* David J. Hill, *The Social Influence of Christianity, with Special Reference to Contemporary Problems* (Boston: Silver, Burdett and Co., 1888), pp. 102–3, 109–21, and *passim.*

30. Hill, "Confidences," pp. 148, 157–59; *College Herald,* May 1880, p. 122; *Lewisburg Chronicle,* Mar. 18, 1880.

31. Hill, "Confidences," pp. 469–93, 518; Hill to Eva Liddell, twenty-two letters, 1884, HC; *University Mirror,* Oct. 1884, p. 10; *Lewisburg Chronicle,* Oct., 2, 1884; unidentified news clippings, HP.

32. Hill, "Confidences," pp. 498, 515–16, 519–32, 539, 545; item from *Williamsport Gazette and Bulletin* reprinted in *Lewisburg Saturday News,* June 5, 1886; *University Mirror,* Apr. 1887, pp. 90, 95; May 1887, pp. 103–4, 108; June 1887, p. 123; July 1887, p. 137; Feb. 1888, p. 63.

33. Hill to M. Anderson, Mar. 24, July 9, 1888, Hill to E. Bright, June 27, 1888, Anderson Papers; M. Anderson to Hill, June 22, 1888, E.H. Johnson to Hill, Jan. 19, 26, June 4, 14, 22, 1888, D.C. Gilman to Hill, June 25, 1888, Hill to C. Bridgman, E. Bright, and J. Rathbone, June 19, 1888, Hill to E. Bright, July 9, 1888, E. Bright to E.H. Johnson, June 22, 1888, E.H. Johnson to Juliet Hill, June 23, 1888, HP.

34. Minutes of the Trustees, June 26, July 18, 1888; D.P. Leas to Hill, July 12, 1888, A.J. Rowland to Hill, July 18, 1888, HP.

35. Hill, "Confidences," pp. 553–68; New York *Examiner,* Dec. 6, 1888, May 8, Aug. 1, 1889; *University Mirror,* Mar. 1889, p. 79; G. Stanley Hall, *Life and Confessions of a Psychologist* (New York: D. Appleton and Co., 1923), p. 275; E. Bright to Hill, May 22, 1889, HP.

CHAPTER 2

1. Jesse L. Rosenberger, *Rochester and Colgate: Historical Backgrounds of the Two Universities* (Chicago: University of Chicago Press, 1925), pp. 13–22, 46–139; Jesse L. Rosenberger, *Rochester, The Making of a University* (Rochester: University of Rochester, 1927), pp. 1–38; Joseph H. Gilmore, *An Outline History of the University of Rochester* (Rochester: Ezra R. Andrews, 1886), pp. 3–9; University of Rochester, Trustees' Records 1 (May 13, 1850): 6–7; (Sept. 16, 1850): 12–20; Martin B. Anderson, *The Ends and Means of a Liberal Education, An Inaugural Delivered July 11, 1854, by M.B. Anderson, President of the University of Rochester* (Rochester: William N. Sage, 1855), pp. 60–64; *Report of the President of the University of Rochester, 1894–1895,* pp. 15–16.

2. Rosenberger, *Rochester,* p. 239; William C. Morey, "The University of Rochester in its Relation to the Educational Movement of the Last Fifty Years," in *Addresses at the Semi-Centennial Anniversary of the Founding of the University of Rochester, June Tenth to Fourteenth, MCM* (Rochester: E.R. Andrews Printing Co., 1901), p. 69; E.H. Johnson to Hill, Jan. 19, June 22, 1888, Myron G. Peck to Hill, July 13, Aug. 17, 1893, Charles M. Williams to Hill, July 1, 1893, John H. Deane to Hill, June 7, 1895, A.W. Tourgee to Hill, Aug. 26, 1893, HP.

3. Anderson, *Inaugural Address,* pp. 49–50; Morey, "University of Rochester," pp. 59–65; Dexter Perkins, "The University of Rochester, Its Place in the Civic Century," in *Centennial History of Rochester, New York* (Rochester: The Rochester Historical Society, 1934), 4: 136–37.

4. University of Rochester, *Catalogues* (1870–71 to 1887–88), *passim;* University of Rochester, Treasurer's Statements (1879 to 1887); John R. Slater, "Small Beginnings: The College for Men, 1850–1899," in *The University of Rochester: the First Hundred Years,* Centennial Issue of the *Alumni-Alumnae Review* (Rochester: University of Rochester,

1950), p. 17; Perkins, "University of Rochester," p. 137; A.W. Tourgee to Hill, Aug. 26, 1893, W.M. Kimball to Hill, Sept. 5, 1892, HP.

5. "David Jayne Hill, LL.D.," University of Rochester, *Interpres* 38 (1897): 115; University of Rochester, *Campus*, May 17, 1893; Hill, "Confidences," p. 493; *Rochester Morning Herald*, June 18, 1891; Rochester *Herald*, June 23, 1893; New York *Examiner*, June 29, 1893; M.W. Cooke to Hill, June 28, 29, July 23, 1891, HP.

6. University of Rochester, Faculty Meeting Records, 2 (Dec. 1889): 233; (May 7, 1890): 266–68, 270, 272; (May 14, 1890): 269, 271; (May 21, 1890): 273–74; University of Rochester, *Catalogue* (1890–91), pp. 67–71; *ibid* (1891–92), pp. 73–77.

7. *Report of the President of the University of Rochester, 1894–1895*, pp. 4–6; *Report of the President of the University of Rochester, 1895–1896*, pp. 8–9; Perkins, "University of Rochester," pp. 145–46; Hill, "Confidences," pp. 693–94; University of Rochester *Catalogue* (1889–90), p. 29; *ibid.* (1890–91), p. 64; *Campus*, Oct. 12, 1894; Trustees' Records, 2 (June 19, 1894): 348–49; (June 18, 1895): 375–76.

8. Henry H. Barstow, "Anderson Hall a Battle Field in Gay 'Nineties," *Rochester Alumni Review* 9 (April–May, 1931): 111–12; Albert Ehrgott, "Dr. Anderson and Dr. Hill—a Contrast," *Rochester Alumni Review* 5 (Dec.–Jan. 1926–27): 41; Philadelphia *National Baptist*, Dec. 10, 1891; *Campus*, Nov. 15, 1889, May 10, Dec. 23, 1890, Mar. 1, 1894, Apr. 19, 1894, Nov. 29, 1895; Hill to Rhees, Oct. 30, 1900, HP; "David Jayne Hill, LL.D.," *Interpres* 38 (1897): 116.

9. David J. Hill, *The American College in Relation to Liberal Education, The Inaugural Address of President David J. Hill, LL.D., Read before the alumni and friends of the University of Rochester, June 19, 1889*, pp. 26–27; *Report of the President of the University of Rochester, 1895–96*, pp. 9–10; Barstow, "Anderson Hall," pp. 111–12; *Rochester Morning Herald*, June 19, 1890; Rochester *Herald*, June 21, 1895; Hill to C. M. Williams, June 24, 1899, HP.

10. Trustees' Records, 2 (June 16, 1891): 272; (June 19, 1894): 349; *ibid.*, 3(June 14, 1898): 25; (June 12, 1900): 69, 71; Hill to C.M. Williams, June 24, 1899, Hill to E.M. Moore, Mar. 23, 1900, HP; Rochester *Post Express*, Sept. 11, 1899, Apr. 21, 1891; *Rochester Morning Herald*, Mar. 15, 1892; Ida Harper, *Life and Work of Susan B. Anthony* (Indianapolis: Hollenbeck Press, 1908), 3: 1221–24.

11. Hill to M.B. Anderson, Oct. 4, 1889, Anderson Papers; Hill, "Confidences," pp. 612–13.

12. Hill to E.H. Johnson, Jan. 27, 1900, F.A. Williams to Hill, Aug. 17, 1893, HP; Hill, *Inaugural Address*, pp. 5–6; Hill, "Confidences," p. 571.

13. Philadelphia *National Baptist*, July 16, Aug. 13, 1891; E. Brown to Hill, June 15, 1891, F.M. Goodchild to Hill, June 24, 1891, J.W.A. Stewart to Hill, Aug. 19, 1891, HP; *Rochester Morning Herald*, June 18, 1891.

14. Trustees' Records, 2 (June 16, 1891): 273; J.P. Townsend to M.W. Cooke, June 1, 1892, J.P. Townsend to Hill, Dec. 15, 1893, HP.

15. Trustees' Records, 2 (June 14, 1892): 300–301, 305; New York *Christian Inquirer*, June 23, 1892; M. W. Cooke to Hill, Apr. 20, Aug. 13, 1895, HP; New York *Examiner*, June 29, 1893.

16. *Campus*, Mar. 8, 1893.

17. Quoted from material prepared by Hill and published in the Rochester *Herald*, Aug. 18, 1893.

18. New York *Examiner*, July 6, 1893; H.C. Vedder to Hill, July 14, 1893, M.G. Peck, to Hill, July 13, 1893, M.W. Cooke to Hill, July 13, 1893, HP.

19. Rochester *Democrat and Chronicle*, June 23, 1893; Rochester *Herald*, Aug. 27, 1893; A.H. Strong to Hill, n.d., A.H. Strong to Hill, July 3, 22, 1893, Hill to A.H. Strong, July 15, 1893, HP.

20. New York *Examiner*, July 27, Aug. 10, 1893.

21. W.C. Morey to Hill, Aug. 13, 1893, H.E. Burton to Hill, Aug. 8, [1893], HP.

22. New York *Examiner*, Aug. 17, 1893.

23. David J. Hill, "The Relative Authority of Scripture and Reason," in *Proceedings of the Tenth Baptist Congress, held in Philadelphia, Pa., May, 1892* (New York: Baptist Publishing Co., 1892).

24. David J. Hill, *Genetic Philosophy* (New York: Macmillan Co., 1893), pp. 1–23, 371–72, and *passim*.

25. *Oxford Magazine* 12 (May 23, 1894): 346–47; Indianapolis *Baptist*, Mar. 22, 1894; Boston *Watchman*, Nov. 23, 1893, May 10, 1894; *New World* 3 (Mar. 1894): 198–200; Philadelphia *National Baptist*, Mar. 15, 1894; New York *Examiner*, Feb. 1, 1894.

26. Hill to H.C. Vedder, Jan. 31, 1894, H.C. Vedder to Hill, Feb. 2, 1894, HP; New York *Examiner*, Mar. 1, 1894.

27. Philadelphia *National Baptist*, Apr. 12, 1894; New York *Examiner*, Apr. 12, 1894; "Syllabus of the Levering Lectures for 1894 on Religion in the Light of Science, Delivered by David Jayne Hill, at the Johns Hopkins University, March 15, 16, 19 and 20, 1894."

28. Macmillan Co. to Hill, July, 3, 1895, HP; Rochester *Democrat and Chronicle*, Jan. 30, 1895.

29. Rochester *Democrat and Chronicle*, Mar. 5, 1895.

30. G.F. Love to Hill, Apr. 3, 1895, H.C. Townley to M.W. Cooke, Apr. 3, 1895, M.W. Cooke to Hill, Apr. 1, 20, June 30, 1895, J.W.A. Stewart to Hill, Mar. 7, 1895, H.H. Hunt to M.W. Cooke, Mar. 26, Apr. 9, 1895, HP; Rochester *Herald*, Apr. 1, 4, Nov. 30, Dec. 11, 1895.

31. University of Rochester, Records of Executive Board, 3 (Apr. 27, 1895): 339–40; *Report of the President of the University of Rochester, 1894–1895*, pp. 7–20; Trustees' Records, 2 (June 18, 1895): 380–81; M.W. Cooke to Hill, Aug. 2, 1895, HP.

32. *Report of the President of the University of Rochester, 1894–1895*, pp. 6, 16.

33. Rochester *Herald*, Dec. 5, 1895; Rochester *Post Express*, Dec. 10, 1895; Hill, "Confidences," p. 813–16; M. G. Peck to Hill, Sept. 11, 1893, M. W. Cooke to Hill, June 30, 1895, H. C. Black to Hill, Nov. 24, 1895, Hill to J. B. Scott, July 24, 1922, HP; New York *Examiner*, Dec. 12, 1895; *Williamsport Gazette and Bulletin*, Jan. 11, 1892.

34. Juliet Hill to A.D. White, Oct. 31, 1895, WP; Trustees' Records, 2 (Dec. 4, 1895): 385–87; Rochester *Democrat and Chronicle*, Nov. 20, Dec. 8, 12, 1895; Rochester *Herald*, Dec. 2, 5, 6, 10, 1895; Rochester *Post Express*, Nov. 21, Dec. 2, 1895.

35. Rochester *Herald*, Dec. 5, 7, 12, 21, 1895, Jan. 2, Mar. 10, 1896; Rochester *Democrat and Chronicle*, Dec. 16, 1895, Jan. 2, Mar. 11, 1896; Rochester *Post Express*, Dec. 27, 1895; New York *Evening Post*, Mar. 10, 1896; Trustees' Records, 2 (June 16, 1896): 401–2. Several years later, when asked about rumors of his becoming president of Columbian (now George Washington) University, another Baptist institution in

financial trouble, Hill retorted that he wouldn't give the proposition a moment's consideration. "It would put me once more into a situation that it took me two or three years to get out of and which, with the Lord's help, I shall never get into again." (Hill to E.H. Johnson, Jan. 27, 1900, HP).

CHAPTER 3

1. Rochester *Democrat and Chronicle,* Mar. 20, 1891; *Rochester Morning Herald,* Mar. 20, 1891.

2. David J. Hill, "Why I Am a Protectionist," *American Economist* 8 (Dec. 18, 1891): 309.

3. New York *Tribune,* Dec. 24, 1895.

4. Rochester *Democrat and Chronicle,* Apr. 10, 1896.

5. Rochester *Post Express,* May 12, 1896; Blake McKelvey, "Rochester's Political Trends, An Historical Review," *Rochester History* 14 (Apr. 1952): 12–14; Hill to McKinley, Apr. 21, May 12, 1896, McKinley to Hill, Apr. 25, 1896, HP.

6. Rochester *Democrat and Chronicle,* June 24, July 2, 3, 1896; Rochester *Post Express,* July 2, 1896; Hill to G.W. Aldridge, July 3, 1896, Aldridge Papers, Rochester (N.Y.) Public Library.

7. Hill to A.D. White, July 11, 1896, WP; White to Hill, July 14, Aug. 8, 1896, HP.

8. Rochester *Democrat and Chronicle,* July 3, 1896; L.P. Ross to Hill, Nov. 25, 1895, HP; Hill to A.D. White, July 11, 1896, WP; F.B. Mitchell to Hill, n.d., C.E. Bostwick to Hill, July 6, 1896, HP.

9. *Nation* 63 (Aug. 20, 1896): 132–33; Robert M. Gordon, "George W. Aldridge; A Study of the Political Career of a Local Boss" (M.A. thesis, University of Rochester, 1927), pp. 40–41; Roscoe C.E. Brown and Ray B. Smith, *Political and Governmental History of the State of New York* (Syracuse: The Syracuse Press, 1922), 4:23.

10. W.A. Sutherland to Hill, Aug. 1, 1896, Hill to Sutherland, n.d., G.F. Danforth to Hill, Aug. 16, 1896, C.E. Bostwick to Hill, Aug. 18, 1896, Hill to Aldridge, Aug. 18, 1896, L.P. Ross to Hill, Apr. 9, 1897, HP; Hill to A.D. White, Aug. 19, 1896, WP; Hill to Aldridge, Aug. 11, 1896; Aldridge Papers; Rochester *Herald,* Aug. 31, 1896.

11. Aldridge to Hill, Aug. 22, 1896 (telegram), L.P. Ross to Hill, Mar. 20, Apr. 9, 1897, HP; Rochester *Post Express,* Aug. 25, 26, 1896; Rochester *Herald,* Aug. 31, 1896.

12. Brown and Smith, *History of the State of New York,* 4: 23–26; Rochester *Herald,* Aug. 11, 1896.

13. *New York Times,* Aug. 28, 1896; C.W. Hackett to Hill, Aug. 4, 1896, P. Clayton to Hill, Aug. 28, Sept. 15, Oct. 13, 1896, C.C. Sackett to Hill, Sept. 7, Oct. 6, 1896, J.S. Kenyon to Hill, Sept. 15, 21, 1896, C.L. Kurtz to Hill, Sept. 24, 1896, L.B. Gleason to Hill, Sept. 26, 1896, N.L. Douglas to Hill, Oct. 9, 1896, HP.

14. W.M. Osborne to Hill, July 21, Aug. 3, Nov. 10, 1896, Hill to C.R. Buckland, June 28, 1900, HP; Brooklyn *Daily Times,* Oct. 27, 1896.

15. A. Crapsey to A.D. White, Nov. 24, 1896, Hill to White, Mar. 6, 25, 1897, WP; "Brief for the Appointment of David Jayne Hill, LL.D., of Rochester, New York, as United States Minister to Belgium," HP. The brief contained about one hundred endorsements. The Hill papers also contain some ninety letters relating to getting testimonials and the help of Brewster and Platt.

16. L.P. Ross to Hill, Mar. 28, 1897, C.N. Bliss to W.A. Butler, Apr. 22, 1897, A.D. White to Hill, Mar. 31, 1897, HP; Hill to A.D. White, Mar. 25, Apr. 6, 1897, Juliet Hill to White, Apr. 24, 1897, WP; Washington *Evening Star,* Apr. 27, 1897.

17. Hill to J. Van Voorhis, Apr. 27, 1898, HP.

18. Hill to J. Van Voorhis, Apr. 27, 1898, Hill to W.M. Osborne, Aug. 30, 1898, Hill to J.B. Scott, July 24, 1922, HP; Hill to A.D. White, Aug. 1, 1898, WP; *New York Critic,* Dec. 25, 1897.

19. J. Van Voorhis to Hill, Dec. 13, 25, 1897, May 10, 1898, L.P. Ross to Hill, Apr. 2, 1898, HP.

20. Hill to Van Voorhis, Apr. 27, 1898, enclosed in Van Voorhis to McKinley, May 28, 1899, William McKinley Papers, Library of Congress, microfilm, series 1, reel 3; J.A. Porter to Van Voorhis, June 16, 1898, HP; Hill to A.D. White, Oct. 6, 1898, WP.

21. Hill to A. D. White, Aug. 1, Oct. 6, 1898, WP; Van Voorhis to Hill, Aug. 16, 1898, Hill to W. M. Osborne, Aug. 30, 1898, Osborne to Hill, Sept. 16, Oct. 4, 1898, H. Porter to Hill, Oct. 4, 1898, Hay to Van Voorhis, Sept. 6, 1898, HP.

22. Hay to Hill, Oct. 2, 1898 (telegram), Hill to Hay, Oct. 4, 1898, HP; Hill to A.D. White, Oct. 6, 1898, WP; *Washington Star,* Oct. 25, 1898.

23. "Who's Who—and Why," *Saturday Evening Post* 180 (May 2, 1908): 19; Hill to Hay, Aug. 3, 1902, W.H. Michael to Hill, Sept. 12, 1899, T. Morrison to Hill, Jan. 3, 1902, HP.

24. Tyler Dennett, *John Hay, From Poetry to Politics* (New York: Dodd, Mead and Co., 1933), pp. 253–55; Howard K. Beale, *Theodore Roosevelt and the Rise of America to World Power* (Baltimore: Johns Hopkins Press, 1956), p. 102; Edward P. Mitchell, *Memoirs of an Editor* (New York: Charles Scribner's Sons, 1924), p. 342.

25. F.W. Holls to Hill, Jan. 31, 1900, HP; Nicholas Murray Butler, *Across the Busy Years* (New York: Charles Scribner's Sons, 1939), 1: 310–11. Butler states that Andrew D. White was present, in his recollections confusing Senator White with the ambassador. A.D. White was at this time in Germany.

26. New York *World,* May 15, 1900.

27. Philadelphia *Press,* Mar. 29, 1908; Hill to M.D. Learned, Dec. 18, 1900, HP. The Hill Papers contain numerous newspaper clippings describing Juliet's receptions and dinners.

28. Hill to Hay, Aug. 8, 1900, Hay to Hill, Aug. 17, 1900, HP.

29. Quoted in Dennett, *John Hay,* p. 201.

30. Graham H. Stuart, *The Department of State: A History of Its Organization, Procedure and Personnel* (New York: Macmillan Co., 1949), pp. 194–96.

31. Hay to Hill, Sept. 6, 1900, HP; *New York Times,* Sept. 4, 1900; *Washington Times,* Sept. 4, 1900.

32. Hay to Hill, Sept. 24, 1900, HP; Juliet Hill to A.D. White, Oct. 14, 1900, WP.

33. Quoted in Alfred L.P. Dennis, *Adventures in American Diplomacy, 1896–1906* (New York: E.P. Dutton & Co., 1928), p. 522.

34. Hay to Hill, Aug. 4, 1902, HP.

35. Hill to Carnegie, Apr. 22, 1909, HP.

CHAPTER 4

1. David J. Hill, *International Justice: With a Plan for Its Permanent Organization*, reprinted from the *Yale Law Journal* 6 (Oct. 1896): 1–19.

2. F.W. Hooper to Hill, Sept. 17, 1896, F. Wayland to Hill, Oct. 1, 1896, HP.

3. James Brown Scott, ed., *The Hague Conventions and Declarations of 1899 and 1907,* 3rd ed. (New York: Oxford University Press, 1918), pp. xv–xvi; Thomas K. Ford, "The Genesis of the First Hague Peace Conference," *Political Science Quarterly* 51 (Sept. 1936): 354–82; Frederick W. Holls, *The Peace Conference at The Hague* (New York: Macmillan Co., 1900), p. 11; Merze Tate, *The Disarmament Illusion: The Movement for a Limitation of Armaments* (New York: Macmillan Co., 1942), pp. 249–78; U.S., Department of State, *Papers Relating to the Foreign Relations of the United States, 1898* (Washington: Government Printing Office, 1901), pp. LXXXI, 547.

4. David J. Hill, *The Problem of a World Court* (New York: Longmans, Green and Co., 1927), pp. 3–5; Scott, *The Hague Conventions,* pp. xvii–xix.

5. Hill to A.D. White, Apr. 7, 1899, WP; James Brown Scott, ed., *Instructions to the American Delegates to the Hague Peace Conferences and Their Official Reports* (New York: Oxford University Press, 1916), pp. 6–9.

6. Scott, *Instructions,* pp. 14–16; Hill to Holls, Apr. 24, 1899, HP.

7. Holls, *Peace Conference,* pp. 328–29; John W. Foster, *Arbitration and The Hague Court* (Boston: Houghton Mifflin Co., 1904), pp. 59–60, 101–2; A.C.F. Beales, *The History of Peace* (New York: Dial Press, 1931), p. 236; Merle Curti, *Peace or War, the American Struggle, 1636–1936* (New York: W.W. Norton and Co., 1936), p. 182; *Memorial of the New York State Bar Association to the President Recommending the Creation of an International Court of Arbitration* (privately printed, n.d.), pp. 3–5; Hill, *Problem of a World Court,* p. 9.

8. Hill to Holls, Jan. 23, Feb. 3, 9, Mar. 22, 1899, Holls to Hill, Feb. 4, 24, Mar. 1, 2, 15, 21, 1899, HP.

9. Hill to A.D. White, Apr. 7, 1899, WP.

10. Andrew D. White, *Autobiography of Andrew Dickson White* (New York: Century Co., 1905), 2: 250–51; A.D. White to Hill, Apr. 21, 1899, Holls to Hill, Mar. 15, 1899, Hay to Hill, July 22, 1901, HP.

11. A.D. White to Hill, Apr. 21, 1899, S. Newel to Hill, Apr. 24, 1899, HP; White, *Autobiography,* 2: 256.

12. Scott, *The Hague Conventions,* pp. 41–81, 100–129, 163–77, 220–28; Scott, *Instructions,* p. 37; A.D. White to Juliet Hill, June 5, 1899, Holls to Hill, May 31, 1899, HP.

13. Holls to Hill, May 31, June 26, 1899, HP; White to Hay, June 2, 1899 (telegram), William McKinley Papers, Library of Congress, microfilm, series 1, reel 7; Holls, *Peace Conference,* pp. 246–51; White, *Autobiography,* 2: 293–321; Margaret Robin-

son, *Arbitration and the Hague Peace Conferences, 1899 and 1907* (Philadelphia: University of Pennsylvania, 1936), pp. 69–83; Calvin D. Davis, *The United States and the First Hague Peace Conference* (Ithaca: Cornell University Press, 1962), pp. 151–61.

14. Holls to Hill, May 31, June 13, 26, 1899, HP; Holls, *Peace Conference*, pp. 228–30; White, *Autobiography*, 2: 259, 263, 266, 280; White to Hay, May 24, 1899 (telegram), William McKinley Papers, Library of Congress, microfilm, series 1, reel 7.

15. A.D. White to Juliet Hill, June 5, 1899, Holls to Hill, June 5, 13, 26, 1899, HP; Scott, *Instructions*, p. 23.

16. Hill to Holls, June 15, 1899, HP; Hill to A.D. White, Sept. 25, 1899, WP.

17. Hill to Hay, Sept. 28, 1899, HP; George H. Ryden, *The Foreign Policy of the United States in Relation to Samoa* (New Haven: Yale University Press, 1933), pp. 558–74; U.S., Department of State, *Papers Relating to the Foreign Relations of the United States, 1899* (Washington: Government Printing Office, 1901), pp. 669–70.

18. Hill to Hay, Sept. 26, 1899, Hay to Hill, Sept. 28, 1899, HP.

19. William M. Malloy, ed., *Treaties, Conventions, International Acts, Protocols and Agreements between the United States of America and other Powers, 1776–1909* (Washington: Government Printing Office, 1910–38), 2: 1589–95; Walter S. Penfield, "The Settlement of the Samoan Cases," *American Journal of International Law* 7 (Oct. 1913): 770.

20. *Foreign Relations, 1899*, p. XXXIV; U.S., Congress, Senate, *Second International Conference of American States*, S. Doc. 330, 57th Cong., 1st sess., 1902, pp. 4, 27–30 (hereinafter referred to as S. Doc. 330); *Second International American Conference* (Mexico City: Government Printing Office, 1902), pp.̇ 3–15 (hereafter referred to as *S.I.A.C.*); John V. Noel, *History of the Second Pan-American Congress* (Baltimore: Guggenheimer, Weil and Co., 1902), pp. 18–26; William S. Dennis, *Tacna and Arica* (New Haven: Yale University Press, 1931), pp. 174–97; Graham H. Stuart, "The Tacna-Arica Dispute," in *World Peace Foundation Pamphlets* 10 (1927): 19–28.

21. This note, not identified by date, is quoted at length in *Pan-American Congress and Arbitration* (a collection of over 100 editorials from some 60 United States newspapers, privately printed, n.d.), pp. 24–26, quoted in part in Noel, *Second Pan-American Congress*, p. 23, and referred to in *S.I.A.C.*, p. 15.

22. New York *Tribune*, May 14, 1901; *S.I.A.C.*, pp. 14–17; Noel, *Second Pan-American Congress*, pp. 27–28.

23. *S.I.A.C.*, pp. 17–20.

24. *Pan-American Congress and Arbitration*, pp. 40–43, 62–64, 67–69, 77–82, 109–19, 124–26, 157–59.

25. New York *Herald*, June 6, 9, 10, 1901; New York *Tribune*, June 22, July 9, 13, 28, 1901.

26. *S.I.A.C.*, pp. 13–14, 16–17; Noel, *Second Pan-American Congress*, p. 29.

27. *Literary Digest* 23 (July 13, 1901): 51; *ibid.* (Nov. 2, 1901): 544; Hay to Hill, Oct. 2, 1901, HP; S. Doc. 330, pp. 31–36.

28. J. Barrett to Hill, Oct. 19, 30, 1901, HP; *S.I.A.C.*, pp. 28–30; Noel, *Second Pan-American Congress*, p. 71; Thomas R. Dawley, Jr., "At the Pan-American Congress," *Outlook* 69 (Dec. 28, 1901): 1067.

29. J. Barrett to Hill, Oct. 19, 30, 1901, HP; S. Doc. 330, pp. 8–9; *Literary Digest*

23 (Dec. 28, 1901): 826; William I. Buchanan, "Latin America and the Mexican Conference," *Annals of the American Academy of Political and Social Sciences* 22 (July 1903): 52; *S.I.A.C.,* pp. 334–35.

30. J. Barrett to Hill, Nov. 19, 20, 1901, HP.

31. S. Doc. 330, pp. 10–11, 36–98 *passim;* Scott, *The Hague Conventions,* pp. xxii–xxxiii; Helen M. Cory, *Compulsory Arbitration of International Disputes* (New York: Columbia University Press, 1932), p. 60.

32. S. Doc. 330, pp. 11–12, 35, 139–43; *S.I.A.C.,* pp. 295–310; J. Barrett to Hill, Dec. 20, 1901, HP; Cory, *Compulsory Arbitration,* p. 61 n.

CHAPTER 5

1. J. Van Voorhis to Hill, Sept. 29, Oct. 6, 1898, Platt to Hill, Oct. 29, 1898 (telegram), B. Odell to Hill, Oct. 29, 1898 (telegram), Hill to Platt, Aug. 30, Oct. 29, 1898, Hill to B. Odell, Oct. 29, 1898, HP.

2. David J. Hill, *Greater America. Address . . . Delivered at the Annual Banquet of the Rochester Chamber of Commerce, December 8, 1898* (Washington, D.C.: Judd & Detweiler, Printers, 1898).

3. Washington *Evening Star,* Dec. 17, 1898; David J. Hill, "The Expansion of Civilization," MS of address delivered to the Baptist Social Union of Washington, Dec. 16, 1898, HP.

4. David J. Hill, "The War and the Extension of Civilization," *Forum* 26 (Feb. 1899): 650–55.

5. See press clippings, HP; H.C. Lodge to Hill, Jan. 7, 1899, HP.

6. David J. Hill, "The Original Territory of the United States," *National Geographic Magazine* 10 (Mar. 1899): 73–92; *Washington Post,* Feb. 22, 1899; David J. Hill, *George Washington as the Interpreter of His Time,* in *Historical Papers of the Society of the Sons of the Ameri can Revolution in the District of Columbia,* no. 2 (1900); *Washington Post,* Dec. 15, 1899; David J. Hill, "The Place of America in World Politics," University of Chicago, *University Record* 5 (Apr. 6, 1900): 1–7.

7. Rochester *Democrat and Chronicle* June 16, 1900.

8. Hill to F.W. Holls, n.d., Hill to L.P. Ross, July 27, 1900, HP.

9. Hill to C. Dick, Apr. 25, 1900, C. Dick to Hay [June?] 1900, Hay to Hill, n.d., Hill to O.P. Austin, July 13, 23, 1900, O.P. Austin to Hill, July 5, 23, 1900, HP.

10. Hill to C.R. Buckland, June 8, 28, 1900, Hill to P.S. Heath, n.d., HP.

11. David J. Hill, *The Vital Issue: An Honest Dollar the Basis of Prosperity* (Chicago: Republican National Committee, [1900]), pp. 1–3; P.S. Heath to Hill, Aug. 15, 31, 1900, J. Boos to Hill, Sept. 8, 1900, HP.

12. David J. Hill, *The Fiction of "Imperialism." The Sovereignty of the Nation the Safeguard of Self-Government* [Republican National Commitee, 1900].

13. P.S. Heath to Hill, Aug. 31, Sept. 1, 1900, Hill to D.T. Hill, Sept. 12, 1900, HP; Thomas A. Bailey, "Was the Presidential Election of 1900 a Mandate on Imperialism?" *Mississippi Valley Historical Review* 24 (June 1937): 43–52.

14. P.S. Heath to Hill, Aug. 27, 1900, C.R. Dean to Heath, Oct. 8, 1900, Heath to Dean, Oct. 10, 1900, HP; Hill to A.D. White, Oct. 14, 1900, WP.

15. Hill to W.F. Aldrich, Mar. 23, 1900, Aldrich to Hill, Mar. 27, 1900, Hill to A.G. Warren, Oct. 21, 1899, Hill to A.J. Ramaker, Feb. 27, 1900, Hill to R.C. Dryer, Mar. 22, 1900, HP; John Barrett, "An American School of Diplomacy," *Harper's Weekly* 44 (Mar. 3, 1900): 194.

16. At the Fourteenth Annual Convention of the Association of Colleges and Preparatory Schools of the Middle States and Maryland, held at the University of Pennsylvania, Nov. 30 and Dec. 1, 1900, Hill spoke on "Preparation for the Administrative and Diplomatic Service of the Government" (Philadelphia *Public Ledger,* Dec. 1, 1900). At the 1902 commencement of Union College he spoke on "The Public Influence of Scholarship," emphasizing preparation for career diplomatic service (*Schenectady Union,* June 11, 1902). To the alumni of Massachusetts Institute of Technology in Dec. 1900, he stressed the necessity of a career consular service (David J. Hill, *Our Commercial Expansion,* reprint from the *Technology Review* 3, no. 2 [Boston: George E. Ellis, Printer, 1901]).

17. M. Caudel, *School of Comparative Jursiprudence and Diplomacy* (translated by Herman Schoenfeld from an article in *Revue Internationale L'Enseignment,* Paris, Oct. 1899; Washington: The Columbian University, [1899]), pp. 1–3; C.W. Needham to Hill, Jan. 12, 24, 27, 1899, HP; *Washington Post,* Nov. 6, 1899.

18. Hill to E.M. Moore, Mar. 23, 1900, Hill to F.T. Gates, Jan. 16, 1902, HP.

19. A.D. White to Hill, Jan. 17, 1902, May 20, 1903, Hill to F.T. Gates, Jan. 31, 1902, HP.

20. Hill to F.T. Gates, Jan. 16, 22, 31, Feb. 13, Oct. 17, 1902, F.T. Gates to Hill, Jan. 17, Oct. 27, Nov. 28, 1902, S.J. Murphy to Hill, Jan. 20, Mar. 4, 17, 20, 24, Apr. 15, May 1, 1902, Hill to S.J. Murphy, Jan. 22, Feb. 12, 13, Mar. 15, 21, 25, Apr. 30, 1902, HP.

21. Hill to Carnegie, Jan. 28, 1903, Hill to R.D. Harlan, Apr. 22, 1907, HP.

22. David J. Hill, *A Plan for a School of the Political Sciences* [published by the George Washington University in 1907 on the occasion of "The George Washington University Movement"]; Hill to A.D. White, Mar. 14, 1909, Hill to W.B. Stephens, Mar. 16, 1925, HP.

CHAPTER 6

1. *Harper's Weekly* 45 (Aug. 10, 1901): 808; New York *World,* May 15, 1900, Feb. 20, 1901; Washington *Post,* June 18, 1899; Juliet Hill to A.D. White, Mar. 15, Oct. 10, 1901, WP; Hill to H.C. Bolton, Dec. 26, 1901, Hill to R. Johnson, Apr. 14, 1902, Hill to O. James, Dec. 28, 1901, HP.

2. Hill to T.R. Platt, July 12, 1901, Hill to D.R. Francis, Aug. 25, 1901, Hay to Hill, Aug. 24, 1901, HP.

3. Hill to Hay, Aug. 25, 1901, HP.

4. Juliet Hill to A.D. White, Feb. 16, 1902, WP; Hill to White, May 22, 1902, Hill to F.W. Holls, Mar. 13, 1902, W.H. Michael to Hill, Mar. 15, 1902, HP.

5. Hill to W.H. Michael, Mar. 24, 1902, F.W. Holls to Hill, Mar. 25, 1902, J.H. Worman to Hill, Mar. 31, 1902, J.H. Worman to L. Abbott, Mar. 31, 1902, W.I. Buchanan to Hill, Apr. 5, 1902, J. Barrett to Hill, Apr. 6, 1902, J. Van Voorhis to

C.N. Bliss, Apr. 7, 1902, Hill to W. I. Buchanan, Apr. 11, 1902, Hill to J.S. Fassett, Apr. 14, 1902, C. Schurz to J. Van Voorhis, Apr. 29, 1902, J. Van Voorhis to Hill, Apr. 30, 1902, O.H. Platt to Juliet Hill, July 31, 1902, HP.

6. Boston *Herald*, Mar. 31, 1902; New York *Sun*, Apr. 15, 1902; F.W. Holls to Hill, Sept. 4, 1902, M.S. Quay and B. Penrose to T. Roosevelt, Aug. 6, 1902 (telegram, copy), HP; F.W. Holls to A.D. White, Apr. 27, 1902, WP.

7. W.H. Michael to Hill, Aug. 1, 1902, HP.

8. Hill to T. Platt, Aug. 4, 1902, J. Van Voorhis to Hill, Aug. 4, 5, 6, 7, 8, 11, Sept. 6, 1902, W.H. Michael to Hill, Aug. 5, 10, 11, 1902, R. Bartholdt to Hill, Aug. 5, 1902, H.C. Lodge to Hill, Aug. 6, 1902, J.T. Morgan to Mrs. Hill, Aug. 6, 1902, G.B. Cortelyou to Hill, Aug. 7, 1902 (telegram), J. Wilson to Mrs. Hill, Aug. 7, 29, 1902, H.S. Boutell to Hill, Aug. 7, 1902, J.J. McCook to Hill, Aug. 8, 1902, J.M. Ives to Hill, Aug. 8, 1902, G.S. Hall to Hill, Aug. 8, 1902, J.A. McCall to W.H. Michael, Aug. 8, 1902, L.P. Ross to Hill, Aug. 9, 1902, C.R. Dean to Hill, Aug. 9, 1902, Armour and Co. to T. Roosevelt, Aug. 11, 1902 (copy), S.M. Cullom to Hill, Aug. 11, 1902, G. Cortelyou to D.B. Henderson, Aug. 12, 1902 (copy), J.B. Foracker to Mrs. Hill, Aug. 14, 1902, HP.

9. Hill to T. Platt, July 12, 1901, H.C. Lodge to Hill, Aug. 6, 1902, R. Bartholdt to T. Roosevelt, Aug. 5, 1902 (copy), T. Brentano to T. Roosevelt, Aug. 6, 1902, Hill to M.D. Learned, Sept. 13, 1900, M.D. Learned to Hill, Sept. 19, 1900, F.W. Holls to Hill, Oct. 9, 1900, HP.

10. Hill to Hay, Aug. 3, 1902, Hay to Hill, Aug. 4, 9, 1902, Roosevelt to Hay, Aug. 7, 1902 (copy), HP. Hay's letter to the President is quoted in Alfred L.P. Dennis, *Adventures in American Diplomacy, 1896-1906* (New York: E.P. Dutton and Co., 1928), p. 522.

11. H.S. Boutell to Hill, Aug. 30, 1902, Armour and Co. to Postmaster-General Payne, Aug. 27, 1902 (telegram), S.M. Cullom to Hay, Aug. 27, 1902 (telegram), C. Stewart to Roosevelt, Aug. 28, 1902 (telegram), F. W. Holls to Hill, Sept. 4, 1902, HP. For "Holland's" article see the Philadelphia *Press*, Sept. 4, 1902.

12. *New York Times*, Sept. 27, 1902.

13. Hill to A.D. White, Oct. 17, 1902, Mar. 5, 1903, F.W. Holls to White, Feb. 3, 1903, WP; Hill to J.M. Lot, Dec. 13, 1902, Hill to J.S. Fassett, Jan. 9, 1903, Holls to Hill, June 22, 1903, HP; New York *Tribune*, Jan. 6, 1903.

14. Hill to L.E. Quigg, Jan. 7, 1903, HP; Hill to A.D. White, Feb. 15, 1903, WP.

15. Memorandum dated Jan. 7, 1903, HP.

16. Hill to Hay, June 12, 1903, No. 16, Diplomatic Despatches, Switzerland, vol. 33, RDS; Hill to A.D. White, May 22, 1903, WP.

17. Hill to A.D. White, Jan. 4, 1904, WP; W.C. Morey quoted from the Rochester *Post Express* in *A History of Europe from the Point of View of the Modern Publicist*, a Longmans, Green and Co. brochure, HP; *American Historical Review* 11 (Jan. 1906): 358–60; *American Journal of International Law* 1 (July 1907): 797–800; *Catholic World* 82 (Nov. 1905): 263–66; New York *Tribune*, Aug. 19, 1905; New York *Sun*, Aug. 13, 1905.

18. *American Historical Review* 12 (Apr. 1907): 617–19; *American Journal of International Law* 1 (Apr. 1907): 556–58; *Catholic World* 85 (May 1907): 258–59; "His Magnum Opus," *American Monthly Review of Reviews* 32 (Aug. 1905): 136–37.

19. Holls to A.D. White, Feb. 3, 1903, WP; Holls to Hill, Jan. 23, Apr. 17, June 22,

1903, A. Shaw to Hill, July 28, 1903, W. Loeb to Hill, Oct. 7, 1904, C.R. Dean to Hill, Oct. 7, 1904, A. Adee to Hill, Oct. 8, 1904, Hill to Hay, Oct. 12, 1904, Hay to Hill, Oct. 21, 1904, A. Shaw to Roosevelt, Oct. 18, 1904 (copy), Shaw to R.W. Patterson, Oct. 18, 1904 (copy), Shaw to W. Loeb, Oct. 27, 1904 (copy), Shaw to Hill, Oct. 22, 28, 1904, HP.

20. Juliet Hill to A.D. White, Nov. 8, 1905, WP.

21. *Ibid.*; Hill to A.D. White, Dec. 2, 1905, WP.

22. Hill to Hay, Mar. 9, 1905 (personal), Hill to Hay, Mar. 10, 1905, no. 70, Diplomatic Despatches, Switzerland, vol. 34 RDS; Hay to Hill, Mar. 9, 1905, no. 71, Diplomatic Instructions, Switzerland, vol. 3, RDS; Chentung Liangcheng to Hay, Mar. 2, 1905 (copy). A. Adee to Hill, Mar. 21, 1905, Hill to Wu Ting-fang, Mar. 21, Apr. 5, 1905, Wu Ting-fang to Hill, May 1, 26, 1905, HP.

23. A. Lysen, *History of the Carnegie Foundation and of the Peace Palace at The Hague,* vol. 28 of *Bibliotheca Visseriana* (Leiden: E.J. Brill, 1934), pp. 2–95; Holls to Hill, Jan. 23, 1903, A.D. White to Hill, May 20, 1903, HP; Holls to White, Feb. 3, 1903, WP.

24. Carnegie to Hill, June 18, 20, 1906, HP.

25. Lysen, *Carnegie Foundation,* pp. 96–97; Carnegie to Hill, July 10, 1906 (two letters), HP.

26. Hill to Carnegie, July 18, 21, 1906, CP.

27. Carnegie to Hill, July 28, Aug. 13, 1906, Feb. 9, 1907, HP; Hill to Carnegie, Jan. 21, 1907, CP.

28. A. Shaw to Hill, May 23, 1906, C.R. Dean to Hill, Apr. 19, 1906, Root to Hill, Apr. 18, 1906, HP.

29. Hill to E. Root, May 2, 1906 (personal), Diplomatic Despatches, Netherlands, vol. 42, RDS; Root to Hill, June 11, 1906, HP.

30. A. Adee to Hill, Jan. 23, 1907, A. Shaw to Hill, Mar. 3, 1907, HP.

31. James B. Scott, ed., *Instructions to the American Delegates to The Hague Peace Conferences and their Official Reports* (New York: Oxford University Press, 1916), p. 88.

32. Hill to A.D. White, July 13, 1907, HP; James B. Scott, *The Hague Peace Conferences of 1899 and 1907* (Baltimore: The Johns Hopkins Press, 1909), 1: 156, 170–71.

33. James B. Scott, ed., *The Proceedings of the Hague Peace Conferences, the Conference of 1907* (New York: Oxford University Press, 1920), 1: 329; 2: 245; New York *Herald,* Mar. 26, 1908; Hill to Carnegie, Oct. 10–13, 1907, CP.

34. Scott, *Instructions,* pp. 77–80; *The Hague Peace Conferences,* 1:330–85, 423–60; Margaret Robinson, *Arbitration and the Hague Peace Conferences, 1899 and 1907* (Philadelphia: University of Pennsylvania, 1936), pp. 52–67, 98–105; James B. Scott, ed, *The Hague Conventions and Declarations of 1899 and 1907,* 3d ed. (New York: Oxford University Press, 1918), pp. 41–219.

35. Hill to Carnegie, Oct. 10–13, 1907, CP.

36. Juliet Hill to A.D. White, Nov. 24, 1907, WP; Hill to C. Tower, Jan. 16, 1908, HP.

CHAPTER 7

1. C.R. Dean to Hill, Jan. 9, 1908, HP; Tower to Root, Mar. 31. 1908 (telegram), file 2582/23, Root to Tower, Mar. 25, 1908 (telegram), file 2401/9, SDNF 1906–10; *New York Times,* Nov. 9, 1907.

2. Tower to Root, Jan. 1, 1908, Despatch no. 1279, file 3371/16, SDNF 1906–10; J.W. Garrett to Hill, Feb. 8, 1908, B.J. Wheeler to C.M. Gayley, Apr. 28, 1908, HP; Hill to Carnegie, Apr. 16, 1908, CP; *New York Times,* Mar. 29, Apr. 5, 1908; Fürst von Bülow, *Denkwürdigkeiten* (Berlin: im verlag Ullstein [1930–31]), 1: 573.

3. Hill to A.D. White, May 3, 1908, WP; Hill to Root, Mar. 10, 1908 (copy), HP; Hill to Root, Apr. 13, 1908, file 2401/32, SDNF 1906–10; New York *Tribune,* Mar. 27, 1908.

4. *New York Times,* Mar. 26, 27, 28, 29, 1908; New York *World,* Mar. 26, 1908; New York *American,* Mar. 26, 1908; New York *Herald,* Mar. 26, 27, 28, 29, 1908; New York *Sun,* Mar. 26, 29, 30, 1908; Boston *Herald,* Mar. 26, 27, 1908; London *Times,* Mar. 28, 29, 1908; "The Lesson of the Hill Muddle," *Literary Digest* 36 (Apr. 11, 1908): 508–10; F.P. Dunne, "Mr. Dooley on Diplomacy," *American Magazine* 66 (June 1908): 109.

5. Lloyd C. Griscom, *Diplomatically Speaking* (Boston: Little, Brown and Co., 1940), pp. 298–301.

6. Tower to Root, Mar. 27, 1908 (telegram), file 2401/15 (portions of letter to Roosevelt on Mar. 16 quoted), Tower to Root, Apr. 3, 1908, Despatch no. 1334, file 2401/26, SDNF 1906–10.

7. Freiherrn von Schoen, *Erlebtes: Beiträge zur politischen Geschichte der neuesten Zeit* (Stuttgart: Deutsche Verlags-Anstalt, 1921), pp. 91–92.

8. Philadelphia *Public Ledger,* June 25, 1921.

9. Tower to Root, Mar. 27, 1908 (telegram), file 2401/15 SDNF 1906–10; Tower to Root, Mar. 21, 1908 (telegram), Root to Tower, Mar. 25, 1908 (telegram), file 2401/9, SDNF 1906–10; *Washington Post,* Mar. 28, 1908.

10. C.R. Dean to Hill, Mar. 31, 1908, HP; New York *Herald,* Mar. 28, 1908; Griscom, *Diplomatically Speaking,* p. 302.

11. Private despatch from Elmer Roberts to Howard N. Thompson, Mar. 26, 1908 (copy), HP; New York *Tribune,* Mar. 27, 1908; New York *Sun,* Mar. 29, 1908; Tower to Root, Apr. 3, 1908, Despatch no. 1334, file 2401/26, SDNF 1906–10.

12. New York *Tribune,* Mar. 31, Apr. 1, 1908; Root to Tower, Mar. 30, 1908 (telegram), file 2401/17, SDNF 1906–10.

13. *New York Times,* May 3, 17, June 15, 1908; Hill to Root, June 13, 1908, Despatch no. 1, file 2401/45, Hill to Root, June 15, 1908, Despatch no. 2, file 2401/46, SDNF 1906–10; Hill to Carnegie, June 16, 1908, CP.

14. David J. Hill, "Die zeitgenossische Entwicklung der Diplomatie," *Neue Revue* 1 (July 2, 1908): 1296–1304; Hill to J.B. Scott, Sept. 21, 1908, HP; C.A. Bratter, *David Jayne Hill und die amerikanische Diplomatie,* Heft 22, Persönlichkeiten (Charlottenberg: Virgil Verlag, [1908]), "The Week," *Nation* 87 (July 16, 1908): 45.

15. Washington *Post,* June 21, 1908; *New York Times,* June 21, Sept. 15, 16, Dec. 3, 1908; New York *Evening Mail,* Sept. 15, 1908; New York *Sun,* Sept. 15, 16, 1908; E. Root to Hill, Nov. 23, 1908, HP.

16. Hill to Carnegie, Dec. 8, 1908, Mar. 12, 13, Apr. 8, Nov. 22, 1909, CP; Hill to R. Bacon, Feb. 18, 1909, file 2401/58, SDNF 1906–10; Root to Hill, Jan. 18, Mar. 27, 1909, HP; Memorandum on Resignation from Berlin, 1911, HP.

17. Hill to Root, Nov. 9, 1908, file 3371/55, SDNF 1906–10; Hill to W. McCarroll, Jan. 20, 1909, HP.

18. See e.g., "The Ambassadorship Muddle," *Nation* 86 (Apr. 2, 1908): 298; "Our Embassies and Their Needs," *American Monthly Review of Reviews* 37 (May 1908): 521.

19. *Congressional Record,* 60th Cong., 1st sess., vol. 42, pt. 5 (Apr. 18, 1908), 4919–28; *Statutes at Large* 36 (1911): 917; "Permanent Housing for Diplomats," *American Monthly Review of Reviews* 43 (June 1911): 690–94; *New York Times*, Sept. 9, 1931.

20. Hill to Root, July 9, 1908, Despatch no. 23, file 3371/44, Hill to Root, July 16, 1908, Despatch no. 30, file 3371/45, Hill to Root, Nov. 9, 1908, file 3371/55, A. Adee to Hill, Sept. 11, 1908, Instruction no. 34, file 3371/45, R. Bacon to Hill, Nov. 16, 1908, file 3371/54, SDNF 1906–10; *New York Times,* Nov. 29, 1908.

21. Hill to Knox, Mar. 19, 1910, Despatch no. 642, file 3371/78, Hill to Knox, Apr. 16, 1910, Despatch no. 668, file 3371/81, SDDF 1910–29; New York *Sun,* Mar. 24, 1910; Memorandum on Resignation, HP.

22. Philip C. Jessup, *Elihu Root* (New York: Dodd, Mead and Co., 1938), 2: 79–80; James B. Scott, ed., *Instructions to the American Delegates to the Hague Peace Conferences and their Official Reports* (New York: Oxford University Press, 1916), p. 79.

23. Root to Tower, Apr. 13, 1908, Instruction no. 813, file 11313/2A, SDNF 1906–10; Memoranda from the German Ambassador to the President, Mar. 5, Apr. 7, 1908, files 11313/1, 11313/2, Root to von Sternburg, Apr. 8, 1908, file 11313/2, SDNF 1906–10.

24. Memorandum from the German Ambassador to the President, Apr. 18, 1908, Root to von Sternburg, May 14, 1908, file 11313/5, von Bernstorff to Root, May 1, 1909 (memorandum relating to the German proposal of the year before enclosed), file 11313/12–13, SDNF 1906–10.

25. Root to Tower, Apr. 13, 1908, Instruction no. 813, file 11313/2A, Tower to Root, June 3, 1908, Despatch no. 1395, file 11313/7, SDNF 1906–10.

26. Hill to Carnegie, June 16, 1908, CP.

27. Hill to Root, July 23, 1908, Despatch no. 33 (memorandum by Kriege on Georgia Railroad case enclosed), file 11313/8–9, Hill to Root, Dec. 10, 1908, Despatch no. 163, file 11313/11, SDNF 1906–10.

28. Root to Hill, Jan. 13, 1909, Instruction no. 85, file 11313/11, SDNF 1906–10.

29. Hill to Carnegie, Feb. 20, 1909, CP.

30. Hill to Carnegie, May 5, 6, 1909, CP; Hill to Root, Oct. 17, 1908, Despatch no. 106, file 11313/10, SDNF 1906–10.

31. Hill to Knox, Apr. 30, 1909, Despatch no. 292, file 11313/14, von Bernstorff to Knox, May 1, 1909 (memorandum enclosed), file 11313/12–13, SDNF 1906–10.

32. Hill to Carnegie, Jan. 18, 1910, CP.

33. Hill to Knox, Feb. 24, 1910, Despatch no. 616, file 11313/18, SDNF 1906–10; David J. Hill, *Impressions of the Kaiser* (New York: Harper and Bros., 1918), pp. 102–3.

34. Hill to Carnegie, June 8, July 1, 1909, CP; Burton J. Hendrick, *The Life of Andrew Carnegie* (Garden City, N.Y.: Doubleday, Doran & Co., 1932), 2: 324–25; Carnegie to Hill, Feb. 12, 1910, HP.

35. Hendrick, *Carnegie,* 2: 325–28; Taft to Carnegie, Dec. 25, 1909 (copy), Carnegie to Hill, Dec. 27, 1909, HP.

36. Hill to Carnegie, Jan. 18, 1910, CP; Hill to Roosevelt, Jan. 19, Feb. 11, 21, 1910 (telegrams), Roosevelt to Hill, Feb. 8, 13, 26, Apr. 14, 1910 (telegrams), Roosevelt to Hill, Feb. [?], Jan. [*sic,* Feb.] 27, Mar. 19, 24, Apr. 11, 14, 15, 29, 30, 1910,

Hill to Roosevelt, Jan. 3, Mar. 10, Apr. 1, 6, 9, 20, 27, May 2, 1910, von Schoen to Hill, Mar. 7, Apr. 1, 9, 1910, HP.

37. Hill to Carnegie, Apr. 22, 1910, CP.

38. T. Roosevelt to G.O. Trevelyan, Oct. 1, 1911, Theodore Roosevelt, *The Letters of Theodore Roosevelt,* ed. Elting E. Morison et al., 8 vols. (Cambridge, Mass.: Harvard University Press, 1954), 7: 376–78; Hendrick, *Carnegie,* 2: 330–31; Joseph C. Grew, *Turbulent Era: A Diplomatic Record of Forty Years, 1904–1945* (Boston: Houghton Mifflin Co., 1952), 1: 64–65; *New York Times,* Apr. 10, 24, 1910; von Schoen, *Erlebtes,* p. 123; Hill to Roosevelt, May 8, 1910 (telegram), HP.

39. Hill to Carnegie, May 17, 1910, CP.

40. Carnegie to Hill, June 7, 1910, HP; T. Roosevelt to G.O. Trevelyan, Oct. 1, 1911, Roosevelt, *Letters,* 7: 377, 378.

41. Carnegie to Hill, Feb. 12, 13, 1910, HP; Hendrick, *Carnegie,* 2: 326, 328–31.

42. Hill to Carnegie, Mar. 26, 1911, CP; Hill to W.H. Carpenter, May 27, 1911, HP.

43. David Jayne Hill, *World Organization as Affected by the Nature of the Modern State* (New York: Columbia University Press, 1911), *passim.*

44. Hill to Carnegie, Jan. 18, 1910, CP.

CHAPTER 8

1. Wilson to Hill, Mar. 6, 1911 (telegram), file 123.H55/81a, SDDF 1910–29; Draft of letter, Hill to Taft, June 1, 1911, marked "not sent," HC.

2. U.S. Department of State, *Papers Relating to the Foreign Relations of the United States, 1911* (Washington: Government Printing Office, 1918), pp. 198–201.

3. *Ibid.,* 204–7.

4. See file 123.H55, SDDF 1910–29.

5. *Foreign Relations, 1911,* pp. 208–16.

6. *Ibid.,* p. 216; J.C. Grew to Hill, July 10, 1910, HP.

7. Hill to Knox, Sept. 22, 1910, Despatch no. 801, file 611.627/140, Davis to Knox, Oct. 4, 1910, file 611.627/145, Davis to Knox, Oct. 12, 1910 (copy of Davis to Sydow, Oct. 11, 1910, enclosed), file 611.627/151, Hill to Knox, Oct. 17, 1910, Despatch no. 822, file 611.627/156, SDDF 1910–29.

8. *Foreign Relations, 1911,* pp. 219, 222, 226; Hill to Knox, Nov. 5, 1910, Despatch no. 834, file 611.627/206, Bradley to Knox, Nov. 8, 1910 (telegram), file 611.627/160, SDDF 1910–29.

9. Hill to G. Scholle, Nov. 17, 1910, G. Scholle to Hill, Nov. 11, 1910, HP.

10. Davis to Knox, Nov. 6, 1910 (telegram), file 611.627/159, Davis to Knox, Nov. 8, 1910, file 611.627/215, SDDF 1910–29; *Foreign Relations, 1911,* pp. 220–21.

11. *Foreign Relations, 1911,* pp. 222–27, 230–33.

12. Memorandum on Resignation from Berlin, 1911, HP; Hill to N.M. Butler, Feb. 15, 1911, HP.

13. Hill to Wilson, Mar. 20, 1911 (telegram), Davis to Wilson, Mar. 20, 1911, file 123.H55/82, Wilson to Hill, Mar. 21, 1911 (telegram), file 123.H55/84a, SDDF 1910–29.

14. Memorandum on Resignation, HP. Hill wrote a briefer account of the events surrounding his resignation in Hill to Knox, July 3, 1911, Despatch no. 993, file 123.H55/95, SDDF 1910–29.

15. Knox to Hill, Mar. 28, 1911, HC.

16. Memorandum on Resignation, HP; Hill to Taft, Apr. 12, 1911, HC; Hill to Knox, Apr. 12, 1911, file 123.H55/86, SDDF 1910–29; *Washington Evening Star*, Apr. 14, 1911; New York *Herald*, Apr. 15, 1911; *New York Times*, Apr. 15, 1911; New York *World*, Apr. 15, 1911; Philadelphia *Public Ledger*, Apr. 15, 1911.

17. Memorandum on Resignation, HP; Taft to Hill, Apr. 14, 1911, HC.

18. Hill to Carnegie, June 11, 1911, CP; Memorandum on Resignation, HP.

19. New York *Tribune,* Apr. 16, 1911; *New York Times,* Apr. 16, 1911; New York *Herald,* Apr. 22, 1911; New York *Evening Post,* May 4, 1911; Memorandum on Resignation, HP.

20. Taft to Hill, May 21, 1911 (copy), file 123.H55/ 86, SDDF 1910–29.

21. Memorandum on Resignation, HP; New York *Sun,* Apr. 25, 1911.

22. Hill to Carnegie, June 3, 11, July 4, 1911, CP.

23. Hill to Carnegie, July 18, 1911, CP.

24. Memorandum dated Holland House, New York City, Nov. 23, 1911, recording Taft's statement as given to Hill by Carnegie on the evening of Carnegie's return from Washington, HP; Memorandum on Resignation, HP.

25. *New York Times,* Aug. 3, 1912; T. St. John Gaffney to Hill, July 30, 1912, HP.

26. Memorandum on Resignation, HP.

27. *Washington Evening Star,* Apr. 14, 1911; New York *Herald,* Apr. 15, 1911; *New York Times,* Apr. 15, 23, 1911; New York *World,* Apr. 15, 16, 22, 1911; New York *American,* May 19, 1911; Boston *Herald,* Apr. 20, May 7, 1911; *Boston Transcript,* Apr. 30, 1911; Philadelphia *Public Ledger,* Apr. 15, 20, 1911; Cincinnati *Inquirer,* Apr. 20, 1911.

28. "Why Ambassador Hill Comes Home," *Literary Digest* 42 (May 13, 1911): 933–34.

29. Joseph C. Grew, *Turbulent Era: A Diplomatic Record of Forty Years, 1904–1945* (Boston: Houghton Mifflin Co., 1952), 1: 64; Hill to Carnegie, June 11, 1911, CP; [W.M.] Sloane to Hill, July 21, 1911, HP.

30. Memorandum, dated Kiel, June 28, 1911, HP.

CHAPTER 9

1. Hill to T. Stanton, Mar. 12, 1909, Hill to J.B. Scott, July 24, 1922, Hill to R.U. Johnson, Feb. 21, 1910, HP.

2. Sidney B. Fay, review of David J. Hill's *Diplomacy of the Age of Absolutism,* in *American Historical Review* 20 (Feb. 1915): 401–2.

3. Hill to J.B. Scott, July 24, 1922, Hill to N.M. Butler, Apr. 8, 1922, J.B. Scott to Hill, June 19, 1922, HP.

4. David J. Hill, "In Memoriam, Doctor Henry Campbell Black, October 17, 1860–March 19, 1927," *Constitutional Review* 11 (Apr. 1927): 70. This statement is also in David J. Hill, "Policy of the Association," *Bulletin of the National Association for Constitutional Government,* no. 13, (Dec. 1929), p. 2.

5. David J. Hill, "The Crisis in Constitutionalism," *North American Review* 198 (Dec. 1913): 769–78; [George Harvey], "For Constitutional Clubs," *ibid.,* p. 763; J.H. Gallinger to Hill, Dec. 17, 1913, F.B. Brandegee to Hill, Feb. 13, 1914, HP. The Hill Papers contain many newspaper clippings on the article.

6. David J. Hill, *The People's Government* (New York: D. Appleton and Co., 1915); David J. Hill, *Americanism: What It Is* (New York: D. Appleton and Co., 1916). In 1914 Houghton Mifflin published *Open Air Politics,* which Hill had written under the pseudonym "Junius Jay." An exposition of political issues ranging from labor questions to women's suffrage, it was cast in the form of the conversations of a varied assortment of people on a wilderness camping trip. Its sales were disappointing (Houghton Mifflin to Hill, Jan. 30, 1915, HP).

7. Hill, *People's Government,* pp. 211–14, 246–75; David J. Hill, "An Impending Danger to the Republic," *North American Review* 202 (Dec. 1915): 810; Hill, *Americanism,* pp. 40–41, 55, 65.

8. Hill, *Americanism,* p. 34.

9. Hill, "Crisis in Constitutionalism," p. 772; David J. Hill, *Our Great Inheritance, An address before the Daughters of the American Revolution, Sons of the Revolution, and Sons of the American Revolution,* Feb. 22, 1919 (Washington: National Association for Constitutional Government [1919]).

10. Hill, *Americanism,* p. 98.

11. Hill, *People's Government,* pp. 150–51.

12. New York *Bookseller,* Dec. 15, 1917, Mar. 15, 1918.

13. P.L., "Books and Things," *New Republic* 7 (July 8, 1916): 255.

14. Chase Osborn, *The Iron Hunter* (New York: Macmillan Co., 1919), p. 260.

15. David J. Hill, "Birthday of the Constitution," *The Review* 1 (Sept. 13, 1919): 382; David J. Hill, *Three Great Traditions, An Address delivered by David Jayne Hill, at Bucknell University on Commencement Day, June 18, 1924* (privately printed, n.d.) The address was also published in part in the *National Republican,* Sept. 27, 1924.

16. Hill, "Crisis in Constitutionalism," p. 778; Hill, "Doctor Black," pp. 71–73. Among the organizers were John W. Foster, George Harvey, Archibald Hopkins, John Edson, Frank W. Hackett, Harvey S. Wiley, Samuel H. Greene, Walter S. Penfield, Charles H. Butler.

17. *Constitution of the National Association for Constitutional Government,* Article II, HP.

18. Hill, "Doctor Black," pp. 73–74; Hill, "Policy of the Association," pp. 4–5; Hill to J.G. Cutler, Jan. 22, 1920, Hill to H.S. Pritchett, Nov. 1, 1926, HP.

19. C.R. Dean to Hill, May 23, June 24, 1914, Aug. 12, 1916, Aug. 30, 1919, Hill to N.M. Butler, Sept. 14, 1918, H.C. Black to C.W. Ames, Aug. 22, 1919 (copy), Hill to S.S. Menken, June 10, 1926, HP; Washington *Herald,* May 7, 1916; *List of Members of the National Association for Constitutional Government, March 1, 1918,* HP; "Approximate Receipts & Disbursements from May 1, 1927, to May 1, 1928," memorandum in HP; Hill to H.F. Atwood, Jan. 2, 1930, HC.

20. Memorandum dated Monday, Feb. 2, 1914, HP.

21. Hill, "Policy of the Association," p. 6; S.J. Murphy to Hill, June 2, 1916, A. Hopkins to Hill, Sept. 7, 1920, Hill to H.S. Pritchett, Nov. 1, 1926, HP.

22. S.S. Menken to Hill, Mar. 31, Apr. 1, 1926, R.L. Bullard to Hill, Apr. 2, 1926, Hill to R.L. Bullard, Apr. 6, 1926, Hill to S.S. Menken, June 10, 1926,

H.F. Atwood to Hill, June 17, Aug. 4, 1927, Hill to H.S. Pritchett, Mar. 26, 1927, HP.

23. Hill, "Policy of the Association," pp. 6–8; Minutes of the Executive Committee of the Association for Constitutional Government, April 25, 1930, HC; Hill to H.F. Atwood, Jan. 2, 21, 1930, H.F. Atwood to Hill, Dec. 2, 1929, Jan. 14, 24, 1930, Hill to members of the Association for Constitutional Government, n.d., Hill to O.K. Hand, Sept. 28, 1930, HC; Hill to E.W. Hamlin, Apr. 2, 1931, HP.

24. Rochester *Post Express,* Mar. 26, 1912; *New York Times,* Sept. 22, 23, 24, 28, 1912; New York *Evening Telegram,* Sept. 25, 1912.

25. Hill to F.B. Mitchell, July 28, 1914, Hill to J.G. Cutler, Aug. 31, 1914, Hill to L.P. Ross, Sept. 2, 1914, Hill to W. Barnes, Oct. 1, 1914, HP.

26. W. Barnes to Hill, June 15, 1914 (telegram), Barnes to Hill, July 1, 1914, Hill to Barnes, Oct. 1, 1914, N.M. Butler to Hill, Sept. 5, 1914 (telegram), Hill to Butler, Sept. 5, 1914 (telegram), Hill to Butler, Sept. 6, 1914, Hill to F.B. Mitchell, Sept. 6, 1914, Hill to J.G. Cutler, Sept. 6, 1914, HP.

27. F.B. Mitchell to Hill, Sept. 8, 1914 (telegram), J.G. Cutler to Hill, Sept. 24, 29, Nov. 2, 1914, Mitchell to Hill, Sept. 30, 1914, Hill to Mitchell, Oct. 1, 1914, Hill to Cutler, Oct. 14, 1914, HP.

28. Hill to C.H. Sherrill, June 13, 1914, HP.

29. George E. Mowry, *Theodore Roosevelt and the Progressive Movement* (Madison: University of Wisconsin Press, 1946), p. 289; W. Dalliba to Hill, June 15, 1914, HP.

30. C.H. Sherrill to Hill, July 11, 1914, HP.

31. Hill to W. Barnes, June 16, 1914, W. Barnes to Hill, July 1, 1914, HP.

32. Mowry, *Roosevelt,* pp. 300–303.

33. Arthur S. Link, *Wilson: The New Freedom* (Princeton: Princeton University Press, 1956), pp. 304–10.

34. Hill to G.H. Lorimer, Apr. 8, 1914, HP; David J. Hill, "The Meaning of the Hay-Pauncefote Treaty," *Saturday Evening Post* 186 (May 16, 1914): 3–4, 81–82. Hill also published a condensed version of this argument in "Supremacy in the Panama Canal," *American Monthly Review of Reviews* 49 (June 1914): 722–25.

35. *Congressional Record,* 63d Cong., 2d sess., vol. 51, pp. 8628–30, and Appendix, pp. 492–94; Link, *Wilson: The New Freedom,* pp. 311–14.

36. Rochester *Post Express,* Dec. 11, 1913.

37. David J. Hill, "Why Do We Have a Diplomatic Service?" *Harper's Magazine* 128 (Jan. 1914): 188–97; "Shall We Standardize Our Diplomatic Service?" *ibid.* (Apr. 1914): 690–98; "Can Our Diplomatic Service be Made More Efficient?" *ibid.* 130 (Jan. 1915); 190–98; "Material Needs of Our Diplomatic Service," *ibid.* (Feb. 1915), 148–56.

38. David J. Hill, "National Defense, An address . . . delivered before the Society of the Genesee, . . . New York, . . . January 22, 1916," HP. On another occasion Hill criticized Wilson for permitting an invasion of at least two states of the Union by armed forces and the shooting down not only of civilians but also uniformed soldiers on our own soil (David J. Hill, *The Essential Elements of Foreign Policy, An Address delivered before the National Conventions of the Navy League of the United States, Washington, D.C., April 10–13, 1916* [Pamphlet no. 47, Navy League of the United States, Washington, D.C.]).

39. David J. Hill, "President Wilson's Administration of Foreign Affairs," *North American Review* 204 (Sept. 1916): 344–61, (Oct. 1916): 550–74.

40. W.R. Willcox to Hill, Sept. 8, 1916, D.S. Barry to Hill, Aug. 8, Sept. 7, 11, 28, 1916, HP; Rochester *Democrat and Chronicle,* Oct. 5, 1916.

41. Hill, *Americanism,* pp. 187–88, 219–220; Hill, "National Defense," HP; David J. Hill, "The Protection of American Citizens," *North American Review* 203 (Mar. 1916): 383–85; David J. Hill, "A Defensible Program of Defense," *American Defense* 1 (Feb. 1916): 42, 56; David J. Hill, "World Politics as Affecting the United States, An address to the National Security Congress, Washington, D.C., January 20–22, 1916, held under the auspices of the National Security League," HP.

42. Hill, *Americanism,* p. 190; David J. Hill, "Address . . . at the Luncheon of the American Defense Society [New York], February 22, 1916," HP.

43. Hill, *Americanism,* pp. 213–14; David J. Hill, "The Aims and Principles of the Sons of the American Revolution," an address before the Sons of the American Revolution, Washington, D.C., January 16, 1918, HP; Hill, "Address . . . at the Luncheon of the American Defense Society [New York], February 22, 1916," HP.

44. David J. Hill, "An Impending Danger to the Republic," *North American Review* 202 (Dec. 1915): 801–11.

45. Boston *Herald,* Oct. 20, 1915; David J. Hill, *Industrial Defense, Address . . . at the Home Market Club Dinner, February 25, 1916* (Boston: Home Market Club, [1916]); David J. Hill and George E. Roberts, *Economic Readjustment in the United States After the European War, Addresses Before The Economic Club of Portland, Maine, February 26, 1916* (Portland: The Economic Club of Portland, 1916), also published in the *National Economic League Quarterly* 1 (May 1916): 49–57; Hill, *Americanism,* pp. 235–68.

46. New York *Journal of Commerce,* Dec. 13, 1915. See also New York *World,* Dec. 12, 1915, and Rochester *Union and Advertiser,* Dec. 11, 1915, for critical comment.

47. See, e.g., *New York Times,* Dec. 4, 1915; New York *Sun,* Dec. 3, 8, 1915; New York *Commercial,* Dec. 3, 1915; New York *American Economist,* Dec. 10, 1915; New York *Globe,* Dec. 11, 1915.

48. Hill, *Americanism,* p. 265; Hill, *Industrial Defense,* p. 8.

49. T.O. Marvin to Hill, Feb. 28, Oct. 7, 1916, C.H. Sherrill to Hill, Oct. 23, 24, 1916, R.F. Griggs to Hill, Oct. 25, 1916, HP; David J. Hill, *American Industrial Defense* (Boston: Home Market Club, [1916]).

50. T.O. Marvin to G. Harvey, Dec. 8, 1915 (copy), Marvin to H.F. Lippit, [Oct. 1916] (copy), Hill to E.B. Hooker, July 26, 1916, HP; Rochester *Times,* Feb. 17, 1916; Albany *Knickerbocker Press,* Feb. 20, 1916; *New York Times,* Feb. 15, 16, 17, 1916.

51. Hill to G. Aldridge, July 20, 26, 1916, HP.

52. G. Aldridge to Hill, July 25, 1916, W. Barnes to Hill, July 28, 1916, Aug. 15, 1916 (telegram), R. Bacon to Hill, Aug. 18, 1916 (telegram), Hill to Bacon, Aug. 18, 1916, HP; *New York Times,* Aug. 21, 1916; New York *Tribune,* Aug. 21, 1916.

53. J.A. Stewart to Hill, June 8, 1918, Hill to Stewart, June 26, 1918, HP.

54. G. Aldridge to Hill, July 11, 1918, Hill to Aldridge, July 17, 1918 (telegram), Aldridge to Hill, July 26 (telegram), Sept. 13, 1918, Hill to Aldridge, July 26, 1918 (telegram), HP.

CHAPTER 10

1. New York *World,* May 30, 1917.

2. "Kaiser and Peace: Analysis of the Guiding Mind in a War-Mad Government Whose Word Has Been Proved Unworthy of Trust," *New York Times Magazine,* Oct. 21, 1917; "The Kaiser's Responsibility," *Current History* 7 (Dec. 1917): 496–505; "The Sources of the Kaiser's Power," *Harper's Magazine* 136 (May 1918): 790–99; "The Kaiser's Method of Personal Control," *ibid.* 137 (June 1918): 29–39; "The Kaiser as a Stage Manager," *ibid.* (July 1918): 220–28; "The Kaiser Under Fire," *ibid.* (Aug. 1918): 377–86. See also, David J. Hill, *The Rebuilding of Europe* (New York: Century Co., 1917), pp. 246–77.

3. David J. Hill, *Impressions of the Kaiser* (New York: Harper and Bros., 1918).

4. David J. Hill, *Present Problems in Foreign Policy* (New York: D. Appleton and Co., 1919), and *American World Policies* (New York: George H. Doran Co., 1920), *passim.*

5. Hill, *Present Problems,* pp. 180–245, *passim;* Hill, *American World Policies,* pp. 168–87.

6. "The Gospel of Good Will; An Influence for the World's Peace," *Homiletic Review* 68 (Sept. 1914): 191–96; "World Organization," a paper read at a symposium of the American Philosophical Society on International Law, *Proceedings of the American Philosophical Society* 55 (1916): 322–29; "The Possible Means of Increasing the Effectiveness of International Law," an address delivered at the tenth annual meeting of the American Society of International Law at Washington, D.C., April 27, 1916, *Proceedings of the American Society of International Law* (1916), pp. 11–17. See also *Americanism: What It Is,* pp. 161–91.

7. Five lectures were also published in *Century Magazine,* May-October 1917.

8. Hill, *Rebuilding of Europe,* pp. 172–87.

9. Hill, "The Possible Means of Increasing the Effectiveness of International Law," p. 16.

10. Hill, *Rebuilding of Europe,* pp. 187–98.

11. *The World Court* 3 (Nov. 1917): 521; *Literary Digest* 55 (Dec. 1, 1917): 42; *North American Review* 207 (Mar. 1918): 458–59; *American Review of Reviews* 56 (Dec. 1917): 662; New York *Tribune,* Oct. 20, 1917; New York *World,* Jan. 13, 1918; Chicago *Post,* Dec. 14, 1917; Philadelphia *Public Ledger,* Dec. 1, 1917; *Christian Science Monitor,* Dec. 12, 1917.

12. Hill, *Present Problems,* pp. ix-x.

13. *Ibid.,* pp. 33–36, 102, 113–20; Hill, *American World Policies,* pp. 93–105.

14. Hill, *American World Policies,* pp. 42–43, 47–48, 166; Hill, *Present Problems,* pp. 97–98, 104–5, 123, 128–31.

15. Hill, *Present Problems,* pp. 132–33; Hill, *American World Policies,* pp. 33, 51–54, 188; Hill, *Rebuilding of Europe,* pp. 115–22.

16. Hill, *Present Problem,* pp. 240–44, 253, 100.

17. *Ibid.,* pp. 110, 244, 247, 258–59; Hill, *American World Policies,* pp. 41–46, 95–97.

18. Hill, *American World Policies,* pp. 97–100, 116–19; Boston *Herald,* Sept. 24, 27, 29, 1920.

19. Hill, *Present Problems,* p. 117.

20. Frederick J. Teggart, "A Jaundiced Ex-Diplomat," review of *Present Problems*

in Foreign Policy, in the *Public* (New York), Aug. 2, 1919; Lord Eustace Percy, "World Politics," review of *American World Policies,* in the New York *Post,* Oct. 2, 1920.

21. Hill, "The Gospel of Good Will," p. 195; Hill, "The Possible Means of Increasing the Effectiveness of International Law," pp. 15–16; David J. Hill, *Our Great Inheritance, An Address before the Daughters of the American Revolution, Sons of the Revolution, and Sons of the American Revolution, Feb. 22, 1919* (Washington: National Association for Constitutional Government, [1919]).

22. Hill, *American World Policies,* pp. 59–61, 106–10, 196.

23. N.M. Booth to Hill, May 12, 1919, W. Collier to Hill, May 24, 28, 1919, HP.

24. The League for the Preservation of American Independence to Hill, n.d. (telegram), H.E. Bowes to Hill, July 21, 1919, Hill to M.E. Gates, Aug. 4, 1919, H.W. Keyes to the Editors of the North American Review, Dec. 22, 1919, HP.

25. C.E. Hughes to Hill, June 26, 1920, E. Cutting to Hill, June 29, 1920, HP.

26. T. Beale to Hill, Aug. 3, 1920 (telegram), C.M. Roe to Hill, Aug. 7, 1920, G.L. Tait to Beale, Oct. 7, 1920, D. Gerould to Hill, Oct. 22, 1920, HP.

27. *New York Times,* July 14, 1920; New York *Tribune,* July 14, 1920.

28. *New York Times,* July 28, 1920; *Address of David Jayne Hill as Temporary Chairman of the Republican State Convention, Saratoga, New York, July 27, 1920* (New York: George H. Doran Co., [1920]); G.A. Glynn to Hill, July 14, 1920, L.B. Gleason to Hill, Sept. 30, 1920, T. Beale to Hill, Sept. 20, 23, 1920, H.C. Lodge to Hill, Aug. 25, 1920, Lodge to Juliet Hill, Aug. 30, 1920, HP.

29. R.V. Sollett to Hill, Sept. 9, 1920, Hill to Sollett, Sept. 24, 1920, T. Beale to Hill, Sept. 23, 25, 1920, HP; David Jayne Hill, *The Peace Family and The League of Nations* (New York: Republican National Committee, [1920]).

30. R.V. Solett to Hill, Oct. 22, 1920, T. Beale to Hill, Oct. 20, 1920, A. Tillinghast to Hill, Oct. 1, 1920, D. Gerould to Hill, Oct. 13, 1920, F.K. Harding to Hill, Oct. 22, 1920, HP.

31. B. King to Hill, Nov. 3, 1920, W.R. Thayer to Hill, Nov. 3, 1920, C. Thomas to Hill, Nov. 6, 1920, J. Wasdworth, Jr., to Hill, Nov. 5, 1920, W. Harding to Hill, Nov. 6, 1920, HP.

32. New York *Tribune,* Dec. 27, 1919; W.M. Collier to G.W. Aldridge, Sept. 17, 1919, Collier to Hill, Nov. 9, 1919, Aldridge to Collier, Sept. 27, 1919, HP.

33. Hill to Harding, Sept. 18, 1920, F.W. Wile to Hill, Jan. 8, 1921, HP; New York *Herald,* Dec. 19, 1919, Nov. 7, 1920; New York *Evening Post,* Nov. 9, 1920, Jan. 3, 1921; New York *Evening World,* Nov. 9, 1920; *New York Times,* Nov. 24, Dec. 29, 31, 1920; *Boston Transcript,* Nov. 10, 13, 24, 1920; Boston *Herald,* Dec. 15, 1920; *Washington Times,* Nov. 15, 24, Dec. 8, 1920; *Washington Star,* Nov. 22, 1920; Philadelphia *Public Ledger,* Dec. 6, 10, 11, 19, 20, 23, 1920; *Baltimore News,* Nov. 13, 1920; *Washington Herald,* Jan. 8, 1921.

34. New York *Evening Post,* Jan. 20, 1921; Butler, *Across the Busy Years,* 1: 403.

35. *New York Times,* Feb. 11, 20, Apr. 23, May 5, 1921; New York *Herald,* Feb. 11, 1921; *Washington Herald,* Jan. 16, 1921; *Washington Times,* May 4, 1921; New York *Tribune,* May 5, 1921; J. Barrett to Hill, Feb. 14, 1921, Hill to W.R. Willcox, Feb. 14, 1921, Willcox to Hill, Feb. 16, 1921, Hill to J. Wadsworth, Mar. 8, 1921, Wadsworth to Hill, Mar. 10, 1921, W. Calder to Hill, Mar. 17, 1921, HP.

36. Memorandum dated Tuesday, May 3, Wednesday, May 4, 1921, HP; *New York Times*, May 11, 1921.

CHAPTER 11

1. Hill to C.E. Hughes, June 22, 29, July 12, 20, 27, Aug. 12, 21, 22, 1921, HP.

2. New York *Tribune*, Oct. 31, Nov. 2, 4, 6, 8, 11, 1921.

3. *Ibid.*, Nov. 14, 17, Dec. 8, 1921.

4. Merlo J. Pusey, *Charles Evans Hughes* (New York: Macmillan Co., 1951), 2: 497–98.

5. New York *Tribune*, Dec. 12, 1921.

6. *Ibid.*, Dec. 17, 22, 1921.

7. *Ibid.*, Jan. 2, 13, 1922.

8. Jusserand to Hill, Jan. 3, 1922, HP; Pusey, *Hughes*, 2: 461, 482–83; New York *Tribune*, Feb. 12, 1922.

9. Jusserand to Hill, Jan. 3, 1922, M. Leon to Hill, Jan. 7, 1922, W. Berry to Hill, Jan. 28, 1922, HP.

10. *New York Times*, Oct. 28, 1922, Jan. 17, 1923; Hill to G. Grassmuck, Jan. 5, 1924, Hill to R.O. Johnson, May 13, 1930, Hill to G.D. Vanamee, Oct. 8, 1930, HP; Hill to R. Rhees, June 11, 1923, Sept. 8, 1925, June 10, 1927, June 11, 1928, June 10, 1929, Oct. 20, 1931, Rush Rhees Papers, University of Rochester Library, Rochester, New York.

11. Letters relating to the General Real Estate and Trust Company dated from June 29, 1922, to June 5, 1925, C. Spring-Rice to Hill, May 24, 1915, J.H. Weaver to Hill, Aug. 28, 1916, Hill to the Minister from Sweden, July 16, 1924, the Italian Ambassador to Hill, Apr. 13, 1927, HP.

12. Manley O. Hudson, *The Permanent Court of International Justice* (New York: Macmillan Co., 1934), pp. 85–121, 161–65, 209–10.

13. Pusey, *Hughes*, 2: 598–99; U.S., Department of State, *Papers Relating to the Foreign Relations of the United States, 1923* (Washington: Government Printing Office, 1938), 1: 10–18.

14. *Congressional Record*, 67th Cong., 4th sess., vol. 64, pt. 5, p. 4632; *ibid.*, pt. 6, pp. 5272–74, 5316.

15. David J. Hill, "The League of Nations, Its Court, And Its Law," *Saturday Evening Post* 196 (Aug. 11, 1923): 8–9, 112–14; David J. Hill, "American Cooperation for World Peace," *ibid.* (Oct. 27, 1923): 29, 148–49, (Nov. 3, 1923): 29, 170–74.

16. W.E. Borah to Hill, Aug. 25, 1923, M. McCormick to Hill, Aug. 13, 1923, J.K. Shields to Hill, Oct. 31, 1923, H.C. Lodge to Hill, Aug. 13, Nov. 20, 1923, HP.

17. *Foreign Relations, 1923*, 1: vii–viii.

18. David J. Hill, "A Real World Court, President's Aim," *Boston Transcript*, Dec. 7, 1923; Hill to Lodge, Dec. 6, 1923, Lodge Papers, Massachusetts Historical Society, Boston, Massachusetts.

19. J.T. Williams, Jr., to Hill, Dec. 8, 1923, Lodge to Hill, Dec. 7, 14, 17, 1923, HP.

20. Hill to Williams, Dec. 11, 1923, HP; "The Legend of the Protocol," *Boston*

Transcript, Dec. 15, 1923; "A Foreign Agency," *ibid.,* Dec. 17, 1923; "Where the United States Comes In," *ibid.,* Dec. 19, 1923; Why the League Wants Its Own Court," *ibid.,* Jan. 14, 1924.

21. Lodge to Hill, Dec. 14, 17, 20, 1923, Jan. 5, Feb. 18, 1924, HP.

22. *Congressional Record,* 68th Cong., 1st sess., vol. 65, pt. 1, pp. 151–52; Hill to Lodge, Feb. 19, 1924, Lodge Papers.

23. G.W. Pepper to Hill, Apr. 23, 1924, Hill to Pepper, Apr. 26, 1924, HP.

24. *Congressional Record,* 68th Cong., 1st sess., vol. 65, pt. 8, pp. 7904, 8084; *ibid.,* pt. 9, pp. 9143–44, 9157–58; U.S., Congress, Senate, *Organization of the World For Peace; A Plan by which the United States May Cooperate with other Nations to Achieve and Preserve the Peace of the World,* by Chandler P. Anderson, S. Doc. 107 to Accompany S. Joint Res. 122, 68th Cong., 1st sess., 1924; Williams to Hill, May 10, 1924 (telegram), Hill to Williams, May 10, 1924 (telegram), HP; *Literary Digest* 81 (May 24, 1924): 12–13; *New York Times,* May 25, 1924.

25. Kirk H. Porter and Donald B. Johnson, eds., *National Party Platforms, 1840–1956* (Urbana: University of Illinois Press, 1956), pp. 251, 260; Memorandum dated Nov. 21, 1924, HP.

26. U.S., Department of State, *Papers Relating to the Foreign Relations of the United States, 1924* (Washington: Government Printing Office, 1939), 1: xxi; *New York Times,* May 25, 1924.

27. *New York Times,* Mar. 1, 1925; *Congressional Record,* 68th Cong., 2d sess., vol. 66, pt. 5, pp. 4860–61.

28. Denna F. Fleming, *The Treaty Veto of the American Senate* (New York: G. P. Putnam's Sons, 1936), pp. 186–88; *Congressional Record,* 68th Cong., 2d sess., vol. 66, pt. 5, pp. 5413–14; *ibid.,* 69th Cong., special sess., vol. 67, pt. 1, pp. 5, 10, 207.

29. U.S., Department of State,*Papers Relating to the Foreign Relations of the United States, 1925* (Washington: Government Printing Office, 1940), 1: xiv-xvii.

30. Hill to Borah, Jan. 7, 1926, Hill to Coolidge, Jan. 14, 1926, HP; *Congressional Record,* 69th Cong., 1st sess., vol. 67, pt. 3, pp. 2647–56.

31. David J. Hill, "The Whole Case of the World Court of Justice," *Saturday Evening Post* 198 (Jan. 16, 1926): 27, 153–62; Hudson, *Permanent Court,* pp. 112–17.

32. Hill to Pepper, Nov. 6, 1925, Hill to Moses, Dec. 31, 1925, Hill to Borah, Jan. 5, 1926, Hill to G.H. Williams, Jan. 16, 18, 1926, HP.

33. Moses to Hill, Dec. 29, 1925, Hill to Moses, Dec. 31, 1925, Hill to Williams, Jan. 16, 18, 1926, Hill to L.R. Wilfley, Jan. 20, 1926, HP; *Congressional Record,* 69th Cong., 1st sess., vol. 67, pt. 3, pp. 2657–58, 2803–6.

34. Borah to Hill, Jan. 27, 1926, HP.

35. Pepper to Hill, Oct. 25, Nov. 7, 1925, HP.

36. Hudson, *Permanent Court,* pp. 212n, 285, 435, 447–48; Memorandum of February 18, 1922, by J.B. Moore, *Congressional Record,* 69th Cong., 1st sess., vol. 67, pt. 2, pp. 1427–31; "Suggestion, for consideration, as to clauses to follow the first two paragraphs (the recitals) of the Draft of Resolution," carbon copy enclosed in Pepper to Hill, Nov. 7, 1925, HP.

37. *Congressional Record,* 69th Cong., 1st sess., vol. 67, pt. 2, pp. 1245–46.

38. The lengthy and scattered chronicle of the debate in the *Congressional Record*

is summarized in Charles P. Howland, comp., *Survey of American Foreign Relations, 1929* (New Haven: Yale University Press for the Council on Foreign Relations, 1929), pp. 351–62; Fleming, *Treaty Veto of the Senate*, pp. 191–212; Denna F. Fleming, *The United States and the World Court* (Garden City, N.Y.: Doubleday, Doran and Company, 1945), pp. 56–65. For Moore's anonymous memorandum see *Congressional Record,* 69th Cong., 1st sess., vol. 67, pt. 2, pp. 2293–94. Two declarations were also added to the Swanson resolution, which provided that the United States would have recourse to the Court only by general or special treaties, and that adherence by the United States was not to be construed to require departure from its traditional policy of noninterference in the political affairs of other states or relinquishment of its traditional attitude toward purely American questions.

39. Hudson, *Permanent Court*, pp. 455–57.

40. *New York Times,* Jan. 28, 1926; *Congressional Record,* 69th Cong., 1st sess., vol. 67, pt. 3, pp. 2656–57.

41. David J. Hill, "The Gentle Art of Learning to Swim Without Going Near the Water," *Saturday Evening Post* 198 (Apr. 3, 1926): 198–210.

42. Borah to Hill, Apr. 16, 1926, HP.

43. The Senate had amended the fourth reservation to provide for unrestricted right of withdrawal from the Court. To balance this the conference proposed that the signatory states should possess the corresponding right to withdraw by a two-thirds vote their acceptance of the American reservations.

44. Howland, *Survey of Foreign Relations, 1929,* pp. 362–69; Hudson, *Permanent Court,* pp. 211–16, 466–67; Fleming, *Treaty Veto of the Senate,* pp. 217–35; Fleming, *World Court,* pp. 68–81.

45. New York *Herald Tribune,* Aug. 19, 1928; David J. Hill, *The Problem of a World Court: The Story of an Unrealized American Idea* (New York: Longmans, Green and Co., 1927), pp. 108–66.

46. London *Saturday Review,* Apr. 30, 1927.

47. David J. Hill, "Briand's Proposal of Perpetual Peace," *Saturday Evening Post* 200 (July 30, 1927): 27, 112; David J. Hill, "America's Influence Preserved by Keeping a Free Hand," *Current History* 27 (Jan. 1928): 463–67; David J. Hill, "The Multilateral Treaty for the Renunciation of War," *American Journal of International Law* 22 (Oct. 1928): 823–26; David J. Hill, "A Constructive Program Against War," *Saturday Evening Post* 197 (Apr. 18, 1925): 173; David J. Hill, "New International Alignments," *Saturday Evening Post* 202 (Nov. 9, 1929): 37, 157–60; David J. Hill, "Camouflage in the Peace Movement," *American Journal of International Law* 23 (July 1929): 617–19; David J. Hill, "The League of Nations and the United States: Against Joining the League, I" *Current History* 31 (Jan. 1930): 668–78; David J. Hill, "The London Naval Conference, How the Result is Viewed in Each Nation: I—The United States," *Current History* 32 (June 1930): 446–49; David J. Hill, "Does the World Want Peace?" *Current History* 33 (Dec. 1930): 321–25.

48. Manley O. Hudson, *The World Court, 1921–1931* (Boston: World Peace Foundation, 1931), pp. 15–18; Hudson, *Permanent Court,* pp. 433–67; John Bassett Moore, *International Law and Some Current Illusions* (New York: Macmillan Co., 1924), p. 131.

49. Secretariat of the League of Nations, *Ten Years of World Cooperation* (1930) pp.

164–75; League of Nations, *Official Journal* 1 (Nov.–Dec. 1920): 20; Arthur K. Kuhn, "Codification of International Law and the Fifth Assembly," *American Journal of International Law* 19 (Jan. 1925): 155–57; George A. Finch, "The Progressive Codification of International Law," *ibid.* (July 1925): 534–36.

50. Finch, "Progressive Codification of International Law," pp. 534–42; Kuhn, "Codification of International Law," pp. 155–57; James W. Garner, "Some Observations on the Codification of International Law," *American Journal of International Law* 19 (Apr. 1925): 327–33; Elihu Root, "The Codification of International Law," *ibid.* (Oct. 1925): 675–84; George A. Finch, "The Annual Meeting of the American Society of International Law," *ibid.* (July 1925): 531; *Washington Post,* Apr. 25, 1925; Hill, *Problem of a World Court,* pp. 34–35.

51. Hudson, *Permanent Court,* pp. 523–42; C. Howard-Ellis, *The Origin, Structure, and Working of the League of Nations* (Boston: Houghton Mifflin Co., 1928), pp. 349–50.

52. *New York Times,* Mar. 3, 1932.

Bibliography of Sources Cited

MANUSCRIPTS

George W. Aldridge Papers, Rochester, New York, Public Library.

Martin B. Anderson Papers, University of Rochester Library.

Andrew Carnegie Papers, Library of Congress.

Department of State Papers, National Archives.

David Jayne Hill Papers, University of Rochester Library.

David Jayne Hill Collection, Bucknell University Library.

Henry Cabot Lodge Papers, Massachusetts Historical Society.

William McKinley Papers on microfilm, Library of Congress.

Rush Rhees Papers, University of Rochester Library.

Andrew D. White Papers, Cornell University Library.

PUBLIC DOCUMENTS

Publications of the United States Government

Congressional Record, vols. 42, 51, 64–67.

Congress. House. *Consular and Embassy and Legation Buildings.* House Report 1564, 60th Cong., 1st sess.

Congress. Senate. *The League of Nations, Its Court, and Its Law; American Cooperation for World Peace,* by David Jayne Hill. Senate Doc. 9, 68th Cong., 1st sess.

Congress. Senate. *Organization of the World for Peace; A Plan by which the United States May Cooperate with other Nations to Achieve and Preserve the Peace of the World,* by Chandler P. Anderson. Senate Doc. 107 to Accompany Senate Joint Res. 122, 68th Cong., 1st sess.

Congress. Senate. *Report . . . of delegates to the Second International Conference of American States, City of Mexico, Oct. 22, 1901–Jan. 22, 1902.* Senate Doc. 330, 57th Cong., 1st sess.

Department of State. *Papers Relating to the Foreign Relations of the United States, 1898.* Washington, 1901.

Department of State. *Papers Relating to the Foreign Relations of the United States, 1899.* Washington, 1901.

Department of State. *Papers Relating to the Foreign Relations of the United States, 1911.* Washington, 1918.

Department of State. *Papers Relating to the Foreign Relations of the United States, 1923.* Washington, 1938.

Department of State. *Papers Relating to the Foreign Relations of the United States, 1924.* Washington, 1939.

Department of State. *Papers Relating to the Foreign Relations of the United States, 1925.* Washington, 1940.

Malloy, William M., ed. *Treaties, Conventions, International Acts, Protocols and Agreements between the United States of America and other Powers, 1776–1909.* Washington, 1910–1938.

Statutes at Large, vol. 36 (1911): 917. *An Act Providing for the Purchase or erection, within certain limits of cost, of embassy, legation, and consular buildings abroad.*

Publications of Foreign Agencies

League of Nations. *Official Journal,* 1. London: Harrison and Sons, Ltd., 1920.

League of Nations, Secretariat. *Ten Years of World Cooperation.* Secretariat of the League of Nations, 1930.

Mexico, General Secretary of the Second International American Conference. *Second International American Conference.* Mexico City: Government Printing Office, 1902.

MISCELLANEOUS DOCUMENTS

Bucknell University. *Catalogues,* 1886–1888.

———. *Memorials of Bucknell University, 1849–1896.* Lewisburg, Pa., 1896.

———. Minutes of the Trustees, 1886–1891.

Memorial of the New York State Bar Association to the President Recommending the Creation of an International Court of Arbitration. Privately printed, n.d.

National Association for Constitutional Government. *Constitution of the National Association for Constitutional Government.* Copy in Hill Papers, University of Rochester Library.

———. *List of Members of the Association for Constitutional Government, March 1, 1918.* Copy in Hill Papers, University of Rochester Library.

———. Minutes of the Executive Committee, April 25, 1930. In Hill Collection, Bucknell University Library.

Oliphant, J. Orin, ed. *The Beginnings of Bucknell University: A Sampling of the Documents.* Lewisburg, Pa.: Bucknell University Press, 1954.

Porter, Kirk H., and Johnson, Donald B., eds. *National Party Platforms, 1840–1956.* Urbana: University of Illinois Press, 1956.

Scott, James Brown, ed. *The Hague Conventions and Declarations of 1899 and 1907.* 3d ed. New York: Oxford University Press, 1918.

———. *Instructions to the American Delegates to The Hague Peace Conferences and Their Official Reports.* New York: Oxford University Press, 1916.

———. *The Proceedings of the Hague Peace Conferences, the Conference of 1907.* 3 vols. New York: Oxford University Press, 1920.

University at Lewisburg. *Abstract of Treasurer's Report, June 1, 1879.*

———. *Catalogues,* 1851–1886.

————. Minutes of the Trustees, 1851–1886.

————, Female Institute. *Catalogue*, 1871.

University of Rochester. *Catalogues*, 1870–1892.

————. Faculty Meeting Records, 1889–1890.

————. Records of Executive Board of the Trustees, 1895.

————. *Reports of the President*, 1894–1895, 1895–1896.

————. Treasurer's Statements, 1879–1887.

————. Trustees' Records, 1850–1900.

COLLECTED CORRESPONDENCE

Roosevelt, Theodore. *The Letters of Theodore Roosevelt.* Edited by Elting E. Morison et al. 8 vols. Cambridge, Mass.: Harvard University Press, 1954.

Thayer, William Roscoe. *The Life and Letters of John Hay.* 2 vols. Boston: Houghton Mifflin Co., 1915.

MEMOIRS AND REMINISCENCES

Barstow, Henry H. "Anderson Hall a Battlefield in Gay 'Nineties." *Rochester Alumni Review*, 9 (April–May 1931): 111–12.

Bartol, William C. "Looking Backward." *Bucknellian*, 31 (Mar. 1, 1928): 7; (Apr. 13, 1928): 7; (Apr. 26, 1928): 7.

Bülow, Fürst von. *Denkwürdigkeiten.* 4 vols. Berlin: im verlag Ullstein, [1930–1931].

Butler, Nicholas Murray. *Across the Busy Years.* 2 vols. New York: Charles Scribner's Sons, 1939.

Ehrgott, Albert. "Dr. Anderson and Dr. Hill—a Contrast." *Rochester Alumni Review*, 5 (Dec.–Jan. 1926–27): 41.

Grew, Joseph C. *Turbulent Era: A Diplomatic Record of Forty Years, 1904–1945.* 2 vols. Boston: Houghton Mifflin Co., 1952.

Griscom, Lloyd C. *Diplomatically Speaking.* Boston: Little, Brown and Co., 1940.

Hall, G. Stanley. *Life and Confessions of a Psychologist.* New York: D. Appleton and Co., 1923.

Hill, David Jayne. "The Ancestry of David Jayne Hill, Compiled for his children, Washington, 1921." Typescript. Hill Collection, Bucknell University Library.

————. "As It Seemed to Me: Confidences Regarding the Inner and Outer Phases of a Varied Life." Also titled: "Confidences of a Grandfather." Typescript memoir to 1896. Hill Collection, Bucknell University Library.

Mitchell, Edward P. *Memoirs of an Editor*. New York: Charles Scribner's Sons, 1924.

[Moore, James, Jr.] "The Original Manuscript Concerning the Founding of the University at Lewisburg by one of the Founders." [April 10, 1878] *Bucknell Mirror*, 16 (Dec. 10, 1896): 49–53.

Osborn, Chase. *The Iron Hunter*. New York: Macmillan Co., 1919.

Schoen, Freiherrn von. *Erlebtes: Beiträge zur politischen Geschichte der neuesten Zeit*. Stuttgart: Deutsche Verlags-Anstalt, 1921.

Taylor, Stephen W. "A Brief History of the Origin of the University at Lewisburg." Manuscript in Treasurer's Office, Bucknell University.

White, Andrew D. *Autobiography of Andrew Dickson White*. 2 vols. New York: Century Co., 1905.

BOOKS BY DAVID JAYNE HILL

American World Policies. New York: George H. Doran Co., 1920.

Americanism: What It Is. New York: D. Appleton and Co., 1916.

The Diplomacy of the Age of Absolutism, vol. 3 of *A History of Diplomacy in the International Development of Europe*. New York and London: Longmans, Green and Co., 1914.

The Elements of Logic. Recast of Jevons, W. Stanley, *Elementary Lessons in Logic*. New York: Sheldon and Company, 1883.

The Elements of Psychology. New York: Sheldon and Company, 1888.

The Elements of Rhetoric and Composition. New York: Sheldon and Company, 1878.

The Establishment of Territorial Sovereignty, vol. 2 of *A History of Diplomacy in the International Development of Europe*. New York and London: Longmans, Green and Co., 1906.

Genetic Philosophy. New York: Macmillan and Co., 1893.

Impressions of the Kaiser. New York: Harper and Bros., 1918.

Open Air Politics. Junius Jay (pseud.). Boston: Houghton Mifflin Co., 1914.

The People's Government. New York: D. Appleton and Co., 1915.

Present Problems in Foreign Policy. New York: D. Appleton and Co., 1919.

The Principles and Fallacies of Socialism. no. 533, *Lovell's Library.* New York: John W. Lovell Co., 1885.

The Problem of a World Court: The Story of an Unrealized American Idea. New York: Longmans, Green and Co., 1927.

The Rebuilding of Europe. New York: Century Co., 1917.

The Science of Rhetoric. New York: Sheldon and Company, 1877.

The Social Influence of Christianity, with Special Reference to Contemporary Problems. Boston: Silver, Burdett and Co., 1888.

The Struggle for Universal Empire, vol. 1 of *A History of Diplomacy in the International Development of Europe.* New York and London: Longmans, Green and Co., 1905.

Washington Irving, vol. 1 of *American Authors.* New York: Sheldon and Company, 1879.

William Cullen Bryant, vol. 2 of *American Authors.* New York: Sheldon and Company, 1879.

World Organization as Affected by the Nature of the Modern State. New York: Columbia University Press, 1911.

ARTICLES, PAMPHLETS AND ADDRESSES BY DAVID JAYNE HILL

Address of David Jayne Hill as Temporary Chairman of the Republican State Convention, Saratoga, New York, July 27, 1920. New York: George H. Doran Co. Also printed as *The League of Nations* by the Republican National Committee.

"Address . . . at the Luncheon of the American Defense Society, [New York] February 22, 1916." Manuscript in the Hill Papers, University of Rochester Library.

"Address to the Baptist Social Union, Philadelphia, Pennsylvania, May 20, 1879." Manuscript in the Hill Collection, Bucknell University Library.

"The Aims and Principles of the Sons of the American Revolution." Address before the Sons of the American Revolution, Washington, D.C., January 16, 1918. Manuscript in the Hill Papers, University of Rochester Library.

The American College in Relation to Liberal Education, The Inaugural Address of President David Jayne Hill, LL.D., Read before the alumni and friends of the University of Rochester, June 19, 1889. Privately printed, n.d.

"American Cooperation for World Peace." *Saturday Evening Post,* 196 (Oct. 27, 1923): 29, 148–49; (Nov. 3, 1923): 29, 170–74. Also printed in *International Conciliation,* no. 194 (Jan. 1924): 23–49.

American Industrial Defense. Address before the Rochester Hughes Business Men's League, Oct. 19, 1916. Boston: Home Market Club, [1916].

"America's Influence Preserved by Keeping a Free Hand." *Current History* 27 (Jan. 1928): 463–67.

"Birthday of the Constitution." *The Review* 1 (Sept. 13, 1919): 381–83.

"Briand's Proposal of Perpetual Peace." *Saturday Evening Post* 200 (July 30, 1927): 27, 112.

"Camouflage In the Peace Movement." *American Journal of International Law* 23 (July 1929): 617–19.

"Can Our Diplomatic Service be Made More Efficient?" *Harper's Magazine* 130 (Jan. 1915): 190–98.

"A Constructive Program Against War." *Saturday Evening Post* 197 (Apr. 18, 1925): 31, 173–74.

The Contemporary Development of Diplomacy. A paper read before the International Congress of Arts and Science, St. Louis, September 23, 1904. Privately printed, n.d. Reprinted, "Die zeitgenössische Entwicklung der Diplomatie." *Neue Revue* 1 (July 2, 1908): 1296–1304.

"The Crisis in Constitutionalism." *North American Review* 198 (Dec. 1913): 769–78.

"A Defensible Program of Defense." *American Defense* 1 (Feb. 1916): 42, 56.

"Does the World Want Peace?" *Current History* 33 (Dec. 1930): 321–25.

"The Elective System." University at Lewisburg *College Herald* 5 (Feb. 1875): 57–58.

The Essential Elements of Foreign Policy. Address before the National Convention of the Navy League of the United States, Washington, D.C., April 10–13, 1916. Pamphlet no. 47 of the Navy League of the United States, Washington, D.C.

"The Expansion of Civilization." Address before the Baptist Social Union, Washington, D.C., December 16, 1898. Manuscript in the Hill Papers, University of Rochester Library.

The Fiction of "Imperialism." The Sovereignty of the Nation the Safeguard of Self-Government. [Republican National Committee, 1900]. Reprinted, *Das Märchen vom Imperialismus. Die Gouveränität unserer Nation ist die Schutzwehr der Selbstregierung.*

"A Foreign Agency." *Boston Transcript,* Dec. 17, 1923.

"The Gentle Art of Learning to Swim Without Going Near the Water." *Saturday Evening Post* 198 (Apr. 3, 1926): 35, 198–210.

George Washington as the Interpreter of His Time. Address before the patriotic societies of Washington, on the hundredth anniversary of the death of George Washington, December 14, 1899. *Historical Papers of the Society of the Sons of the American Revolution in the District of Columbia,* no. 2, 1900.

"The Gospel of Good Will: An Influence for the World's Peace." *Homiletic Review* 68 (Sept. 1914): 191–96.

Greater America, Address . . . Delivered at the Annual Banquet of the Rochester Chamber of Commerce, December 8, 1898. Washington: Judd & Detweiler, Printers, 1898.

"An Impending Danger to the Republic." *North American Review* 202 (Dec. 1915): 801–11.

"In Memoriam, Doctor Henry Campbell Black, October 17, 1860–March 19, 1927." *Constitutional Review* 11 (Apr. 1927): 67–76.

"Inaugural Address of President David J. Hill." Philadelphia *National Baptist,* July 10, 1879.

Industrial Defense, Address . . . at the Home Market Club Dinner, February 25, 1916. Boston: The Home Market Club, [1916]. Also printed as *Economic Readjustment in the United States After the European War, Addresses Before the Economic Club of Portland, Maine, on February 26, 1916,* by David Jayne Hill and George E. Roberts. Portland, Maine: The Economic Club of Portland, 1916. Also printed in the *National Economic League Quarterly* 1 (May 1916): 49–57.

"International Justice; with a Plan for its Permanent Organization." *Yale Law Journal* 6 (Oct. 1896): 1–19.

"Kaiser and Peace: Analysis of the Guiding Mind in a War-Mad Government Whose Word Had Been Proved Unworthy of Trust." *New York Times Magazine,* Oct. 21, 1917.

"The Kaiser as a Stage Manager." *Harper's Magazine* 137 (July 1918): 220–28.

"The Kaiser Under Fire," *Harper's Magazine* 137 (Aug. 1918): 377–86.

"The Kaiser's Method of Personal Control," *Harper's Magazine* 137 (June 1918): 29–39.

"The Kaiser's Responsibility." *Current History* 7 (Dec. 1917): 496–505.

"The League of Nations and the United States: Against Joining the League, I." *Current History* 31 (Jan. 1930): 668–78.

"The League of Nations, Its Court, And Its Law." *Saturday Evening Post* 196 (Aug. 11, 1923): 8–9, 112–14.

"The Legend of the Protocol." *Boston Transcript,* Dec. 15, 1923.

"The London Naval Conference, How the Result is Viewed in Each Nation: I—The United States." *Current History* 32 (June 1930): 446–49.

"Material Needs of Our Diplomatic Service." *Harper's Magazine* 130 (Feb. 1915): 448–56.

"The Meaning of the Hay-Pauncefote Treaty." *Saturday Evening Post* 186 (May 16, 1914): 3–4, 81–82.

"The Multilateral Treaty for the Renunciation of War." *American Journal of International Law* 22 (Oct. 1928): 823–26.

"National Defense, an address . . . delivered before the Society of the Genesee, . . . New York, . . . January 22, 1916." Manuscript in the Hill Papers, University of Rochester Library.

"New International Alignment." *Saturday Evening Post* 202 (Nov. 9, 1929): 37, 157–60.

"The Original Territory of the United States." Lecture before the National Geographic Society, Washington, D.C., February 21, 1899. *National Geographic Magazine* 10 (Mar. 1899): 73–92.

Our Commercial Expansion. Address before the alumni of the Massachusetts Institute of Technology. Reprint from the *Technology Review* 3. Boston: George E. Ellis, Printer, 1901.

Our Great Inheritance, An Address before the Daughters of the American Revolution, Sons of the Revolution, and the Sons of the American Revolution, Feb. 22, 1919. Washington: National Association for Constitutional Government, [1919].

The Peace Family and The League of Nations. New York: Republican National Committee, [1920].

"The Place of America in World Politics." Convocation Address delivered on the occasion of the Thirty-second Convocation of the University of Chicago, April 2, 1900. *University* (of Chicago) *Record* 5 (Apr. 6, 1900): 1–17.

A Plan for A School of the Political Sciences. Published by the George Washington University in 1907 on the occasion of "The George Washington University Movement."

"Policy of the Association." *Bulletin of the National Association for Constitutional Government,* no. 13, December 1929. Washington: National Association for Constitutional Government, 1929.

"The Possible Means of Increasing the Effectiveness of International Law." Address before the Tenth Annual Meeting of the American Society of International Law, Washington, D.C., April 27, 1916.

Proceedings of the American Society of International Law, 1916, pp. 11–17. Washington: American Society of International Law, 1916.

"Preparation for the Administrative and Diplomatic Service." *Proceedings of the 14th Annual Convention of the Association of Colleges and Preparatory Schools of the Middle States and Maryland, 1900,* pp. 66–76. Albany: University of the State of New York, 1901.

"President Wilson's Administration of Foreign Affairs." *North American Review* 204 (Sept. 1916): 344–61; (Oct. 1916): 550–74. Reprinted as *The Un-American Foreign Policy of the Wilson Administration.* Republican National Committee, 1916.

A Primer of Finance: An Honest Dollar the Basis of Prosperity. New York: National Republican Executive Committee, 1896.

"The Protection of American Citizens." *North American Review* 203 (Mar. 1916): 381–87.

"A Real World Court, President's Aim." *Boston Transcript,* Dec. 7, 1923.

"The Relation of the United States to the Permanent Court of

International Justice." *American Journal of International Law* 20 (Apr. 1926): 326–30.

"The Relative Authority of Scripture and Reason." *Proceedings of the Tenth Baptist Congress, Held in Philadelphia, Penna., May, 1892.*

"Shall we Standardize Our Diplomatic Service?" *Harper's Magazine* 128 (Apr. 1914): 690–98.

"Socialism: False and True." *Proceedings of the Fourth Baptist Congress, Held in the City of New York, Nov. 1885,* pp. 23–28. New York: Century Co., 1886.

"The Sources of the Kaiser's Power." *Harper's Magazine* 136 (May 1918): 790–99.

"Supremacy in the Panama Canal." *American Monthly Review of Reviews* 49 (June 1914): 722–25.

Syllabus of the Levering Lectures for 1894 on Religion in the Light of Science, Delivered by David Jayne Hill, at the Johns Hopkins University, March 15, 16, 19 and 20, 1894. [Johns Hopkins University, 1894].

Three Great Traditions, An Address delivered . . . at Bucknell University on Commencement Day, June 18, 1924. Privately printed, n.d.

"A Typical Preacher of the Nineteenth Century," Address at the Centenary of the First Baptist Church of Plainfield, New Jersey, November 25, 1918. *Centenary, First Baptist Church, Plainfield, New Jersey, 1818–1918, November 24th, 25th, 1918.* Privately printed, n.d.

"University Extension." Rochester *Democrat and Chronicle,* Mar. 15, 1892.

The Vital Issue: An Honest Dollar the Basis of Prosperity. Chicago: Republican National Committee, [1900]. Reprinted, *Die Haupt-Streitfrage: Der Vollwerthige Dollar die Grundlage der Prosperitat.*

"The War and the Extension of Civilization." *Forum* 26 (Feb. 1899): 650–55.

"Where the United States Comes In." *Boston Transcript,* Dec. 19, 1923.

"The Whole Case of the World Court of Justice." *Saturday Evening Post* 198 (Jan. 9, 1926): 43, 162–70; (Jan. 16, 1926): 27, 153–62.

"Why Do We Have a Diplomatic Service?" *Harper's Magazine* 127 (Jan. 1914): 188–97.

"Why I Am a Protectionist." *American Economist* 8 (Dec. 18, 1891): 309. Reprinted in part in "A College President's Reason." Boston *Home Market Bulletin* 3 (Jan. 1892): 3.

"Why the League Wants Its Own Court." *Boston Transcript*, Jan. 14, 1924.

"World Organization." Paper read at a symposium of the American Philosophical Society on International Law. *Proceedings of the American Philosophical Society* 55 (1916): 322–29.

"World Politics as Affecting the United States, An Address to the National Security Congress, Washington, D.C., January 20–22, 1916, held under the auspices of the National Security League. Manuscript in the Hill Papers, University of Rochester.

REVIEWS OF HILL'S BOOKS

American World Policies. Percy, Lord Eustace, "World Politics." New York *Post,* Oct. 2, 1920.

Americanism: What It Is. [Littell, Philip] P. L., "Books and Things." *New Republic* 7 (July 8, 1916): 255.

The Diplomacy of the Age of Absolutism, vol. 3 of *A History of Diplomacy in the International Development of Europe*. Fay, Sidney B. *American Historical Review* 20 (Feb. 1915): 401–2.

The Establishment of Territorial Sovereignty, vol. 2 of *A History of Diplomacy in the International Development of Europe*. Burr, George L. *American Historical Review* 12 (Apr. 1907): 617–19.

———. *The Catholic World* 85 (May 1907): 258–59.

———. Needham, Charles W. *American Journal of International Law* 1 (Apr. 1907): 556–58.

Genetic Philosophy. Boston *Watchman,* Nov. 23, 1893.

———. Hovey, Alvah. Boston *Watchman,* May 10, 1894.

———. Indianapolis *Baptist,* Mar. 22, 1894.

———. Johnson, Elias. Philadelphia *National Baptist,* Mar. 15, 1894.

———. Johnson, F. H. *New World* 3 (Mar. 1894): 198–200.

———. *Oxford Magazine* 12 (May 23, 1894): 346–47.

———. Vedder, Henry C. New York *Examiner,* Feb. 1, 1894.

Present Problems in Foreign Policy. Teggart, Frederick J., "A Jaundiced Ex-Diplomat." *The Public* (New York) 22 (Aug. 2, 1919): 830–31.

The Problem of a World Court. London *Saturday Review,* Apr. 30, 1927.

———. New York *Herald Tribune,* Aug. 19, 1928.

The Rebuilding of Europe. American Review of Reviews 56 (Dec. 1917): 662.

———. Boston *Christian Science Monitor,* Dec. 12, 1917.

———. Chicago *Post,* Dec. 14, 1917.

———. *Literary Digest* 55 (Dec. 1, 1917): 42.

———. New York *Tribune,* Oct. 20, 1917.

———. New York *World,* Jan. 13, 1918.

———. *North American Review* 207 (Mar. 1918): 458–59.

———. Philadelphia *Public Ledger,* Dec. 1, 1917.

———. *The World Court* 3 (Nov. 1917): 521.

The Struggle for Universal Empire, vol. 1 of *A History of Diplomacy in the International Development of Europe.* Burr, George L. *American Historical Review* 11 (Jan. 1906): 358–60.

———. *The Catholic World* 132 (Nov. 1905): 263–66.

———. Needham, Charles W. *American Journal of International Law* 1 (July 1907): 797–800.

———. [Shaw, Albert]. "His Magnum Opus." *American Monthly Review of Reviews* 32 (Aug. 1905): 136–37.

———. New York *Sun,* Aug. 13, 1905.

———. New York *Tribune,* Aug. 19, 1905.

———. Morey, William C. Quoted from the Rochester *Post Express* in *A History of Europe from the Point of View of the Modern Publicist,* a Longmans, Green and Co. brochure.

CONTEMPORARY WORKS AND ARTICLES

"The Ambassadorship Muddle." *Nation* 86 (Apr. 2, 1908): 298.

Anderson, Martin B. *The Ends and Means of a Liberal Education, An*

Inaugural Address Delivered July 11, 1854, by M. B. Anderson, President of the University of Rochester. Rochester, N.Y.: William N. Sage, 1855.

Barrett, John. "An American School of Diplomacy." *Harper's Weekly* 44 (Mar. 3, 1900): 193–94.

Bratter, C. A., *David Jayne Hill und die amerikanische Diplomatie*, Heft 22, *Persönlichkeiten*. Charlottenburg: Virgil Verlag, [1908].

Buchanan, William I. "Latin America and the Mexican Conference." *Annals of the American Academy of Political and Social Science* 22 (July 1903): 47–55.

Caudel, M. *School of Comparative Jurisprudence and Diplomacy.* Translated by Hermann Schoenfeld from an article in *Revue International de L'Enseignment,* Paris, Oct. 1899. Washington: The Columbian University, [1899].

"David Jayne Hill and the Panama Tolls." *Outlook* 107 (May 30, 1914): 218–20.

"David Jayne Hill, LL.D." University of Rochester *Interpres* 38 (1897): 115–16.

Dawley, Thomas R., Jr. "At the Pan-American Congress." *Outlook* 69 (Dec. 28, 1901): 1067–69.

"Dr. David Jayne Hill." Elmira (New York) *Journal* 1 (June 1894): 1.

Dunne, Finley Peter. "Mr. Dooley on Diplomacy." *American Magazine* 66 (June 1908): 107–11.

Finch, George A. "The Annual Meeting of the American Society of International Law." *American Journal of International Law* 19 (July 1925): 530–34.

———. "The Progressive Codification of International Law." *American Journal of International Law* 19 (July 1925): 534–42.

Foster, John W. *Arbitration and The Hague Court.* Boston: Houghton Mifflin Co., 1904.

Garner, James W. "Some Observations on the Codification of International Law." *American Journal of International Law* 19 (Apr. 1925): 327–33.

Gilmore, Joseph Henry. *An Outline History of the University of Rochester.* Rochester, N.Y.: Ezra R. Andrews, 1886.

Gretzinger, Wm. C., and Walker, Chas. A., eds. *An Historical Sketch of Bucknell University, Lewisburg, Pa.* Printed for the editors, 1890.

"The Growth of Our University." Bucknell *University Mirror* 7 (June 1888): 112.

[Harvey, George]. "For Constitutional Clubs." *North American Review* 198 (Dec. 1913): 763.

Holls, Frederick W. *The Peace Conference at The Hague.* New York: Macmillan Co., 1900.

Howard-Ellis, C. *The Origin, Structure, and Working of the League of Nations.* Boston: Houghton Mifflin Co., 1928.

"In Memoriam, William Bucknell." Bucknell *University Mirror* 9 (April 1890): 211.

Kuhn, Arthur K. "Codification of International Law and the Fifth Assembly." *American Journal of International Law* 19 (Jan. 1925): 155–57.

"The Lesson of the Hill Muddle." *Literary Digest* 36 (Apr. 11, 1908): 508–10.

"Lodge's Plan for a New World Court." *Literary Digest* 81 (May 24, 1924): 12–13.

Moore, John Bassett. *International Law and Some Current Illusions.* New York: Macmillan Co., 1924.

Morey, William Carey. "David Jayne Hill." University of Rochester *Interpres* 50 (1909): 9–11.

———. "The University of Rochester in its Relation to the Educational Movement of the Last Fifty Years." *Addresses at the Semi-Centennial Anniversary of the Founding of the University of Rochester, June Tenth to Fourteenth, MCM.* Rochester, N.Y.: E. R. Andrews Printing Co., 1901.

Noel, John V. *A History of the Second Pan-American Congress.* Baltimore: Guggenheimer, Weil and Co., 1902.

"Our Embassies and Their Needs," *American Monthly Review of Reviews* 37 (May 1908): 521.

The Pan-American Congress and Arbitration. A collection of over one hundred editorials from some sixty United States newspapers. Privately printed, n.d.

"Permanent Housing for Diplomats." *American Monthly Review of Reviews* 43 (June 1911): 690–94.

"Personalities." *Harper's Weekly* 45 (Aug. 10, 1901): 808.

Root, Elihu. "The Codification of International Law." *American Journal of International Law* 19 (Oct. 1925): 675–84.

Scott, James B. *The Hague Peace Conferences of 1899 and 1907*. 2 vols. Baltimore: The Johns Hopkins Press, 1909.

"Sketch of the Life of David Jayne Hill, LL.D." Bucknell University *L'Agenda* 1 (1888): 80–83.

Spratt, O. W. *The University at Lewisburg, Report of the Twenty-Fourth Annual Commencement, Lewisburg, Pa., June 19–24, 1874*. Philadelphia, 1874.

————. ed. *Historical Sketch of the University at Lewisburg, and Report of the Twenty-Sixth Annual Commencement, Lewisburg, Pa., June 23–28, 1876*. Published by the Society of the Alumni, Philadelphia, 1877.

"University History." University of Rochester *Interpres* 35 (1894): 19–32.

"The Week." *Nation* 87 (July 16, 1908): 45.

"Who's Who—and Why." *Saturday Evening Post* 180 (May 2, 1908): 19.

"Why Ambassador Hill Comes Home." *Literary Digest* 42 (May 13, 1911): 933–34.

NEWSPAPERS

Albany *Knickerbocker Press*, 1916.

Baltimore News, 1920.

Boston *Herald*, 1902, 1908, 1911, 1915, 1920–1921.

Boston Transcript, 1911, 1920, 1923.

Brooklyn *Daily Times*, 1896.

Cincinnati *Inquirer*, 1911.

Lewisburg (Pennsylvania) *Chronicle*, 1879–1880, 1884.

Lewisburg (Pennsylvania) *Saturday News*, 1886.

London *Times*, 1908.

New York *American*, 1908, 1911.

New York *American Economist*, 1915.

New York *Christian Inquirer*, 1892.

New York *Commercial*, 1915.

New York Critic, 1897.

New York *Evening Mail*, 1908.

New York *Evening Post*, 1896, 1911, 1920–1921.

New York *Evening Telegram*, 1912.

New York *Evening World*, 1920.

New York *Examiner*, 1888–1889, 1893–1895.

New York *Globe*, 1915.

New York *Herald*, 1902, 1908, 1911, 1919–1921.

New York *Journal of Commerce*, 1915.

New York *Sun*, 1902, 1905, 1908, 1910–1911, 1915.

New York Times, 1896, 1900, 1902, 1907–1908, 1911–1912, 1915–1916, 1920–1922, 1924–1926, 1931–1932.

New York *Tribune*, 1895, 1901–1903, 1905, 1908, 1911, 1916, 1919–1922.

New York *World*, 1900, 1908, 1911, 1915–1917, 1921.

Philadelphia *Inquirer*, 1879, 1911.

Philadelphia *National Baptist*, 1879, 1881, 1883, 1891, 1894.

Philadelphia *Press*, 1902, 1908.

Philadelphia *Public Ledger*, 1911, 1920–1921.

Rochester (New York) *Democrat and Chronicle*, 1889–1896, 1900, 1916.

Rochester (New York) *Herald*, 1893, 1895–1896.

Rochester (New York) *Morning Herald*, 1890–1892.

Rochester (New York) *Post Express*, 1889, 1895–1896, 1912–1913.

Rochester (New York) *Times*, 1916.

Rochester (New York) *Union and Advertiser*, 1915.

Schenectady *Union*, 1902.

University at Lewisburg *College Herald*, 1872, 1880.

University at Lewisburg (after 1886 Bucknell University) *University Mirror*, 1884, 1887–1890.

University of Rochester *Campus*, 1889, 1893–1895.

Williamsport (Pennsylvania) *Gazette and Bulletin*, 1892.

Washington Evening Star, 1897–1898, 1911.

Washington *Herald*, 1916, 1921.

Washington Post, 1899, 1908.

Washington Star, 1898, 1920.

Washington Times, 1900, 1920–1921.

SECONDARY WORKS AND ARTICLES

Bailey, Thomas A. "Was the Presidential Election of 1900 a Mandate on Imperialism?" *Mississippi Valley Historical Review* 24 (June 1937): 43–52.

Beale, Howard K. *Theodore Roosevelt and the Rise of America to World Power*. Baltimore: Johns Hopkins Press, 1956.

Beales, A. C. F. *The History of Peace*. New York: Dial Press, 1931.

Brown, Roscoe C. E., and Smith, Ray B. *Political and Governmental History of the State of New York*. 6 vols. Syracuse: Syracuse Press, 1922.

Bryson, Gladys. "The Comparable Interests of the Old Moral Philosophy and the Modern Social Sciences." *Social Forces* 11 (Oct. 1932): 19–27.

Cory, Helen May. *Compulsory Arbitration of International Disputes*. New York: Columbia University Press, 1932.

Curti, Merle. *Peace or War, the American Struggle, 1636–1936*. New York: W. W. Norton and Co., 1936.

Davis, Calvin DeArmond. *The United States and the First Hague Peace Conference*. Ithaca: Cornell University Press, 1962.

Dennett, Tyler. *John Hay: From Poetry to Politics*. New York: Dodd, Mead & Co., 1933.

Dennis, Alfred L. P. *Adventures in American Diplomacy, 1896–1906*. New York: E. P. Dutton & Co., 1928.

———. "John Hay." *The American Secretaries of State and*

Their Diplomacy, vol. 9. Samuel Flagg Bemis, ed. 10 vols. New York: Alfred A. Knopf, 1929.

Dennis, William J. *Tacna and Arica.* New Haven: Yale University Press, 1931.

Earnest, Ernest. *Academic Procession: An Informal History of the American College, 1636–1953.* Indianapolis: Bobbs-Merrill, 1953.

Fleming, Denna F. *The Treaty Veto of the American Senate.* New York: G. P. Putnam's Sons, 1936.

———— *The United States and the World Court.* Garden City, N.Y.: Doubleday, Doran and Co., 1945.

Ford, Thomas K. "The Genesis of the First Hague Peace Conference." *Political Science Quarterly* 51 (Sept. 1936): 354–82.

Gordon, Robert M. "George W. Aldridge: A Study of the Political Career of a Local Boss," M. A. thesis, 1927, University of Rochester.

Harper, Ida. *The Life and Work of Susan B. Anthony.* 3 vols. Indianapolis: Hollenbeck Press, 1908.

Hendrick, Burton J. *The Life of Andrew Carnegie.* 2 vols. Garden City, N.Y.: Doubleday, Doran & Co., 1932.

Hopkins, Charles H. *The Rise of the Social Gospel in American Protestantism, 1865–1915.* New Haven: Yale University Press, 1940.

Howland, Charles P., comp. *Survey of American Foreign Relations, 1929.* New Haven: Yale University Press for the Council on Foreign Relations, 1929.

Hudson, Manley O. *The Permanent Court of International Justice.* New York: Macmillan Co., 1934.

————. *The World Court, 1921–1931.* Boston: World Peace Foundation, 1931.

Jessup, Philip C. *Elihu Root.* 2 vols. New York: Dodd, Mead and Co., 1938.

Link, Arthur S. *Wilson: The New Freedom.* Princeton: Princeton University Press, 1956.

Lysen, A. *History of the Carnegie Foundation and of the Peace Palace at The Hague.* vol. 28 of *Bibliotheca Visseriana.* Leiden: E. J. Brill, 1934.

McKelvey, Blake. "Rochester's Political Trends: An Historical Review." *Rochester History* 14 (Apr. 1952).

Mowry, George E. *Theodore Roosevelt and the Progressive Movement.* Madison: University of Wisconsin Press, 1946.

Oliphant, J. Orin. *The Library of Bucknell University.* Lewisburg, Pa.: Bucknell University Press, 1962.

————. *The Rise of Bucknell University.* New York: Appleton-Century-Crofts, 1965.

Penfield, Walter S. "The Settlement of the Samoan Cases." *American Journal of International Law* 7 (Oct. 1913): 767–73.

Perkins, Dexter. "The University of Rochester, Its Place in the Civic Century." *Centennial History of Rochester, New York,* vol. 4. Edward R. Foreman, ed. Rochester, N.Y.: Rochester Historical Society, 1934.

Pusey, Merlo J. *Charles Evans Hughes.* 2 vols. New York: Macmillan Co., 1951.

Robinson, Margaret. *Arbitration and the Hague Peace Conferences, 1899 and 1907.* Philadelphia: University of Pennsylvania, 1936.

Rosenberger, Jesse Leonard. *Rochester and Colgate: Historical Backgrounds of the Two Universities.* Chicago: University of Chicago Press, 1925.

————. *Rochester, The Making of a University.* Rochester, N.Y.: University of Rochester, 1927.

Ryden, George H. *The Foreign Policy of the United States in Relation to Samoa.* New Haven: Yale University Press, 1933.

Schmidt, George P. *The Old Time College President.* New York: Columbia University Press, 1930.

Slater, John R. *Rhees of Rochester.* New York: Harper & Brothers, 1946.

————. "Small Beginnings: The College for Men, 1850–1899. *The University of Rochester, The First Hundred Years.* Contennial Issue of the *Alumni-Alumnae Review* Commemorating the University's One Hundredth Anniversary. Rochester, N.Y.: University of Rochester, 1950.

Stuart, Graham H. *The Department of State: A History of Its Organiza-*

tion, Procedure and Personnel. New York: Macmillan Co., 1949.

———— ."The   Tacna-Arica   Dispute."   *World   Peace   Foundation Pamphlets,* 10. Boston: World Peace Foundation, 1927.

Tate, Merze. *The Disarmament Illusion: The Movement for a Limitation of Armaments*. New York: Macmillan Co., 1942.

Theiss, Lewis E. *Centennial History of Bucknell University, 1846–1946*. Lewisburg, Pa.: Bucknell University, 1946.

Theiss, Mary Bartol. "In the Beginning; the intimate personal story of the founding of the University at Lewisburg and the sacrifice and devotion of its founders." Bucknell *Alumni Monthly* 9 (Nov. 1924): 11–16.

Works, Articles, and Addresses by David Jayne Hill, Not Cited

"An Address . . . Before the Section on International Law at the Second Pan-American Scientific Congress, 1915–1916." Manuscript in the Hill Papers, University of Rochester Library.

Address of Hon. David Jayne Hill . . . Banquet of the American Chamber of Commerce in France . . . July 4, 1922. Paris: The Lecram Press, n.d.

"The Aims and Purposes of the National Association for Constitutional Government." Address delivered at the First Annual Dinner of the Association, Washington, D.C., May 6, 1916. Manuscript in the Hill Papers, University of Rochester Library.

"The American Conception of the State." Address before Brown University, Feb. 22, 1915, and Syracuse University, Mar. 12, 1915. Manuscript in the Hill Papers, University of Rochester Library.

"Americanizing the Treaty." *North American Review* 120 (Aug. 1919): 155–71.

The Authority of International Law. The Annual Address to the New

York State Bar Association, New York, January 17, 1919. Privately printed, n.d.

"Autocracy by Plebiscite." *North American Review* 211 (Apr. 1920): 457–71.

"The Betrayal of the Monroe Doctrine." *North American Review* 212 (Nov. 1920): 577–93.

"Can Treaty-Making Commit Us to the League of Nations." *League of Nations Magazine* 5 (May 1919): 302–9.

"Civil and Religious Freedom in America: A Tradition that Deserves to Be Jealously Guarded." *The National Republican,* Sept. 27, 1924, pp. 3, 5.

"The Classification of Diplomatic Agents." *American Journal of International Law* 21 (Oct. 1927): 737–42.

"The Cost of Universities." *Forum* (Nov. 1889), pp. 297–304.

"The Commemoration of Grotius. *American Journal of International Law* 19 (Jan. 1925): 118–22.

The Conception and Realization of Neutrality. Paper read before the American Social Science Association at Washington, April 23, 1902. Boston: Privately printed, 1902.

"The Correspondence Regarding the S.S. Sussex," *American Journal of International Law* 10 (July 1916): 556–60.

"The Covenant or the Constitution?" *North American Review* 211 (Mar. 1920): 321–31.

"The Debacle of Dogmatism." *North American Review* 209 (May 1919): 583–99.

"The Default of Democracy." *North American Review* 212 (Sept. 1920): 289–300.

"A Defense of the Constitution." *North American Review* 205 (Mar. 1917): 389–97.

"Democracy." Address before the City Club, Boston, February 4, 1915. Manuscript in the Hill Papers, University of Rochester Library.

"Dual Citizenship in the German Imperial and State Citizenship Law." *American Journal of International Law* 12 (Apr. 1918): 356–63.

"The Eclipse of Peace." *North American Review* 211 (Feb. 1920): 165–78.

"Economic Imperialism." *Century Magazine* 94 (July 1917): 356–63.

"The Entente of Free Nations." *North American Review* 209 (Jan. 1919): 13–28.

"The Ethical Function of the Historian." Address delivered at the opening of the International Congress for Historical Sciences, Berlin, August 8, 1908. *American Historical Review* 14 (Oct. 1908): 2–21. Also published, "Der ethische Beruf des Geschichts-schreibers." *Neue Revue* 1 (Aug. 2, 1908): 1452–64.

"Europe's Heritage of Evil." *Century Magazine* 94 (May 1917): 7–15.

"The Festival Development of Art." *Popular Science Monthly* 42 (Apr. 1893): 734–49.

"Fondation Theirs." *American Monthly Review of Reviews* 48 (Oct. 1913): 449–53.

"The Foundation of the State." *North American Review* 199 (Feb. 1914): 199–204.

"The German Plot and Democracy's Future." *Century Magazine* 94 (Oct. 1917): 863–70.

"Germany After the War." *Scientific Monthly* 7 (Apr. 1919): 311–20.

"Germany's Pose for an Advantageous Peace." *North American Review* 209 (Feb. 1919): 161–74.

"Guarding Our Heritage." Address before the Annual Congress of the Daughters of the American Revolution, Washington, D.C., April 23, 1920. Manuscript in the Hill Papers, University of Rochester Library.

Have We a Philosophy of Government? Address before the Iota Chapter of the Phi Beta Kappa Fraternity, University of Rochester, June 15, 1924. Rochester, N.Y.: The Iota Chapter of Phi Beta Kappa, 1924.

"The Heart of the Covenant." *Boston Transcript*, Sept. 18, 1920.

"Herbert Spencer's Postscript to Man vs. the State," *Forum* 55 (Feb. 1916): 243–50.

Human Nature in the Constitution. The Fifth Lecture of the Cutler Foundation of the University of Rochester, April 23, 1926. Rochester, N.Y.: University of Rochester, 1926.

"The Illusions of Genoa." *North American Review* 216 (Aug. 1922): 154–64.

"Impressions of the Kaiser." *Harper's Magazine* 136 (May 1918): 790–99; 137 (June–Aug. 1918): 29–39, 220–28, 377–86.

"In the Valley of Decision." *North American Review* 210 (July 1919): 18–28.

"International Ideals." *Century Magazine* 94 (June 1917): 260–67.

"International Law and International Policy," *North American Review* 209 (Mar. 1919): 315–29.

"International Law as an Expression of International Life." *Proceedings of the American Society of International Law, 1916,* pp. 144–49. Washington: American Society of International Law, 1916.

"International Morality." *North American Review* 201 (June 1915): 853–59.

"The Issues at Stake." *North American Review* 212 (Aug. 1920): 145–55.

"The Janina-Corfu Affair." *American Journal of International Law* 18 (Jan. 1924): 98–104.

"A League of Insincerity." *North American Review* 210 (Sept. 1919): 297–311.

"Legal Limitations Upon the Initiation of Military Action." *Proceedings of the American Society of International Law, 1925,* pp. 95–102. Washington: American Society of International Law, 1925.

"The Luxburg Secret Correspondence." *American Journal of International Law* 12 (Jan. 1918): 135–40.

"A Missing Chapter of Franco-American History," Paper read before the American Historical Association, Washington, D.C., December 30, 1915. *American Historical Review* 21 (July 1916): 709–19.

"Mr. Balfour Explained." *Bookman* 53 (Apr. 1921): 165–68.

The National Association for Constitutional Government: A Statement of

Its Aims and Purposes. Washington: National Association for Constitutional Government, n.d.

"National Sovereignty in its Relation to International Law." *Proceedings of the American Society of International Law, 1916*, pp. 144–49.

"The Nations and the Law." *North American Review* 110 (Oct. 1919): 439–55.

"The Net Results at The Hague." *American Monthly Review of Reviews* 36 (Dec. 1907): 727–30.

"The New Age and the New Task." Address delivered at the Commencement of Clark University, June 23, 1918. *Clark College Record* 14 (July 1919): 191–206. Reprinted in part as "No Place for German Ideas in the United States," *American Defense* (July 14, 21, 1919).

"The Obstruction of Peace." *North American Review* 209 (Apr. 1919): 453–71.

Our National Development. Address before the Alumni of the University of Pennsylvania, June 17, 1902. Philadelphia: Avil Printing Co., 1902.

Our Place Among the Nations. Address before the Union League of Philadelphia, January 26, 1901. Privately printed, n.d.

"The Peace with Germany." Address delivered at the Eighteenth Annual Banquet of the Navy League of the United States, March 5, 1921. *Sea Power* 10 (Apr. 1921): 163.

"The Permanent Court of International Justice." *American Journal of International Law* 14 (July 1920): 387–92.

"The Powers of Government." Address before the New Jersey Historical Society, Newark, N.J., May 12, 1920, and before the National Wholesale Lumber Dealers Association, Washington, D.C., March 24, 1920. Manuscript in the Hill Papers, University of Rochester Library.

"Present Economic and Social Problems." Address before the Section of Social and Economic Science of the American Association for the Advancement of Science, St. Louis, December 29, 1919. *Scientific Monthly* 10 (June 1920): 381–88.

"The President's Attack on the Senate." *North American Review* 210 (Nov. 1919): 587–603.

"The President's Challenge to the Senate." *North American Review* 209 (June 1919): 737–54.

"Projects of the American Institute of International Law on Measures of Repression and Conquest." *American Journal of International Law* 21 (Jan. 1927): 145–46.

"Psychogenesis." *Philosophical Review* 1 (Sept. 1892): 481–503.

"The Purpose of Government," *American Legion Weekly* 3 (May 13, 1921): 9, 18–19.

"A Question of Honor." *North American Review* 212 (Oct. 1920): 433–48.

"Remarks of David J. Hill at the First Annual Dinner of the National Association for Constitutional Government, May 6th, 1916." Manuscript in the Hill Papers, University of Rochester Library.

"Representative Government." Address before the Lawyers' Club of New York, January 13, 1917. Manuscript in the Hill Papers, University of Rochester Library.

"Republics—The Ladder to Liberty." *National Geographic Magazine* 31 (Mar. 1917): 240–54.

"Rights of the Civil Population in a Territory Occupied By a Belligerent." *American Journal of International Law* 11 (Jan. 1917): 133–37.

"The Second Assembly of the League of Nations." *American Journal of International Law* 16 (Jan. 1922): 59–65.

"The Second Peace Conference at the The Hague." *American Journal of International Law* 1 (July 1907): 671–91.

"The Senate's Service to the Nations." *North American Review* 211 (Jan. 1920): 1–16.

"A Sentinel on Guard." *North American Review* 217 (Feb. 1923): 166–80.

"Some Preliminaries of Peace." Address of the President and Chairman of the Social and Economic Science Section of the American Association for the Advancement of Science,

Chicago, December 28, 1920. *Scientific Monthly* 12 (Mar. 1921): 223–27.

"Speech at the Authors' Club." *Unpopular Review* 9 (Jan. 1918): 7–15.

"The State and the Citizen." *North American Review* 200 (Aug. 1914): 185–93.

"Taking Soundings." *North American Review* 199 (May 1914): 673–83.

"The Test of Democracy." Address before the Brown University Alumni of Boston, February 9, 1916. Manuscript in the Hill Papers, University of Rochester Library.

"The Third Assembly of the League of Nations." *American Journal of International Law* 17 (Jan. 1923): 77–82.

The Training Period for American Independence. Address before the Society of Colonial Wars in the District of Columbia, April 11, 1922. *Historical Papers of the Society of Colonial Wars in the District of Columbia*, no. 9 (1925).

Two Lectures on The Revised Covenant of The League of Nations. Addresses before the George Washington University, April 28–29, 1919. *George Washington University Bulletin* 18 (Mar. 1919).

"A Vision of a Commonwealth." *Century Magazine* 94 (Sept. 1917): 740–47.

A Vision of the World and Other Verses. Washington: The Crane Co. (printed but not published), 1923.

Washington as a Citizen. Address before the Washington Association of New Jersey, at Washington's Headquarters in Morristown, New Jersey, February 22, 1922. Privately printed, n.d.

"Why 'Americanism'?" *Hughes Campaign Services*, Bulletin no. 6 (Sept. 14, 1916), p. 1.

Index

Hill, David Jayne (cont.)

advocated for governorship of New York (1912), 165–66; entered in New York senatorial primaries (1914), 166–67; initiates fusion of Progressive and Republican parties (1914), 167–70; opposes repeal of Panama Canal Act, 170–71; attacks Wilson's foreign policies, 171–74; urges measures for military and industrial defense, 174–78; friendship with Roosevelt costs place at Republican National Convention (1916), 178–79; declines to run in 1916 and 1918 New York senatorial primaries, 179–80, 199; declines congressional nomination (1918), 181; attacks Germany and the Kaiser, 182–83; opposes joining League of Nations, 183–98; criticisms of League, 183–84, 189–95; attacks Wilson's advocacy of League, 184–85; urges society of states based on law, 185–89; contributes anti-League and 1920 election campaign material, 183, 195–98; considered for secretary of state, 198–200; seeks appointment to Paris, 200; declines appointment to Tokyo, 200–201; goes to Europe to care for David, Jr., 200, 202; reports conditions in Europe to Secretary Hughes, 202–4; covers Washington Conference for New York *Tribune,* 204–7; private life after death of Juliet, 208; opposes joining World Court, 209–23; criticisms of World Court, 209–11, 212–13, 216–17, 222–23; contributions to senatorial opponents of World Court, 211–12, 213–14, 216, 217–18; advises President Coolidge on World Court, 214–15; continues to write on questions of foreign policy, 223; fails to be objective in writings, 223–25; death, 225

VIEWS ON:

amendments to the Constitution, 158–59; American system of govern-

Hill, David Jayne (cont.)

ment, 157–58; armaments limitation, 74, 140–41, 203, 204–5; Bryan's conciliation treaties, 172–73, 223; coeducation at the University of Rochester, 40–41; college athletics, 29, 40; consular service, 101; denominational colleges, 41–42; elective studies, 27; "Entente of Free Nations," 189–92; "Entente of the Pacific," 203–5; expansionism, 91–96; Four Power Treaty, 205–6; German attitude toward arbitration, 134–35; Hague Conferences, results of, 80–81, 118–19; immigration, 58–59; imperialism, charges of 98–99; initiative, referendum, and recall, 158; international law, 185–91, 210; League of Nations, 183–84, 190–95; League to Enforce Peace, 185–86; military preparedness, 174–75; money issue, 59, 61, 97; organized minorities, 161; Panama Canal Act, 170–71; peace advocates, 175–76; postwar economic rivalries, 176–78; postwar Europe, 202–3; primary campaigns, 166, 180–81; progressivism, 156–59; religion and science, 16–17, 28–29, 49–51; residences for U.S. diplomats, 127–28; socialism, 31–32; Taft's reasons for demanding his resignation, 147–53; tariffs, 57–58, 176–78; Washington Conference, 203–7; Wilhelm II, 136, 183; Woodrow Wilson, 172, 173–74, 184–85; Wilson's Mexican policy, 172; Wilson's neutrality policy, 173–74; World Court, 203, 209–17, 222–23; world organization under law, 140–41, 185–89, 210, 223

PUBLICATIONS:

American World Policies, 183, 191–92, 196; *Americanism: What It Is,* 157, 159; "Americanizing the Treaty," 196; "Betrayal of the Monroe Doctrine, The," 198; "Corporate Character of the League of Nations, The," 195;

10/08